Academic
Literacies

Academic Literacies

The Public and Private Discourse of University Students

With a Foreword by Denny Taylor

Elizabeth Chiseri-Strater

Boynton/Cook Publishers
Heinemann
Portsmouth, NH

Boynton/Cook Publishers
A Subsidiary of
Heinemann Educational Books, Inc.
361 Hanover Street   Portsmouth, NH 03801–3959
Offices and agents throughout the world

Library of Congress Cataloging-in-Publication Data

Chiseri-Strater, Elizabeth.
    Academic literacies: the public and private discourse of university students/Elizabeth Chiseri-Strater.
        p.   cm.
Includes bibliographical references.
ISBN 0–435–08540–9
1. Education. Higher—United States—Aims and Objectives.
2. Literacy—United States.   3. College students—United States—Intellectual life.   4. Culture   I. Title.
LA227.3.C474   1991
378'.01'0973—dc20   90–42400
                                                        CIP

Designed by Maria Szmauz
Printed in the United States of America
91 92 93 94 95   10 9 8 7 6 5 4 3 2 1

To my Family:
My daughters, Tosca and Alisha, and my husband, Minshall

Contents

Foreword

In Brueghel's Icarus, *for instance: how everything turns away*
Quite leisurely from the disaster; the ploughman may
Have heard the splash, the forsaken cry,
But for him it was not an important failure; the sun shone
As it had to on the white legs disappearing into the green
Water; and the expensive delicate ship that must have seen
Something amazing, a boy falling out of the sky,
Had somewhere to get to and sailed calmly on.

W. H. Auden
"Musée des Beaux Arts"

*E*lizabeth Chiseri-Strater's beautifully written book is quietly revolutionary and will be applauded loudly by those who read it. It is a book in which personal knowledge matters. Through her disciplined and systematic ethnographic study of the academic lives of two undergraduate students, Anna and Nick, Elizabeth makes visible how literacy is defined in different academic settings. Private ways of knowing become public and create new perspectives on learning that take into account the social, cultural, intellectual, and political contexts in which students live their academic lives.

In *Academic Literacies*, Elizabeth Chiseri-Strater confronts popular beliefs about cultural literacy and the decline of literate knowledge. She makes clear that the reconstruction of literacy into some simplistic book of lists is an intellectual form of censorship that creates artificial boundaries that obscure the complexities of literacy in the academic lives of the students whom we study and teach. Elizabeth shows us that we have learned to turn away quite leisurely from the impending disaster that this view of literacy has on the lives of students. No one hears Nick cry, "Critical analysis may slaughter me, in the end. It has smote me furiously already." A boy is falling out of the sky, but the academy does not see him as he hits the water. No one reads him when he writes, "I've tried to convince myself that the ferocious assignments racing past me down the lives of the dead were of the sincerest emergency.... [But now] I'm convinced of two things: school and school work are contrived and, overall inconsequential."

Chiseri-Strater, like Auden in *Musée des Beaux Arts*, draws our attention to the tragedy that has occurred. The literate lives of Anna and Nick have become lost in what she refers to as the "impersonal, hierarchical, singular, competitive, and self-centered" learning of the academy. Language is stripped to abstraction, and literacy is manipulated in ways that hide the complexities of the intellectual functions and uses of print in the personal lives of Anna and Nick. It is through Anna that we become aware that the price that is paid by students for this artificial form of individualism is ultimately the loss of themselves as individuals. In a paper triggered by an essay written by Richard Rodriguez, Anna expresses concern that in the university she will be left without her own ideas, unable to think beyond the text. This time it is Anna who drops out of the sky, but her fall is an unimportant failure, hidden from the expensive, delicate academy by hard work and good grades.

Moving beyond the official text, Elizabeth Chiseri-Strater introduces us to the multiple literacies of the students of the academy. She makes us aware that undergraduate university life is experienced differently by men and women. Through Elizabeth we get to know Anna and Nick. We become aware of the wide range of ways in which they use print in their everyday lives, and their individual and shared literacy configurations become known to us. Elizabeth makes it possible for us to learn from them, but she would not have been able to do such a remarkable job without the help of Donna Qualley, who teaches prose writing at the university. It is in Donna's class that the lives of Nick and Anna become connected and where private ways of knowing become communal. Through her observations in Donna's prose writing course, Elizabeth makes visible the importance of the multiple discourse communities to which Anna and Nick belong, and she helps us to understand the complexities of alternate and exploratory discourse forms that are continually recreated when men and women enter the academy.

Academic Literacies is both passionate and eloquent, and it is a much needed antidote to the fashionably pedantic, boring cries of those who would artificially simplify literacy in ways that stop us from seeing when learning is taking place, or from knowing when we ourselves are the ones who are falling out of the sky.

Denny Taylor

Acknowledgments

Writing a book is often described as a lonely experience: the writer scribbling in her barren garret; the rebel revising his life in the cold cell. This has not been my "scene" for writing. While I will not pretend that I never felt alone or imprisoned before my uncompassionate computer, I also recall that for all the isolation that writing involves, it invites a new kind of companionship. As you write, and I think this is more true of a book than articles or chapters, you feel connected to all those others like you who have tried to shape their ideas through language into a cohesive and meaningful manuscript. Piled in my distinguishably messy study are the dissertations of my friends which are now published books—Lorri Neilsen's *Literacy and Living*, Ruth Hubbard's *Authors of Pictures, Draughtsmen of Words*, Cinthia Gannett's work on journals and gender (SUNY Press, 1991), as well as the new book of my thesis director, Thomas Newkirk, *More Than Stories*. These drafts comfort me because I know those authors personally and have witnessed the seeds of their projects—arguments being compiled, stories being shared—finally germinate into full books.

There are scholars elsewhere working in the same territory whose work has bolstered me: Lucille McCarthy's dissertation, "A Stranger in Strange Lands," was very influential as was her initial encouragement of my project. Patricia Bizzell, whose work on academic discourse communities has been seminal, offered a very thoughtful and constructive reading of my manuscript, which guided my revisions.

Part of my support system was invisible. In still another pile — which grew higher as I wrote — stood my favorite dogeared books from scholars I do not know personally but whose voices have powerfully influenced me to the point that I feel connected to them. These include anthropologist Clifford Geertz, ethnographer Linda Brodkey, educator Maxine Greene, developmental psychologists Mary Belenky and her colleagues, rhetorician Karen Burke LeFevre, reader response theorist Louise Rosenblatt, social scientist Donald Schön. So many resources guide the writing life.

Aside from all these compatible books, there was the telephone connection, through which I could get support from one of my New Hampshire colleagues: Donna Qualley and Cinthia Gannett were tirelessly available for comment on the many revisions of my chapters; Judy Fueyo often lent her ear and eye; Don Murray and Don Graves — "the Dons" as they are referred to at the University of New Hampshire — were ever willing to share advice about writing. Denny Taylor, ethnographer and researcher, was just a phone call away as were Jane Hansen, Sharon Oja, and Robert Connors, all colleagues whose advice was practical and purposeful. I bring all these voices, books, and people together to celebrate the process of writing.

My greatest thanks goes to the young woman and man who allowed me into their lives as I conducted my research. I am sure that neither they nor I really understood to what extent their cooperation would shape this project. When Anna[1] read the first draft of her chapter, she said that it felt "weird" reading about herself, that she didn't realize how very "revealing" it would be. Nick's initial response to his chapter was that he thought it was a fairly "accurate portrait" of himself. Not everyone who reads this book will agree, however, with the perspective offered here, particularly with my affirmation of my informants' viewpoints. As Linda Brodkey (1987b, 99) has recently pointed out, "the academy has a limited tolerance for lived experience," which they regard as "stories," thereby dismissing the ethnographic narrative.

I want to thank those who initially encouraged me with my

[1] The names of all students and university professors in the book — aside from Donna Qualley — have been changed.

dissertation and left me unfettered as I wrote. The original manu-script was written as a dissertation in my makeshift underground office among the musty mops, the turned-over dog-food bags, the sand and grit from garden and beach, as I hid from family and friends in the early morning hours. My chapters were well received by my committee who reaffirmed my waning ego by urging me to seek publication. One of the nicest compliments came from my dissertation chair, Tom Newkirk, who remarked about my chapter on Nick that he read it straight through like a detective story. Tom has always provided my strongest intellectual guidance and to him I am ever grateful.

My original study was rewritten a year later among a circle of women colleagues and critics who provided the final glue, the support, the iron tissue of will to rework the research, while enduring the family interruptions, the emergency phone calls, the Girl Scout nature walk and the three-times-a-week ballet lessons, the writing across the curriculum grant work, the revised course syllabi, the teaching and paper grading, the in-service teacher workshops, the grocery shopping, and the wash folding. My writing group includes Cinthia Gannett, Sherrie Gradin, Donna Qualley, Pat Sullivan, and Bonnie Sunstein, my colleagues at the University of New Hampshire who meet regularly to offer one another re-sponse and community.

Thanks go to my editors at Heinemann, Toby Gordon and Dawne Boyer, as well as to the entire Heinemann staff who supported me in the publication process. I was somewhat amazed when Toby suggested that one of my original chapters interrupted the flow of my argument: I never considered my book as an argument. But the more I worked on this manuscript, the more I understood that she was right. I realized that I am arguing against the way that the academy excludes and marginalizes all students who do not fit into the mainstream of thinking, perceiving, and performing.

I want to thank the University of New Hampshire for a disser-tation fellowship, which supported my entire year of research, as well as a smaller grant to help with my transcriptions.

Finally I must thank my family who in the end see more of the "underlife" in this process than anyone else: the frustrations, the depressions, the blocked writing, and the enormous chunks of time involved. Thanks go to Tosca, who is forever a realist, to Alisha, who is ever cheerful, and to my husband, Minshall, who has agreed to navigate with this messy crew.

Introduction
Circles of Literacy

This book celebrates what college students know. It explores what students know about their educations, what they know about the world outside of the academy, and most of all what they know about themselves. Recent book-length commentaries specifically targeting contemporary college students have described them as "closed-minded and impoverished of soul," as "culturally illiterate" and lacking in "background knowledge" (Hirsch 1987; Bloom 1987). Surely these disparaging appraisals must feed into the cyclic American anxiety over our democratic goal of mass postsecondary schooling, an educational opportunity not available in most other nations. Curiously, by holding up college students for close scrutiny, we somehow avoid seeing ourselves, as if our universities bear no relationship to the culture at large. But the eager public acceptance of these recent educational critiques and their unexpected popularization clearly implicate more than just college students in this ongoing debate over what "every American needs to know."

Reductive arguments like those of Bloom and Hirsch encourage a very narrow view of what it means to know by focusing on highly particularized pieces of information, on restricted and exclusionary knowledge rather than on the wide range of literacies needed for living in our pluralistic culture. One student whose voice will become familiar in this study put it this way: "How can you define cultural literacy? How can there be one culture in America? We don't all share the same culture." Reactionary responses like competency testing of teachers or the mechanistic back-to-basics movement deflect productive thought about the goals and problems of higher education. Most of all, such hollow generalizations about a whole population of students do little to help us examine the actual experiences of university students' intellectual lives. In this book, I will try to confront this debate from a different vantage point, with a set of voices that has essentially gone unheard in this literacy argument.

I invite the participation of college students themselves into a consideration of the meaning of a university education, using their perspective to generate what I hope to be a provocative conversation about how literacy and learning take place in the academy. As I trail after college students across the curriculum while they read, write, and talk in different disciplines, I am interested in listening to *them* talk about what it means to be initiated into the culture of a university, what it means to *them* to learn the discourse of a particular discipline, what their interpretation is for literacy. And while I do attempt to slice off one aspect—academic discourse—to examine, I find other factors outside of the academy seep through this boundary to inform me of the holistic nature of literacy. Academic literacies, I discover, cannot be untied from a student's overall literacy: the package comes complete.

The college student of the eighties did not seem all that different from students in the sixties, when I attended college. The life problems so much the center stage of college experiences resonate with familiar questions: "Who am I and where do I belong in this world?" College students continue to struggle with untangling the web of their young adult issues and feelings: about education and career choices, about the need for creativity and intimacy in their lives. Whether we view them through the lenses of gender, class, ethnicity, politics, or religion, students wrestle during their college years with conflicting personal, intellectual, and moral values or decisions.

And even though the developmental and intellectual concerns of traditional college students remain somewhat alike, students evoke a wide range of literacies to make meaning of these experiences. Many, if not most, of the aesthetic responses students have to art, music, and dance remain untapped and do not find their way into our university curricula. Like the Russian Matreska dolls that nest neatly inside one another, students' intimate, imaginative feelings about what they read or write remain hidden, covered by their larger more public selves. Therefore students' personal gifts, their singular ways of interpreting the world, go unnoticed by educators as the lines are drawn between private imaginative experiences and public academic expression. These multiple literacies, the layers of the self that contribute to personal knowing, mirror the many ways of being literate in this world, ways that Maxine Greene acknowledges as critical to the freedom of the classroom climate, if not essential for what she calls the "remaking of a democratic community":

There must of course be a new commitment to intelligence, a new fidelity in communication, a new regard for imagination. It would mean fresh and sometimes startling winds blowing through the classrooms of the nation. It would mean the granting of audibility to numerous voices seldom heard before and, at once, an involvement with all sorts of young people being provoked to make their own the multilinguality needed for structuring of contemporary experience and thematizing lived worlds. (1988, 126–27)

Perhaps because college students possess such "multilinguality," they do not share an absolute set of ideals or common goals about what a college education should entail, except that it should somehow be meaningful. Admittedly, many career-oriented students are highly responsive to the skill demands of their chosen professions but this is largely a reflection of our society. The theme of education, surprisingly, became one of the strong undercurrents in the writing class considered in this study, where students both talk and write extensively on this topic. Students in the writing course raised questions on different occasions about educational values—questions that arose from the assigned readings and sometimes reproduced the debate between absolutism and cultural relativism reflected in both Bloom and Hirsch's works. At different junctures in the writing course, two students offered organic metaphors to describe very different positions on the value of learning in college. These polar views, which I call "the bush and the eagle," served as emblematic metaphors for this study of academic literacy.

The Bush and the Eagle: The Literacy Spectrum

The bush image entered the writing class discussion after reading Paulo Freire's chapter "The Banking Concept of Education" from *Pedagogy of the Oppressed* (1970). In the conversation, Randy spontaneously offered this analogy about literacy and learning from his coursework: "I have an analogy from my landscape class. You can trim a bush back or you can let it grow wild. When you trim a bush back, the roots get deeper. The basic fundamentals in education need to be strong." This quote suggests that Randy agrees with the necessity of what E. D. Hirsch has called "shared background knowledge," and what liberatory educator Paulo Freire decries as the "banking" mode of learning.

Another class session also raised questions about the goals of education, this time after reading Loren Eiseley's "The Brown Wasps," in which the writer reflects on his feelings toward change in his life. During the discussion, Neil attempted to understand the symbolism of the absent cottonwood tree in the essay and, like Randy, struggled with the value of learning in general. Also pulling on an organic image from a course in wildlife ecology, Neil says: "I'm taking an ecology course where we learn that one of the values of wildlife is its aesthetic value. How many of us have seen a bald eagle? Very few, but the knowledge of its existence is why we pour millions of dollars into this conservation project." Neil's response indicates that he sees learning as aesthetically based and historically situated, and looks to his present community's evolving values toward ecology to create his own norms.

Interestingly enough, both these students are concerned with cultural knowledge in different ways: Randy with the product, and Neil with the process. Randy is most interested in control of knowledge so that our educational heritage will produce uniform students, shaping them to fit neatly into the landscape of society. Neil values learning for its intangible potential, for the experience of thinking, not so much for the end result. Many other voices join these to consider what it means to be literate in the expansive setting of a state university. Perhaps the most succinct snapshot for this study can be provided by briefly looking at the University of New Hampshire to anchor readers in a specific setting.

The University of New Hampshire: A Community of Scholars

The University of New Hampshire (UNH) is situated in the small New England town of Durham, a community that stored gunpowder and flint during the revolutionary war, hosted the visits of both President James Monroe and General Lafayette, and formed an antislavery society with sixty-three members long before the Civil War (Durham Historic Society 1976).

Durham retains a semirural quality with its small-town population; even when school is in session the population barely reaches seventeen thousand. The university today, reflecting its agricultural roots, is bordered by three thousand acres of woods, farmland, and fields. Students protest physical changes to the university, such as a recent proposal to replace horse trails with much needed dormitory space. There remains a casual ambience on campus, which, in part, reflects the kind of student who chooses to study here. Clusters of forestry students might gather around trees and study identification features; engineering students could meet on the front lawns with their surveying instruments; ROTC students might appear in uniform in their transition from training to classes. In good weather a group of students is usually assembled on the front lawn of Hamilton-Smith (the English department headquarters and entrance point of this study), writing in their journals or reading papers aloud to one another.

The predecessor of UNH at Durham was the New Hampshire College of Agriculture and the Mechanical Arts, a two-year school established at Hanover in 1868, sharing buildings and equipment with Dartmouth College (Bardwell, 1984). The original tuition for the college was $15 a year with ten men enrolled (11). The college was moved from Hanover to Durham by 1883 but not until after World War I did it officially adopt the title of "university," incorporating the many divisions of the college into a state institution (65).

UNH is the only public university in the state. Although there are other public colleges such as Keene or Plymouth, students who seek majors that only a university can provide or those who desire the setting of a large institution are attracted to UNH. According to the Office of Admissions, approximately 75 percent of the incoming freshman student body is drawn from New Hampshire residents, with out-of-state acceptance quite competitive. Students who attended the University of New Hampshire in 1987 to 1988, when this research was conducted, paid approximately $6,000 for in-state tuition, including room and board — modest fees by most standards.

The outstanding departments at the university mirror its geography and heritage as an agricultural and technical college: engineering, and the life, marine, and animal sciences all maintain quality programs of study. Although there continues to be at UNH, as in the nation as a whole, a steady interest in business as a major, the university is witnessing a shift in the applicant pool away from technical and professional training back to the liberal arts. The Office of Admissions reports that "liberal arts applications at UNH have increased 31 percent in the past two years alone" (University of New Hampshire, Office of Admissions 1987). In a state university that accepted only 42 percent of its 1988–89 applicant pool, this trend toward the liberal arts represents a historical pattern seen by the Office of Admissions in other stable decades because "when there is a strong economy as there is today, students are under less pressure to pursue technical training and are more free to consider the arts, sciences, and humanities" (*Admissions News* 1987). It is interesting that the criticism aimed at students' lack of knowledge in the humanities comes at a time when students are turning away from professional education back toward the more traditional liberal arts.

At the time this research was being conducted, the president of UNH announced that the university's mission was to create "a community of scholars." This institutional goal is very much related to the theme of this research, which is devoted to exposing, from the point of view not of the faculty or administration but of the students, what it means to be part of an academic setting described as "a community of scholars."

The use of the term "community" to describe disciplines or a group of scholars working together is currently being reexamined by composition scholars. Joseph Harris and Linda Brodkey both agree with Raymond Williams's challenge of the "warmly persuasive" quality of this word. Williams suggest that our understanding of the concept of community is limited by having no opposing or negative term.[1] In this study I will examine, from the students' perspective, what an academic community is and what it is not.

The Ethnographic Perspective: "The Lived Experience"

Every research method carries with it a worldview. As academics and researchers we choose our topics and our methods because of our belief systems and personalities. My own history as a teacher of writing, combined with the shifts in my personal life over the past twenty years, is encoded in this study. As a young white teacher in an all black school in Bedford Stuyvesant during the height of the black power movement, I learned that deficit

---

[1] Linda Brodkey (1987b, Ch. 1) and Joseph Harris (1989) have both drawn on Raymond Williams's discussions of community (1976; 1973). In a less formal way Donald Graves (1989) has also critiqued the orthodoxies of writing-process communities.

educational models do not work. The shift in focus in the late sixties from a model of cultural deprivation to that of cultural power allowed both learner and teacher to reconfigure the weaknesses attributed to black students into a source of strength. My current interest in another deficit model of literacy naturally draws on my earlier experiences with this worldview.

Years and experiences later I lived outside of New York City in the Connecticut suburbs as a thirty-year-old widow and single mother, codirecting a writing program at an urban Catholic commuter college. Within my remedial college classrooms, I worked with basic writing students like those whom Mike Rose so movingly describes in his award-winning book, *Lives on the Boundary* (1989). What Rose says of his experiences teaching the underprepared college student echoes my own: "How much we don't see when we look only for deficiency, when we tally up all that people can't do" (1989, 222).

Now, remarried and with two children, I have studied, taught, and researched composition at a state university in a rural setting where many innovative qualitative researchers concern themselves with a wide range of issues in literacy education. It is within this community of researchers that I chose my topic and conducted my research: it is no accident that I decided to look at college students' literacies, or that my research paradigm is ethnographic. Both my personal perspective as a composition scholar and my training as an ethnographer are woven into the texture of this study.

Ethnography does not masquerade as a neutral approach; it does not pretend to generalize or predict. Linda Brodkey describes the almost theatrical and most certainly dramatic methodology of ethnography: "Accordingly, ethnographers study individuals as if their lives were mounted on a cultural proscenium—in full view of an audience" (1987a, 25). The two students who are featured as case studies in this book, in fact, constitute the main players against the backdrop of the state university as they enact scenes in different academic disciplines. When you are finished reading about them, it is my hope that you will know these students as you might know characters in a play or as you know students in your own particular classrooms.

The major concern of ethnography lies with "the study of lived experience" (Brodkey 1987a, 25). One of my case study informants—Nick—described this perspective in an essay: "Experience is most useful when it is lived through; it is not a by-product of living." An ethnographic account gives you then, the lived-through experience of informants' lives, by means of the ethnographer's lens.

The methodological/ethical/aesthetic questions of ethnography become then: What exactly is the ethnographer's lens? To what extent does the researcher's perspective reveal that of the informants? How does this double lens attach to reality? and finally, Does the construction of the ethnographic perspective take place in the writing or in the research? The act of writing about people and settings, as ethnographers finally do, must involve some degree of distortion, some manipulation of descriptions and interview data in order to present it. Clifford Geertz has recently disclosed his feeling that in the end "all ethnographical descriptions are homemade, that they are the describer's descriptions, not those of the described" (1988, 145). And yet that is necessarily so, since field notes, interviews, life histories, or historical documents do not contain the "reality" of the informants' lives. They must be interpreted by the ethnographer whose understandings are often shared with the informants. Geertz (1988) has disclaimed "thick descriptions" alone as the means by which ethnographies create verisimilitude. Instead, he suggests, the credibility of ethnography comes from the reader's acceptance of the ethnographer's ability to depict having been there, having captured the drama of the participants' everyday scenes.

Readers of ethnographic accounts feel as if they are participating in the very texture of the informants' lives, because, I think, ethnography, like literature, yields a different kind of reality, another type of knowledge. Ethnography provides, just as literature does, a sense of the universality in life, as well as the feeling of "being there," of having participated in an experience. And at the same time ethnography provides instances of the particular, of instructive cases and situations, as does the work of Erikson, Freud, and Piaget. Thus this field-based naturalistic research captures both the universal and the specific, granting this methodology a double seam of scholarship.

Circles of Literacy

This vertical view of reality is a lie ... We live in a circle, not along a line.
Cheatham & Powell
This Way Daybreak Comes

The research for this book takes place within overlapping and interrelated contexts that blur the boundaries between the history of the university and the life stories of the students, between public and private discourse, between learning and literacy, between researching then and writing now.

The first chapter, "Anatomy of a Discourse Community: Prose Writing," describes a process-oriented, college writing course at UNH taught by my colleague Donna Qualley. Prose Writing class provided the entry point of my research, where I asked the ethnographer's question, What goes on here? In this classroom context I located two willing participants to help me pursue the research questions that ripple throughout the study. The two case studies of Anna and Nick constitute the heart of this book. In these chapters, I look at both informants in the concentric contexts of a writing course and their major fields of art history and political science. The final chapter, "The Discourse of Discourse Communities," is devoted to a discussion and comparison of the literacy practices in the three academic settings where I did my research. In the final chapter I also offer my overall observations about literacy in higher education and outline some suggested directions for further research. As the quotation for this section suggests, the dominant learning pattern in the university reinforces a hierarchical and vertical pedagogical paradigm that needs considerable rethinking.

In any ethnography there are overlapping matrices, circles within circles within circles of discourse. In this study there is a juxtaposition of literature and composition; of art history and studio art; of political science and politics. But mainly there is a conflict between the public and private discourses of the two key informants, Anna and Nick. I hope you will find this account of literacy and learning in a university setting as rich and complex as it is in the actual lives of those whose stories you will share.

Anatomy of a Discourse Community

1

Prose Writing

Yet only through communication can human life hold meaning. The teacher's thinking is authenticated only by the authenticity of the students' thinking. The teacher cannot think for his students, nor can he impose his thought on them. Authentic thinking, thinking that is concerned about reality, does not take place in ivory tower isolation, but only in communication.

Paulo Freire

Pedagogy of the Oppressed

*I*ntroduction to Prose Writing (English 501) does not begin as a cohesive community; with few exceptions students do not know one another before the course starts, nor do they have common majors. As juniors and seniors in a university setting, however, the students do share speech habits and classroom behaviors that distinguish them from many other language communities, from their noncollegiate high school contemporaries, for example. Within a few days and within the fairly artificial context of a college classroom, the Prose Writing instructor and the students construct a discourse community, an extended family unit that functions as a support system for students' exploration of personal and intellectual literacy development.

One Teacher Scholar: Donna Qualley

The teacher for Prose Writing—Donna Qualley—is part of the English department's composition staff, which includes twelve nontenured but renewable instructorships. This core faculty, along with the English department's many teaching assistants, assumes the work load of introductory writing courses. Only occasionally do tenured faculty teach the two beginning writing courses (Freshman English or Prose Writing).

Donna's office is located in Hamilton-Smith Hall on the third floor, which can only be reached by climbing the back, not the central, stairs in the building, an indication of the marginal status of composition as a subdiscipline in this department. Still other composition staff members are tucked away in small basement offices or converted spaces.

Greeting the students who work with the third-floor composition staff are two tin buckets, which catch dripping water from a leak in the building's ceiling so old that rust has formed on the surrounding wall area. A flurry of administrative memos suggests some remorse over this indecorous condition. The last memo promises that when funds are found, the leak will be fixed. Composition teachers share one hall phone which receives only incoming calls and rings constantly with messages for the twenty or more instructors who have offices there. The regular tenure-track English faculty all have phones, personal computers, and private offices.

In spite of the low pay, high student contact hours, and crowded conditions, the morale of the composition staff is enthusiastic and familial. In between the eight to sixteen hours of weekly student conferences (depending on the number of courses taught), doors fly open and colleagues seek one another for advice, for feedback on student papers, and for relief from the intensity of conferencing. Students waiting to have their writing conferences line the narrow hallways throughout the English department building, lounging on the floor with their backpacks as they reread their drafts.

Donna prefers teaching morning classes and can be found in her office as early as seven o'clock, drinking coffee and reading student papers. An energetic "thirty-something" woman who wears colorful, informal clothes, Donna is both playful and serious. Well known for her vigorous laugh and good sense of humor, she can also be caught fingering her mouth lightly as she prepares for her classes or chewing sugarless cinnamon gum, nervous mannerisms she attributes to her former chain smoking. At the Australian high school where she taught for nine years, students voted her at various times in their yearbook as Best-Looking, Best-Dressed, Best Sense of Humor, and Loudest-Voiced Female.

Donna's graduate education is not in literature nor in creative writing, the more traditional training of this composition staff; instead she holds an M.S.T. in English from the University of New Hampshire, a degree that allows flexibility in selecting graduate coursework in writing, language, education, and literature. Donna has received excellent evaluations in the three years she has been an instructor and keeps up with her field through reading, writing, and attending and presenting papers at professional conferences. Prior to her graduate work, when Donna taught English in Morwell High School in Victoria, Australia, she proposed a language and learning policy for her school and was the faculty adviser for the student newspaper.

It was in Australia that Donna was first attracted to the process approach to teaching writing through the work of Donald Graves. Because Donna lived in a communal household in Australia, she agrees that Graves's emphasis on "a community of learners" initially appealed to her. When she returned to America, studying with Graves became one of her main reasons for coming to the University of New Hampshire to further her education. Initially the works of both Donald Graves and Donald Murray were the major influences on Donna's thinking as a college-level writing teacher. Over time she has folded many other new ideas into her writing curriculum.

Introduction to Prose Writing: The Curriculum

Prose Writing was originally designed as a new course by Donald Murray at the request of his departmental chair in 1966. Its purpose was to offer students further experiences in writing exposition after their mandated freshman writing course. In its inception, Introduction to Prose Writing incorporated all the innovations that Murray's process approach to teaching writing heralded: frequent conferences, student writing as the major text instead of professional rhetorics or readers, peer-feedback workshops, and extensive revision.

Prose Writing is now an English department prerequisite for all advanced coursework in writing. There are never enough sections of this sophomore-level course offered to satisfy student requests because so many other departments at the university require their majors to take it—outdoor education, wildlife management, business, and communication just to name a few. As a result, Prose Writing is often enrolled with upperclass men and women instead of sophomores. And in spite of its demand across the curriculum, Prose Writing is a fairly undefined course, not explicitly serving to enculturate students into writing for other disciplines as many other universities have accomplished by creating "writing-intensive" courses.

Although special sections of this course are offered in technical, persuasive, research, and critical writing, it is left up to writing instructors rather than the English department to seek approval for these topics. Donna Qualley did not offer her course as a "special section," but the summer before she taught it, she did some rigorous rethinking about the Prose Writing course under consideration here.

Much of her reflection came after reading Bartholomae and Petrosky's book, *Facts, Artifacts and Counterfacts* (1986), which describes and discusses a college-level, integrated reading and writing curriculum. Donna subsequently chose to add Bartholomae and Petrosky's student anthology, *Ways of Reading* (1987), to her Prose Writing course to encourage students to draw on the readings for framing their weekly papers. This decision is explained in her paper written for a graduate seminar ("A New Beginning Place: theory/Theory" 1987). Here Donna expresses a need to challenge the assumption held by some University of New Hampshire writing teachers that open topics *automatically* foster independence. By not offering students some structure for their weekly writing, Donna suggests "we might just be shackling them with a different kind of manacle" (1987, 6). Donna's solution to students overconcern with finding paper topics was to experiment with introducing a reader in her writing course.

Ways of Reading includes a wide range of challenging modern essays and short stories (Berger, "Ways of Seeing"; Dillard, "The Fixed"; Rodriguez, "The Achievement of Desire"; Freire, "The Banking Concept of Education") as well as contemporary fiction (Carver, "What We Talk About When We Talk About Love"; Oates, "Theft"; Bellow, "A Silver Dish"—just to list a few of the writers included in this anthology).

Donna's redesigned course syllabus for Prose Writing (see Appendix A) encourages students to connect their reading and writing: She states, "We will use reading and writing to find out what we have to say—what we think about a subject." Her syllabus also reveals a very tightly constructed course with four major pedagogical strands—reading, writing, rhetorical forms, and collaboration—to be accomplished within three feedback structures—group work, individual conferences, and journal writing. This model for engagement with reading and writing reflects a social view of literacy which Donna also spells out ("this class will work through interaction") and underscores with her attendance rule that "two unexcused class absences lower the grade by a full letter."

Such interactive social processes are woven into the course in the form of small reading and writing groups, which meet eight times during the semester, and into the final writing assignment of a collaborative group paper. A dialogue between teacher and student is built into the course through bimonthly fifteen-minute conferences and through student journal responses, which are read and returned on an alternating weekly schedule. From the one-on-one conference to peer group work, from informal hand-written journals to formal revised papers, from open paper topics to assigned essay reflections, from teacher evaluation to self-evaluation, Donna invites many learning styles and provides diverse opportunities for developing literacy in this university classroom.

Opening Moves: "Queen for a Day"

On a typical day, students who arrive early for class read news-papers, drink coffee or sodas, but mainly talk with one another. Nick enters wearing jeans torn at the knees, a red bandanna covering his head, and a single earring—portraying the image of a modern-day pirate. Anna has on a rumpled skirt, a long unbelted blouse that matches the green of her eyes, sandals, and a turquoise ribbon around her neck, making her seem carelessly arty. These two students, who become the key informants, display distinctive dress styles, which reflect the distinctive writing voices you will later hear.

The class meets in an irregularly shaped room where students assemble around a series of square tables pulled together in the middle. Fixed carrels line the perimeters of the room to provide space for students to write in privacy. Overall, the room is well set up, with ample space and moveable furniture for the group work that characterizes this course. Terri, who is reading hor-oscopes aloud from the *Boston Globe*, asks Carlos, a Russian studies major, if he knows what "obsequious" means. Without missing a beat, Carlos replies, "submissive and willing to serve," and then turns to Anna to show her a sketch he's drawn. Anna, who's an art history major, cradles her hot coffee as she comments on the drawing. Nick, a political science major, fiddles with the cartridge for his fountain pen, an instrument critical for the writing and drawing he executes with great care.

As students trickle into the classroom, they talk about the possibility of war with Iran, a fairly removed political issue for these New England students.

"Iran declared war against us."

"Is there going to be a draft?"

"The stock market crashed. If we have a war, that will help the economy."

"How can you say that we need a war? That's sick."

"There couldn't be a war with Iran. It would be over in a week. They're right on the Soviet border."

"We wouldn't need troops, we'd use air power."

Donna enters the room smiling. She's wearing loose red cotton pants, a multicolored flowered shirt, high-topped red tennis shoes and an emblematic ceramic pig pin from her hog-raising days in Australia. She carries an armload of student journals and papers, plops it down, picks up a copy of a paper left from a previous class, and reads the title aloud to no one in particular: "'My Sister Survived the Rapids.' That sounds like your trip, Laurie." Laurie, an exchange student from Chico State, laughs, remembering her recent dunking on a canoe trip.

Donna tells nearby students that Alexandria is entered in the Miss New Hampshire beauty pageant and that if it didn't cost $25 a head to go, she'd arrange a field trip to offer moral support. When students ask Allie about the contest, she tells them that this is her second try, that last year the judges had asked her a sexist question about her ideal man which she found offensive.

Tina ends a side discussion of being carded: "And then they asked if I was in the eighth grade!" Donna picks up on this thread by saying she loves to be carded since it makes her feel young. Tim, a former football player and bouncer at a local bar, suggests, "Come to Harry's on Tuesday night and I'll card you, Donna." Sarah tells the students around her that she saw Donna on Saturday night at Bayside Seafood in her red and blue waitressing uniform, balancing trays. For the many students in this class who also hold part-time jobs—both of my key informants—Donna's waitressing in order to support her "habit" of teaching composition lends her real-world credibility.

There is some juggling of papers and hurried board work before the class "officially" begins. Alisha rushes in, out-of-breath, harassed, and somewhat embarrassed. "I have a story," she claims, and the class gets ready for her "Queen-for-a-Day" narrative.

"Queen for a Day" was a 1950s afternoon game show hosted by Bess Meyerson and Jack Bailey in which housewives shared their hard-luck stories. The most unfortunate sat on a fake throne telling their tales while the audience cheered: the winner, judged by meter applause, briefly paraded down a runway in a mink stole and rhinestone tiara. This language event entered Donna's Prose Writing class when she invited students who had been put on the waiting list for the class to explain why they needed to add Prose Writing to their schedules. Although there were some basic rules to her "Queen-for-a-Day" game — graduating seniors required to take Prose Writing had priority — the better the narration of the story, the better the chance the student had of adding the course. After the first class session, Donna found notes stuck to her door relating desperate situations: "I have crew practice every morning, afternoon, and evening and can only fit in your section of Prose Writing" or "The computer closed me out of all preregistered courses and I will lose my scholarship tommorow if I can't get into your section."

Alisha ends her narrative with a rush of explanations: "And they were about to tow my car but George saved me and then I had to move it and I then couldn't find a new space, and then I was late." Students clap for George's heroism and make room for Alisha as she organizes her overstuffed bags on the floor.

Donna remarks, "Your life is made up of Queen-for-a-Day stories." Alisha retorts, "You should live it."

Agenda for the Day: Collaboration

Following the opening moves of the class, students typically engage in a variety of reading and writing activities: in-class writing, journal responses, peer editing groups, or whole-class discussions, just to mention a few. This day's agenda centers around collaborative writing projects, an activity that came during the last third of the course when all the routines and rituals were well established for this group of learners. For the collaborative writing assignment each group of students was required to find a triggering article from the library for a paper topic, negotiate a way of working together, and develop a strategy for drafting the paper as a group.

Students have inquired about the collaborative project earlier in the term; their questions, such as "Will we get to choose who we want to work with?" reveal that they're anxious about being paired with someone they may not get along with well. Donna negotiates this potential problem by having them each submit several partner choices, making sure that everyone gets at least one of their selections. When Carlos asks, "Will I have to clean my apartment?" he anticipates the intimacy that some of the collaborative groups, particularly his own, will experience. The question "How will it be graded?" exposes the way that college students allot time to projects according to the grade potential. Donna assigns a group grade for the paper and an individual grade for the collaborative journal that accompanies it. She describes the journal as a kind of "safety net" for them, since students hypothetically could earn a C on the group paper but an A on their individual journals.

When Donna presents the format of the project (see Appendix B for collaborative writing project description), she suggests that it has two agendas. One, she tells students, is the "hidden curriculum" of getting them into the library, looking through selected newspapers, journals, and literary magazines for an article to "trigger" the group paper. But the more explicit agenda of collaborative writing, she says, is an exercise in "working with people" and in "problem solving." Donna explains that the image of writers struggling in their garrets, immersed and lonely for the sake of art is not the only way people write. "We're going to see what it's like to write together," Donna challenges them.

Donna announces that for the remainder of this class period students will be involved with their collaborative group work. In a scraping of chairs, squeaking of tennis shoes, and shuffling of backpacks, students find spaces to form groups to begin work. Tim's sniffle from his allergies carries across the room. Everyone turns toward Donna whenever she lets forth her wild laugh. Nick straddles two chairs, settling his worn-out boots on one. Connie takes to the floor. Linda, almost six feet tall, always looks like a kindergartener in these chairs. Randy wears his baseball cap during the whole class. George has on his camouflage ROTC pants. Before the group work begins, Alisha and Terri, the glamour girls, sneak in a few snips of gossip. Neil comments on the latest music groups and Laurie reports on her surfer boyfriend. Within this hum of activity and diversity of personalities, these students show amazing concentration for learning about reading and writing through group work.

As Donna mills around, dropping in on different groups, I join Connie, David, and Anna's group. They're busy discussing the theme common to their articles: the dehumanization of man.

Their plan is to write a short story in which three people face a problem situation, such as being trapped in an elevator, and show how the characters were unable to solve the problem of getting out. (Is their plan, I speculate, a reflection of how they face the collaborative project as three strangers trying to work their way out of a problem?) Anna asks what kind of handicap one character should be given in order to suggest a new type of intelligence, a kind of caring that the other characters couldn't share. David notes that the character of the robotics company executive will have to speak with highly technical language. When they try to decide what sex to make each character, Connie says, "Make them all genderless." The group's running so smoothly that I am not surprised later when I learn that they write every word of their paper together in front of a computer. But this very lack of group tension later becomes an issue that Connie addresses in her journal:

Our group process was pretty smooth. There were no stressful moments that created anxiety, so there was nothing exciting to reflect on and try to reframe. For some strange reason, I believe that people learn best when faced with stressful situations that create dissonance. By striving to adapt to disharmony, one learns.

I cause the only dissonance for this group and my researcher interference was noted by both Anna and Connie in their journals. Connie wrote: "Unfortunately I don't think we got very much accomplished today. It seems like we spent most of the time going over everything so that Elizabeth could understand it all. I think that it was good in one way."

When I wander over and sit in on another group, that of Tim, Laurie, and Alisha, I enter a wasps' nest of arguing, cranky students. Although they have selected a topic—how to tell the terminally ill that they are dying—they seem sulky about it and can't get a grip on how to proceed from topic choice to the next stage. (I wonder if this reflects the complexity of the decision-making process within their topic). Alisha wants them to do library research: She writes in her journal, "I mean how the hell can you form an opinion without knowing your subject?" Laurie would prefer to go off and write the whole paper on her own. "I've never experienced such a difficult process," she records in her journal, "Writing a paper on my own is so much easier and a great deal more fun. ... When I write a paper by myself I just sit down and write what's on my mind and later organize. ... Working in a group entails organizing ourselves *before* we write." Tim, who wanted to write about the candidates for the presidential primary, ends up valuing the experience more than his two partners because he sees in it an application to future situations: "I call this collaboration project hands-on training. This has been the best orientation to a businesslike setting I have gone through so far in my education. Our education tends to be so individualistic."

A fairly sour combination turns out to be Mary, Randy, and George, a group that can't agree on a triggering article from among the twelve they have read. Instead, they decide to wrap the paper around song lyrics, a consensual decision that is counter to the outline of the project description because Donna stated explicitly that students must use a written text (periodical article, literature, trade or textbook) to trigger the topic. Randy seems earnest about group work but, according to the student journals, has tried too hard to assume leadership. Mary writes that Randy "wanted to run the show, be the leader." George, a fine writer, became a resistant collaborator who saw the major problem as one of time management: "As time is used up understanding how each person thinks, time for the project slips away. The result will usually be a product that is passed in, while still in transition, to meet the deadline ... I really can't see how this paper will say anything" (George's journal).

I watch Nick, Tina, and Neil working intently on a computer diagram of male-female relationships that emerged from the combined ideas of their triggering essays. Once the diagram is accomplished, the paper will explain the model, they tell me. Journal entries reveal that this system of working has both stimulated and inhibited their paper. Nick writes:

Great. Now we've got a systematic model, incorporating the various aspects of the love "orbit." So ... What's the paper actually about? Er ... well ... As Tina asserted three or four times, correctly, we haven't figured out what, why, or how to begin writing anything useful. She pointed out our distinct lack of theme: We've nothing of importance to say.

Neil, the inventor of the model, feels that it has symbolized the collaborative process: "When I look at the diagram we constructed I realize why the most amazing discoveries are usually made by teams of people ... the interaction between us is better than the sum of our individual ideas" (Neil's journal).

Allie and Terri approach me to borrow my tape recorder for the weekend. They've decided that they want to capture their own talk about the articles and then try to rework their real dialogue into a fictionalized conversation like a Raymond Carver story, a piece they've shared in reading groups. Their problem later becomes similar to that of Connie's group: too much agreement, in their case over the topic of birth control. Allie writes that "the project was dying in its birth" because of their total agreement with one another. Terri suggests in hindsight that they could have "created a conflict right from the beginning instead of when we hit a dead end" (Terri's journal).

A duo that appears to be working well is Sarah and Carlos, whom I do *not* interrupt. I know that Sarah was the only student in class who volunteered to work with Carlos and that most students feel intimidated by his intensity. This group's topic is mate expectations, triggered by an Aldous Huxley article and Raymond Carver short story. Sarah is intent on trying to understand Carlos: "I've never met someone so confident and yet so unsure of himself," she writes. Carlos initially sees himself on the defensive: "I don't trust her, her me, and in this somehow we trust each other? No, nothing makes sense" (Carlos's journal).

The final group of three women — Jane, Linda, and Sarah — has agreed on a short story to trigger the idea of whether or not people are actually restricted by their circumstances or if people trap themselves. This group, too, has been influenced by the format of Carver's short story and they've decided to write a three-way fictionalized conversation among college roommates about being trapped.

The journal entries from this group indicate that each student wrote a complete draft separately and then came together to collaborate. This is where the problem of writing together surfaced: "As I was writing ... I would put myself into each character and try to see who they were from what they were saying ... but the problem was that it didn't fit in with Sarah or Linda's paper" (Jane's journal).

For the three-week period while students work on their writing projects, collaborative group sessions take the majority of class time. After working together, the class usually reconvenes with Donna to discuss where they're headed. After she reviews due dates for journals, new papers, peer writing responses, and reading-group selections, she adds: "I realize you have to orchestrate a lot of things here but I like to have a complex class."

Literacy Structures

So far we've considered how this particular community is formed through literacy opportunities that are available in most college classrooms. From an analysis of what went on in Donna's class over the course of one semester, there emerge four processes that support learning and undergird students' membership in this discourse community: (1) how talk supports learning; (2) how texts support learning; (3) how writing supports learning; (4) how discipline-specific thinking supports learning. Academic discourse communities provide only temporary settings for learning to occur, yet if the literacy opportunities are explicit and meaningful, when the community disbands, those literacy structures will serve as intellectual scaffolds for students' academic work in other disciplines. A further analysis of these classroom literacy supports will suggest that the more conscious students are of the reading, writing, talking, and habits of mind that characterize a discipline, the more articulate they become, not only about *what* they are learning but of *how* they are learning as well.

How Talk Is Used: Narrative Conversations ■ Much of the talk that went on in Donna's section of Prose Writing can be described as informal, collaborative, and narrative; as growing out of and relating back to stories about students' lives. Narrative thinking, Jerome Bruner (1986) asserts, is distinguished from logico-scientific thought and constructs an entirely different worldview. Narrative conversations that infuse university classrooms like Donna's assume a very different view of academic literacy from that of the traditional lecture model.

The narrative discourse style of this class exemplified in its "Queen-for-a-Day" stories suggests that language can be appropriated by a particular group for its own use. "Queen-for-a-Day" stories marked the rituals of the course. When students had problems with submitting papers, being late to class, or showing up for conferences, they needed a good story. Not all students desired the "Queen-for-a-Day" label. Tim, for example, wrote a note on one of his papers: "There is no queen story—this is just late." This language story was singular to this community, with the term "Queen for a Day" part of the insider language system, the origin of which is impenetrable to outsiders. This informal language event also bound the class together by inviting stories and personal narratives into the classroom because, as Joan Didion suggests, "We tell stories in order to live."

A narrative conversational style sets the tone of the course as a place where students could speak without inhibition about their personal lives. Tim puts it this way: "I don't think anyone is scared to speak out in Donna's class." For a learning-disabled student such as Tim—who needed a note taker for his political science lecture courses — a chance both to talk and to listen meant a welcome change.

This narrative conversational style contrasts dramatically with the interrogative model that dominates schooling. Here's the only moment recorded in my field notes in which Donna uses the "cheerleading chant" of questioning. When she asks, "What you decide to write about is called what?" her students choral response is, "the triggering subject." When she then asks, "What you actually write about is called what?" her students all chime, "the real subject." In this speech event, both the students and Donna know that there is a single answer for her cheer.

In contrast, Donna uses a more cooperative but still interrogative style of talk as recorded here:

Donna: What's the purpose of education in our society? Is it to ensure the dominant values?
Allie: Sure. It's connected with patriotism. I remember saluting the flag and writing an essay in eighth grade on "What Memorial Day Means to Me."

In the second exchange, there's still a question-and-answer model, but with no one right response. Further, Allie feels free to embellish her answer with a personal anecdote.

In the following class discussion of Paulo Freire's "The Banking Concept of Education" (Bartholomae and Petrosky 1987), notice the narrative layering of this conversation, clearly not a planned "lesson." Donna initiates some open-ended questions but her students have the most turns talking. Notice too how the affective response to the reading is fostered, how students are encouraged to discuss what Louise Rosenblatt calls the "lived-through experience of reading" before talking about what they have learned or what they take away in terms of concepts.[1]

Donna: Was this [Freire] hard to read?
Randy: I thought it was redundant.
Tina: I didn't have any problem at all.
Donna: Why was it easier for you?
Tina: I could relate to it. It had a lot to say.

---

[1] Rosenblatt has adapted this phrase from a poem by Keats, "On Sitting Down To Read King Lear Once Again," in which the poet refers to the "burned through experience of reading King Lear" (1978, 26–27).

Anna: I got the main idea in the first two pages and then he repeated himself.

Neil: I identified with it.

Alisha: I thought that in a sense Freire was making a mockery of students. He was criticizing students as much as teachers. "You're too stupid to see this," he says.

Allie: I was taken by Freire's categorizing everyone as a man. We're using his essay in another class. I'm not a feminist but I wondered why he kept addressing everyone as "man." Why is that?

Donna: It can put you off after a while.

Tony: It didn't bother me at all.

Allie: That's because you're a man.

Some students imply here that the repetitive, almost redundant and sexist tone of Freire's essay has bothered them while others say they "identified" or "related" to it. Without siding with either response, Donna accepts both and, like many women engaged in conversation, uses questions to keep the class discussion going.[2]

As students further explore Freire's essay, they uncover the key ideas of "problem posing" and "banking" and yet the affective issue in reading the essay is never entirely left behind. David's comments echo Alisha's earlier concern that Friere is mocking students in his essay:

David: I didn't like this reading the first time. I thought it was making fun of how I had been educated.

Donna: How did it make you feel?

David: It made me feel hostile as I read it.

Donna: Why?

David: I understood his position the second time I read it and I didn't feel so hostile. And I did understand why he was exiled for sixteen years. These are radical ideas.

Neil: Remember that he criticized a method of education that made him what he became. He went through this system himself.

David: He called for a liberating education through acts of cognition. How do you get this education without a formal basis?

---

[2] Cambridge (1987), and Ginet-McConnell (1989) have written review articles synthesizing the research on gender and communication. Although there is no consensus of findings because of differences in samples, contexts, and purposes for the research, some studies suggest that women use questions to maintain conversations, while men regard them as informational requests.

After David expresses his feelings about reading the essay, he tries to put his finger on just why he had those personal responses. But it is Nick, not Donna, who assumes the leadership role in answering David's question, responding with an illustrative narrative from his childhood:

Little kids are always picking up things and thinking about it. My mom let me make associations by myself. I understand what he means by problem posing. He doesn't describe it but characterizes it. I learned to think through my mom. I understand that kind of one-on-one interplay. Maybe it's impossible to do this in school education. But it's two people together. It's a consciousness of consciousness, being aware of directing your own thinking. You can direct it yourself. You don't need a formal education.

Donna and her class continue to weigh the two pedagogical extremes that emerge in many of the class readings: education as dialectical interplay and education as banking. As this whole class conversation continues, Donna encourages students to draw on their own lives, to tell stories, like Nick has, about their educational experiences. She draws them out by asking what they think of their lecture courses in college.

Alisha: I think you could be learning but not know it. For instance, you can choose to be an observer or a sponge, but I don't think that's learning. This semester I'm taking entomology, which is the study of bugs. I had to overcome my fear of touching them. I find now that I'm learning, I'm interested in it, and the course is giving me some knowledge.

Donna: So it's not just that information is deposited in us that Freire is arguing against then; it's that we don't do anything with it?

Nick: As a kid I was curious about everything. This guy [Freire] would say that our curiosity is stagnated. A lot of people don't get to go to college and get the chance to feel curiosity again. This is the privilege of a college education.

Linda: Yes, this class is more like problem posing. In high school I had this chemistry teacher who intimidated me—he'd say, "This is the easiest question I will ever ask you." But then I had this vocabulary class called Words, Words, Words, and we talked about words and meanings and it was open like this class.

Neil: I find courses in college a lot more interesting.

Mary: Is that because you're paying for them?

Neil: Yes, but you're encouraged to think more. They could have done more with my biology course in high school. The teacher gave us ten phylum to memorize and on the test were ten blanks to fill in. I can't remember any of it now.

In the previous conversation, Donna's open, affective question about college courses ("How do you feel . . . ?") encouraged Alisha, Nick, Linda, and Neil to contribute more narratives about their schooling, stories that reflect on and critique their previous and ongoing learning experiences. Tina offers the final story from this section of the transcript:

> I went to a private school and it was so different. I made so many connections. We were forced to think. Some of my high school classes make college look like nothing. He [Freire] mentions in his essay that we don't teach teachers to learn from students. I remember that I showed one of my high school teachers how to do a trig proof and he was really grateful. I taught him something. The purpose of school is that you're not so much learning what they are teaching. Our teachers were there to *teach us the process—not the banking concept, but how to make connections.* (emphasis added)

Most students in this particular section of the Prose Writing course attest that they have not had another college class (except for Freshman Composition) where they were allowed to talk in an unstructured, conversational way. Tim compares Prose Writing with his political science classes: "The banking concept is so boring. Being able to speak your mind, and having something to speak your mind about makes this class so much more interesting."

Donna's classroom provides many occasions for students to talk in small and large groups about their reading and writing processes, often reinforced by journal reflections. These layers of narrative talk help shape students' ways of thinking and eventually shape what they will write. Douglas Barnes has argued for the cooperative power of talk and writing within the curriculum: "Not only is talking and writing a major means by which people learn, but what they learn can often hardly be distinguished from the ability to communicate it. Learning to communicate is at the heart of education" (1976, 20).

Like all academic disciplines, then, this community is bound primarily through language, which serves as both the subject of study and the process through which learning takes place. With language as the center of this writing classroom, much of the learning comes through talk. From the outset of this Prose Writing course students use talk, along with writing, to reflect, to describe and narrate, to explicate and analyze, to persuade and argue, and to construct meaning.

Response forums: public, peer, private   One of the ways this community works is through the spiral of response forums that includes whole-group public talk, small peer-group talk, and private conversations—either one-on-one conferences with Donna or a written dialogue through journal responses. In the following conversation, Donna poses a question to the class about the differences between "essaying and storytelling" based on a series of shared class readings. She opens the discussion with a question: "Stories, you suggest, help us make sense of our lives. Is this just true of fiction or does that fit essays too?" Students offer the following possible suggestions to explain the difference between the two rhetorical forms:

Randy: There's more of an outer self in an essay. Essays are just a different way of telling the story.

Anna: Some things can be the same but stories are more an explanation of the soul. But in both stories and essays, ideas can be explored.

Alisha: Stories give the whole picture and essays a selection of the picture.

Donna: Is an essay more organized then?

Anna: A story allows you to personalize more. There are more observations in fiction. When you read an essay you read what one person saw. But a reader can make a story your own more easily because it doesn't belong so much to one writer.

Randy: The essay is more like one mind to another. The story is more heart-to-heart.

Nick: You can't argue in a story but you can argue in an essay.

Donna: The line is shaky then?

In this public, collaborative conversation, Donna accepts all responses as she pulls through the thread of student contributions to the discussion to point out that the distinctions among rhetorical forms are "shaky," what anthropologist Clifford Geertz refers to as the "blurring of genres" (1983). Donna weaves as many voices as possible into her class discussion.

Small peer-group discussions reveal students continuing to focus on the topic of form in writing, an influence carried over from whole-group talks. Here's a snippet of peer conversation from a reading group about Bellow's short story "The Silver Dish," with Anna, Carlos, and Mary in the group.

Mary: This is easier reading than an essay. It reads quicker.

Carlos: You get just as much out of them, don't you think?

Anna: Well, I like reading short stories but it's much harder for me to react and say just how I reacted and these are the connections I made. When I read short stories, I usually get images and stuff. I usually don't take that much out. Maybe because I don't study them.

Mary: I think with short stories, you don't need to study them because sometimes they are a lot lighter, you know?

Anna: I think they are much heavier.

Mary: Oh, you think so?

Anna: Because you have to search for things. Essays are like, "This is what I think and this is the way I see it." And there's a point and you can take it or leave it. But with a short story, I mean, I can guess at the meaning but I don't know. You know what I mean?

In peer-group discussions, students do not always agree with one another. Clearly, Anna disagrees with Mary about fiction being easier to read, and with Carlos about her getting just as much out of a short story. All three students, however, use the model of an open question format much like Donna's in their small-group talks.

The private conversation in this class—a dialogue between student and teacher—occurs either in the written journal exchange or orally in the biweekly conferences. For instance, David considered the purpose of the essay genre in a journal entry. Since he had previously turned in two fiction pieces to Donna—a form unacceptable for a prose-writing class—David had personal reasons to reflect on the differences in rhetorical forms. In this journal entry, he's responding to Donna's previous comments:

In one of your journal comments, you stated that essayists write for an elite group of readers. This fact is becoming apparent in the selections from Bartholomae (*Ways of Reading*) that we are reading. ... You never completely get these essays because that's one of the things reflective bodies of writing do best. They suggest an area or topic and you the reader, log the information into your own mind, then filter an opinion that's pertinent to your understanding. My favorite line: "What essayists do; they observe minutely and reflect deeply."

Through this circle of public and private conversations, often reinforced with reflective journal writing, students first discuss literacy concepts together and then pull some of these ideas into their peer and private responses. What seem to be meandering classroom conversations assume particular shapes as students draw from the large-group talk for the conversations in their small groups, their teacher conferences, and their journal writing.

Demonstrations: Writing-Response Groups ■ In addition to learning through collaborative conversations and response groups, students also learn new literacy concepts through teacher-led classroom demonstrations, what Nancie Atwell calls the mini-lesson (1987). These modeling sessions may cover useful writing skills such as Donna's lesson on "leads as a kind of window-shopping," followed by some practice on lead writing, or her demonstration of "revision as re-seeing," followed by an examination of multiple drafts of student papers. In the following classroom episode, Donna demonstrates a way for her students to participate in their writing groups.

Modeling in conference   Donna sets up the modeling session ahead of time by suggesting that "the purpose of a writing group is feedback, not a critique. You give feedback to a work in progress." She then asks for a student to volunteer a draft in progress for the next class session. Carlos comes forward with a paper Donna hasn't read yet, titled *Oblomov*.[3] When Donna later reads the paper before copying it for the workshop demonstration, she wonders why Carlos wants to share it and further wonders what the paper is really about. So obscure is the Russian reference in his paper's title that Donna at first thinks Carlos has confused "oblomov" with the word "obelisk."

The paper is about the Russian novel *Oblomov*, which has a main character by the same name. However, Carlos does not tell the reader who this Oblomov is but presents a modern interpretation of this Russian character's personality on the assumption that the reader already knows the novel. Carlos, who's also enrolled in a Russian literature survey course, writes in this paper:

Let's look at a twentieth century Oblomov: Perhaps you have found yourself in dire need of some company because you don't like to go out alone. You're aware of how you look to the opposite sex alone: threatening. So you call up that one friend you know will look good next to you ..."

Coincidentally, before the class demonstration, Donna holds her regularly scheduled writing conference with Carlos, in which she explains her difficulty in reading his paper. While praising his efforts — "I applaud what you are trying to do with this; I'm sitting here in this cheering section saying, "Go to it, Carlos" — Donna admits that she can be an audience for his paper only to a certain extent because: "I don't have this background knowledge. I don't have that particular knowledge, not having read this particular Russian novel."

In this conference, Carlos finally agrees that the class will need some background information on the novel in order to

---

[3] *Oblomov* is the title of a novel by Ivan Goncharov, Russian author 1812–1891.

understand his paper. But he badgers Donna by implying that she should be able to understand his highly personalized reinterpretation of the novel. Donna responds in this conference by being very specific about where she's having trouble with his text:

Donna: But here in this part, I don't know what the narrator is remembering. [*Reads from his paper*] "A wedding that never took place, a love affair that went askew ..."

Carlos: Jesus, Donna, you call yourself a woman and you can't put that together? Come on. I left a lot of things out purposefully.

Donna: What does this have to do with my womanhood, the fact that I can't put this together?

Modeling in class   Carlos is an older returning student who often assumed a defensive attitude in class and conference and takes such a stance in the subsequent class discussion of his "Oblomov" paper. After reading the paper, the class members wrestle, as Donna had, to provide a context for what he has written. Even after Carlos summarizes the novel for them, some students wear quizzical looks. Connie is the first to indicate to Carlos that she is stumped in some places:

Connie: I think I got out of it what I was supposed to. But in the last page, I got kind of lost there.

Carlos: That's me. That's where I turn my attention away from my friend and write about me and why I'm like him. And I purposely used that part there because that's the truth, that's my own experience and I related to it; if you'd read *Oblomov*, you'd know that.

Donna: Okay. So they haven't.

Connie: I kind of get that part — that you're turning it back but *if you could expand on that part* ...[4]

Carlos: Everybody goes through an experience ...

Donna: Whoa. You're *justifying* and I want you just to *acknowledge*.

Carlos: Oh. I just wanted to clear it up. She asked me a question.

Donna: She said, "Can you expand?" And as the writer you can take that away and think about it. I'm butting in here. If it turns into the writer saying "What I'm trying to do here," no one will get feedback because you'll be explaining your paper. What the readers are saying is that whatever your intentions are for the paper, it's not working

---

[4] There are a number of transcript conventions used by linguists to indicate interruptions in the flow of conversation (see, for example, West and Zimmerman in *Language, Gender and Society* 102–17). Here, following the work of Dale Spender in *Man Made Language* (1985, 85–90), I am using three dots to show interruptions in the conversation.

for me. Just take that comment and go back and do with it whatever you wish.

In this minilesson, Donna's demonstrating how students are to respond in their small writing groups where, as members of this writing community, they give *considered response* and *acknowledge* feedback, but don't *justify* their writing.

Subsequent journal responses to this class session indicate that students felt shut out by Carlos's paper: "I have no idea what the lines about having someone around to boost your ego mean" (Alisha's journal). This original confusion is later turned into a friendly reference point for some class members. Nick jokingly says to Carlos during a reading group later in the semester: "I read that 'Oblomov' paper again this morning. It's like a romp through a thesaurus really."

How Texts Are Used: The Triggering Subject ■ Donna introduces the concept of a "triggering subject" early in the semester with Richard Hugo's "Writing Off the Subject" (1979). In his chapter, Hugo invites writers to get off track, forget the original focus, and let new ideas trigger other ideas. After reading Hugo, students subsequently begin to locate the triggering subjects for their weekly papers.

It would be almost impossible for an outsider to uncover the various influences that published readings had on subsequent student writing. When, for example, Connie writes a paper, "Blinking Lights," about celebrating Christmas without her brother who was killed on his high school graduation night, only Connie and those in her writing group know that she was *triggered* to write this paper by reading Eiseley's essay, "The Brown Wasps." Since there is no explicit reference in her paper to Eiseley's piece, Donna comes to learn about this connection through reading Connie's journal.

By working in reading and writing groups, students begin to see that their ideas are never generated totally in isolation, but that other texts—oral and written—serve as subtexts to help writers produce new meanings. Students come to a tacit understanding of intertextuality—the idea that all texts, all signs, arise from what Vygotsky has called "the web of meaning" (1978). As James Porter has pointed out, the idea of intertextuality moves "our attention away from the writer as individual" so that the focus becomes "more on the sources and social contexts from which the writer's discourse arises" (1986, 34–35).

The community exchange encourages students to see that borrowing from their readings and from one another does not constitute plagiarism, but characterizes the process of academic thinking. In the following journal entry, titled "Monkey Read, Monkey Think," Allie articulately describes the concept of intertextuality and its development in her own writing as she drew from the class readings. Allie connects Rodriguez and Freire's published texts, my dissertation-in-progress, and her own ongoing writing.

Monkey Read, Monkey Think

> *He lifts an opinion from Coleridge, takes something else from Frye or Empson or Leavis. He even repeats exactly his professor's earlier comment. All of his ideas are clearly borrowed. He seems to have no thought of his own.*
>
> Rodriguez
> *"The Achievement of Desire"*

Indeed we do borrow ideas from other people, and we even form some of our opinions by reading the opinions of other people. We see the world through our past experiences. An example of this would be Elizabeth's thesis on the recurrence of words and ideas in a class. She found that the idea of "triggering" reoccurred throughout our class. The use of this concept was applied by many students after our workshop but not before. This is a representation of how we get ideas from our professors and other classmates, and express them as our own ideas when we are analyzing, for instance, our own writing.

After looking through my journal, I could see that I was much like the "scholarship boy" as he is described. I, too, have developed many ideas from authors, and from previous classes. These ideas have shed their light on several essays that I read, thought about, and learned from this class. There were journal entries which clearly demonstrated my use of "borrowed ideas." These were responses to "The Achievement of Desire" and "The Banking Concept of Education."

My reactions to "The Achievement of Desire" were related to ideas and concepts I had learned in a previous class about race and ethnicity. Because my mind was conditioned to respond to situations like Rodriguez's as an ethnic situation, this is what I related to as a reader, and what I referred to as a thinker and writer in my journal.

My response to "The Banking Concept of Education" was colored by my experience as a student in a women's studies class. This class I was taking the same semester as my English course, so I was being conditioned to respond to the use of masculine language rather than a genderless form. It wasn't so much that Freire touched my nerve, but I knew he'd touched a nerve with my other professor, therefore, I responded in a defensive manner.

In this class, and in my journal, I brought with me many "borrowed ideas." I was able to relate concepts that I had previously learned with entirely new situations and examples. We are all carriers of different ideas and viewpoints which made the class as successful as it was. In fact, we have omitted some ideas, and developed others which makes Rodriguez's statement about the scholarship boy having no ideas of his own questionable. We all do develop our own ideas, even if they are triggered by someone else's thoughts ...

In considering her own process of intertextuality, Allie also describes the process of becoming educated, of realizing, unlike Rodriguez, that borrowing from the ideas of others need not isolate students but can rather draw them into a collaborative conversation with other academic minds.

Donna's goal of using the class readings to trigger student writing was easily achieved. When Donna combines open paper topics with a series of triggering texts, what results is that many students "choose" to use the readings to help them frame and reframe their own experiences. The students' lives, their personal and/or intellectual experiences remain as the central view displayed in the writing: the new addition is the frame of published readings, which adds further support to that window.

Intertextuality: "The storytelling animal"   As Allie's journal entry suggests, the class became aware of what Donald Murray has described as the "ghost text" or the "intertext" created by what the writer reads, and what the writer then writes. Murray urges composition teachers to invite students "not only to understand the text they are reading, but to allow that text to spark other texts, ghost texts ... that are born because of the communication between the written text and the experience of the reader" (1984, 244).

Sarah drafts a paper that is born of such a ghost text. When the whole class discusses an essay by Kathryn Morton (1984) called "The Storytelling Animal," Sarah comments in class that "man is separated by his storytelling," an observation underscored by the essayist. Sarah files the Morton essay in her mind and writes a paper called "Harmony," which describes her experience on a New Hampshire lake where she watches the loons on the water at night while listening to a phantom flutist play. Donna encourages Sarah to find the deeper meaning of this experience through multiple drafting.

While Sarah's busy reworking "Harmony," Donna shares a draft of her own work-in-progress called "A Rock by Any Other Name." Donna's essay is about stumbling on a piece of granite in the New Hampshire woods that reminds her of Australia. Sarah interrupts her own writing after hearing Donna's paper and starts a new essay comparing her experiences on Squam Lake with Donna's encounter in the woods. Sarah's new paper, "The Tale Bearer," is written in third person and describes both herself and Donna as writers attempting to impose meaning on their accidental encounters with nature: for Donna it's a piece of New Hampshire stone and for Sarah it's the flutist's sound on the deserted Squam Lake.

Less explicit, but clearly the intertext that allows Sarah to compare her work with Donna's, is the Morton essay discussed by the class. Sarah's essay shows that she understands how both writers are struggling to make meaning from what is found in nature through the frame of storying or myth making. Sarah writes in "Harmony":

> Myth-assembling people continue to thrive, recreating new worlds from the notions stimulated by their average experiences. They lead an exciting fictitious life; one they will willingly share if given the opportunity, around an open fire or on a piece of paper ...

The mystery of the ghost text disappears upon a closer inspection of how it is achieved. By writing her paper about Donna's work, Sarah conveys a strong communal message as well—that they are both writers in this business of storying together.

How Thinking Is Presented: Collaborative Learning ■ Donna creates a supportive and nurturing context, which assumes that knowledge is socially, not individually, constructed.[5] For learners in this community, understanding about literacy does not reside "in" the subject matter but is constructed by students themselves as they work within what Fish (1980) has called the "interpretive community." Such an epistemology shifts power from the teacher as outside authority to inside members of the community.

Donna's writing class offers a way of knowing quite different from that of mainstream education, a way of learning that values *sharing* over the traditional *presentational* mode. Watson and Potter (1962) describe this sharing interaction as collaborative and empathic to another's point of view. But university education has traditionally favored the presentational style with its lecture format

---

[5] Donna noted that although she accepted my descriptions of her as a "nurturing" teacher to be accurate, she questioned the equation embedded in some feminist work between female understanding/intuition and motherhood. Donna was comfortable then with my assertion that her class functioned like a family unit, but she did not see herself as a mother figure.

and impersonal, hierarchical, singular, competitive, and self-centered learning. The literacy/learning model of Donna's class favors what can be described as a female way of knowing and understanding (see Belenky et al. 1986).[6]

The collaborative writing project most easily illustrates how thinking in this discipline is presented. Collaboration offers Donna's students an alternative way of learning and a critique on the dominant patriarchal discourse of the academy. Students in Donna's class find collaborative writing very challenging and describe it as a "process of negotiation." They face two practical problems as they write their collaborative projects: how to negotiate the group dynamics, and how actually to compose the paper. "Frustration" is a key word that colors students' journal entries as they talk about the struggle of the collaborative process: "I'm not going to lie and say it was wonderful ... it wasn't terrible but it was very frustrating" (Mary's journal).

What students articulate about writing and learning together is captured mainly in their individual collaborative journals, which Donna reads and evaluates. Excerpts of student journal responses indicate two kinds of learning that take place. One echoes Dewey's intentions for placing the individual in a group whereby the group processes heighten the members' awareness of their own individual learning (1938; 1963). Paradoxically, when students relinquish some of their own individualism, they start to gain in self-knowledge; in Anna's words, the group experiences the "gain of the individual and the loss of individualism."

The gains made to balance this loss of individualism include the externalization of what have previously been primarily internal processes. In her journal, Allie describes how collaboration has intensified her thinking process, which previously had remained unconscious: "It takes collaboration to see how much actually goes into the writing process ... it took this collaboration project to show me how much thinking I do in English class. ... We are immune to some of our thinking patterns because we take them

---

[6] During this research project, Donna and I both read *Women's Ways of Knowing* and discussed how ideas from this book on women's epistemological development informed our own understanding of college students' thinking processes and provided new directions for further research in composition studies (see Flynn 1988). I found the work of Belenky and her colleagues illuminating in ways similar to C. Gilligan's early frame on women's development of "voice." Although I was constantly testing these developmental schemes against my own data, it was impossible for me to ignore their importance and influence on my own research.

for granted." Neil, another great advocate of collaboration, expresses this process of making explicit what had previously been implicit thought:

The same process which occurs *inside* my head on a paper that just I am doing occurred in the construction of the collaborative paper. Instead of asking myself questions and drawing on strands of thought found within my head, we had three heads to use ... The only difference was that it occurred *externally* as opposed to *internally* ... the process was slower when the process was externalized or transferred from inside the mind to the outside world (Neil's journal).

Gender and collaboration: "I'm turning into a woman." In addition to making students conscious of their reading and writing processes, the context of the group writing situation also pulls on different sides of the self, which, regardless of actual gender, take on stereotypical gendered responses. Some students learn from collaboration how to play what Elbow (1973) has called "the believing game" or what Belenky and her colleagues have termed "connected knowing" (1986). This learning style contrasts with the individual, product-oriented thinking usually required for success in academia, as exemplified in Elbow's "doubting game" (1973). In collaborative writing, the conflict arises between the individual's need for mutuality, acceptance, and reciprocity, and the equally strong desire for ownership, autonomy, and power.

George voices the "male" need for control in the group project, an issue that emerged in many students' journals:

I do not feel comfortable holding someone else to my standards of appropriate form and content ... this results in a group paper I think I could have written better myself. I essentially detest group or committee decisions/productions. Groups have a useful purpose in suggesting solutions and theorizing but problems are solved by executive action that a group is unable to take. The necessity of compromise will dilute and mediocritize the product. ... I do not like the dilution a group causes in a strong idea ... groups are more apt to avoid a tough decision. ... Group writing teaches certain skills but they tend to be diplomatic skills such as compromise, tact, and courtesy more than actual writing skills (George's journal).

The power of solitary thinking and writing, of executive action, and of a superior product—all emphasized by George—are also the dominant modes of thinking in the university setting. While George recognizes that there are social skills that he can learn through writing with others, he values the product too much to sacrifice his individual voice for what he sees will become a necessarily mediocre group effort.

It is not just males, however, for whom this group situation is problematic. Sue, for example, in the individualistic male manner, worries in her journal about depending upon others for her evaluation: "I've never had to rely on someone else doing their work for my grade." And some males' journals reflect the "feminine" learning model. David writes that control is no longer an important issue for him: "It's a struggle to keep personalities, persuasions, frames/windows, and styles on an even keel. The question I find myself asking: Should we even try to *govern* the struggle?"

In general, however, female thinkers feel more comfortable with group work because it draws on their prior collaborative skills, which are not often recognized in college learning situations. Anna discusses in her journal how the group efforts provided her with the support to write in an entirely new form she wouldn't try on her own—fiction writing: "It seemed like it [the paper] just fell into fiction. So it was exploring a completely new medium for me. And it didn't feel odd. I was comfortable in it. In that way, the group gave me a sort of strength."

In Carlos's case, the collaborative journal he kept provides a fascinating contrast to that of his partner, Sarah (see Figure 1–1 for Sarah and Carlos's separate collaborative journals). Read together, these journals expose the different styles of working that are often considered male and female. For example, at the outset of the journal, Sarah is concerned with understanding Carlos as a person, in making a connection with his thinking process, no matter how foreign it may seem to her: "My thoughts may not be too complicated to decipher, but Carlos's ideas are more clearly understood if one has background information. ... I really shouldn't try but I am able to follow his train of thought, thus I can communicate."

Carlos, on the other hand, suspicious of the whole collaborative process, starts drawing boundaries on the project by making outlines and definitions: "To set up an outline in which our thoughts are to be kept bounded in. Our first meeting is essentially to define how we are going to let our triggering subject lead us; or better yet, define an area to lead us."

After writing a rough draft, Sarah wants to expand the audience beyond themselves so that the paper will communicate to others: "I want to create an essay that everyone can pick up and relate to." Carlos feels satisfied with the "coolness and detachment" of their draft and does not care if others really understand it.

Gradually, both students begin to recognize the role that gender is playing in their collaborative effort. Sarah feels that their thoughts "repel" one another because "Carlos had come to the dreadful realization that I am a girl, and the opposite sexes can't always

Figure 1–1 ■ *Collaborative Paper Journals*

SARAH'S JOURNAL

11/24 Winding along Route 1, Carlos's truck carries us beneath skeletal limbs of trees and by the most beautiful estates ever built. The coast tour serves as food for thought. Stopping at an occasional scenic spot, a lighthouse, civil war artillery ground, or beach, we are inspired by the life and beauty that is somehow thriving despite the cold wind and frozen ground. I listen to Carlos's voice as it drops and lifts with emotion. I've never met anyone so confident and yet so unsure of himself.

Anyway—our ocean view from the time-truck capsule was an ideal way for two people in the process of producing a masterpiece together to become familiar with one another's mind processes. My thoughts may not be too complicated to decipher, but Carlos's ideas are more clearly understood if one has background information. Actually, I shouldn't flatter myself by saying I understand—I couldn't possibly begin to figure him out, and I really shouldn't try but I am able to follow his train of thought, thus I can communicate. In turn, I will be able to assemble our two contrasting (yet similar) personality traits into a project of our combined insights.

AFTER A CONFERENCE WITH DONNA

I know what we want to present in "Mate Expectations" but I'm torn between presenting personal case histories and generalized hypotheses about people and love. Your insight helped us to see where ideas were too introspective and unclear. Heavy theory upon theory weighs the paper down—making the paper difficult to read. I know that I know there's nothing I hate more than an essay that *preaches*—I dread the thought of accidently creating one myself.

CARLOS'S JOURNAL

11/22 So young to be a cynic! My partner and I cruised the coast road going to all those spots I used to go to with "old flames." How ironic: To set up an outline in which our thoughts are to be kept bounded in. Our first meeting is essentially to define how we are going to let our triggering subject lead us; or better yet define an area to lead us. We both agreed on [mate] expectations as our theme to focus on. Now what we will do is to take our outline, write within its bounds, compare, and then start a first draft.

We were both successful in determining that we are cynics. I don't trust her, her me, and in this somehow we trust each other. No, nothing makes sense.

AFTER A CONFERENCE WITH DONNA

I read the first draft of "Mate Expectations" and I think I might be able to see where Donna was leading us. I think it reads too much like a Norman Vincent Peale self-help psychology book. If these ideas were taken and smoothed out, provided with some examples, a tad bit of humours digressions, and the Tolstoyian forces are left out, it can float.

Figure 1–1 ■ *continued*

SARAH BEGINS TO CONSIDER A LARGER AUDIENCE FOR THE PAPER
11/24

I don't think Carlos is too sure about the psycho-analytic frame we've put our words into. He has some alternate ideas but he keeps pumping back to a therapeutic type of paper. We can't escape it. Finally he said that if people can't relate to our depth of thought and experience of interpretation, then they can put the paper down. I want to create an essay that everyone can and will want to pick up and relate to. The topic should be able to attract people of all types, sex, and ages and hold them. Carlos and I are different in all categories, and we can relate. I believe that's proof enough to assume that others can/will too.

12/1
Our paper was struggling to find the balance between personal love-experiences, repercussions, and results. I had believed that we had great communication ability but apparently Carlos had come to the dreadful realization that I am a girl, and the opposite sexes can't always collaborate because our thoughts repel one another.

FINAL ENTRIES

We review our combined efforts and I feel good. I laugh, I contemplate, I question, I look up words in the dictionary, and most importantly . . . I feel.

I will take Carlos's advice to the point of no return. We will create and recreate until we get it right. I know the final sculpture lies waiting beneath this mound of moldable words. We communicate again, not with words but smiles — the true sign of understanding. That's what it takes to collaborate successfully.

CARLOS FEELS SATISFACTION WITH THIS MIDDLE DRAFT
11/30

This new draft is just like my life. Chekhov would be proud. This draft is the culmination of all my life's reasoning but I don't know how Sarah will receive and perceive it. It's so smooth, cool, and detached, the way I've always known I could be. But Sarah? I think Sarah still has to spin her wheels first before she decides to switch to a snow tire. She needs a few more bad experiences before reality can come back around to her.

12/3
Sarah is extremely cooperative and corrigible. That doesn't mean I can get her to agree to what I think and believe; but I can get her to appreciate it. She's helped me to be that way a lot just by working with her. Men aren't usually so corrigible. Oh Christ, I'm turning into a woman, it's a conspiracy!

FINAL ENTRIES

Our collaboration — Eureka — was like a relationship (Oh Christ that's all I need). We thought that we had something in common but found out we didn't, and reconciled to each other's real identity. I wonder if everybody worked this way? This paper was more learning about ourselves as people than as writers.

I don't know if anyone of the general public (the class?) will realize all the pain we went through to make this work both in our personal life and as collaborators.

Figure 1–1   ■   continued

FINAL ENTRIES

Formulating a product from two contrasting, often opposing forces is a difficult and frustrating job. It's as if you have been told to make north and south meet at the equator.
I don't believe the product of the collaborative process is the primary goal striven for. Whether the product is a paper, ceramic vase, Oldsmobile, or building the procedure taken to get there is the vitality of the creation in the end. Collaboration is a test of your character.
Nothing can be duplicated that is formulated from group effort: everyone has added their own spice, if the recipe is ever minus that one ingredient (individual) then the product will never again occur. That which is unique should be treasured. This understanding provides a lifetime of experiencing new possibilities and creations. Such is the self-made magic of the collaborative project.

FINAL ENTRIES

That's what our paper's about: accepting each other for who we are. That's what collaboration means: accepting another writer for that they value. When writing alone you have only to accept your own way of thinking. You only develop it through your own frame. Collaboration allows you to view your work on her work through different frames.

Social intercourse . . . sexual intercourse, intellectual intercourse. This is why we collaborate. To feel better about our abilities by recognizing others. It is a way to gauge ourselves other than the usual, "What did you get in Mrs. Faquar's class?" Other examples of intellectual intercourse: Student A: "I read so and so's paper and it sucked" or "Professor Despot stands up and expounds his view of asparagus and doesn't let me stick in my two cents." These examples involve little interaction and reciprocity.

---

collaborate because our thoughts repel one another." But Carlos begins to see the advantages to working with another viewpoint and recognizes his possibility for reform and change through Sarah: "She's helped me a lot just by working with her. Men aren't usually so corrigible. Oh Christ, I'm turning into a woman. It's a conspiracy!"

When they evaluate their final collaborative effort Sarah is proud of having learned to communicate with Carlos, applauding the process of collaboration over the final product: "I don't believe the product of the collaborative process is the primary goal striven for. Whether the product is a paper, ceramic vase, Oldsmobile or building, the procedure taken to get there is the vitality of the creation in the end." Carlos too, is able to understand by the end of the project that in addition to the paper, the value of collaboration was mainly in the relationship they formed, which allowed them a larger perspective on the topic than they would have had on their own.

Carlos's final entry echoes the thinking of sociologist Charles Horton Cooley that "the life of the mind is essentially a life of intercourse" (1964, 97). Carlos writes: "Social intercourse, sexual intercourse, intellectual intercourse. This is why we collaborate. To feel better about our abilities by recognizing others." Collaboration exposes a tension between process and product and between the parts of the self that some students have not experienced before. Through collaborative writing, students gain a new set of understandings about literacy and learning that most university writing projects do not afford. For Donna, who wants students to confront a problem-posing writing situation, the process *is* the product in collaborative writing.

Rhetorician Karen Burke LeFevre assigns an even greater value to collaboration: "Learning to invent in communities will do more than enable success in classrooms or careers. It is absolutely essential to achieving peace and indeed, maintaining life on this earth and beyond" (1987, 129). If we believe that what we learn is embedded in how we learn, collaborative writing projects in this classroom involve a new perspective on knowing.

In this Prose Writing classroom Donna built a learning context in which personal narratives and personal knowledge matter, carefully modeled group work encourages discussion and response, outside readings trigger new ideas and new texts, and collaboration fosters risk taking and fresh understandings of the thinking process. Donna established this kind of context through literacy opportunities for her students, what Donald Graves has called "literate occasions," which are available to all college instructors.

From this Prose Writing course, I follow two students, Anna and Nick, into classes in their majors. Their voices as part of this overall classroom description of Prose Writing will become stronger—sometimes almost strident—as we accompany them into other college classrooms. We will consider how talk, texts, and thinking are valued elsewhere in the university and we will see how literacy is defined in different academic disciplines.

Anna's Literacy

The Academic Dance

2

W ords and images from my research journals on Anna sift to the top and are not forgotten: her turquoise ribbon and the dripping ice cream cones, the modern dancer and the emergent artist, her aversion to piercing ears, her love of studying foreign languages. Anna's own hesitant but powerful words surround me as I write: "I hate it when I judge people from my impressions."

Researcher Journal Entries

Anna as both me and not me. Anna as an idealized younger version of myself, literate but not always articulate, artistic but seldom confident.

As ethnographer I enter a world of subjectivity trying to put into words, what I cannot always say in words. That a student's life happens all at once. That this slice of recorded time is so influenced with the background noise of the personal, the social, the cerebral, only sometimes the academic.

As a writer I worry over how to represent psychological time and space on the linear page. Where to begin and where to stop ... how to break out of, or into, formal writing. In writing, my words serve as boundaries for her events, her images that struggle to remain mute. This translation of Anna's silent meaning becomes my own issue as I write.

It takes me some time to understand how important dance is to Anna. One Saturday evening in spring, I attend the university's dance concert where I know she'll be performing. My researcher image of her shreds as a new Anna appears on stage: she's a whirl of lime green in a Chinese worker costume, a fluid, flopsy modern dancer. Communicating through spatial configuration and body tensions, her torso's limp and pliant as it cooperates to convey the pull of emotional energy in the group dance called "Progressions." I am amazed at her ability.

Why include all this? Why not just pick a point and begin? To establish the intersubjectivity between her life and mine, between writing now and observing then, to situate myself as both ethnographer and writer within the frame of this narrative.

Our relationship develops over time from that of researcher and student in an office setting with the tape recorder whirring in the background, to friends and confidantes in a variety of encounters: I order books from her, many of them about art history or women's studies, at the local "alternative" bookstore where she works; we have tea and muffins or coffee and bagels — depending on our mood — after her avant-garde art class; or we walk along together after classes with her dripping ice cream cones. I write her letters of recommendations, first to go on a dig in Greece and then for a summer art internship in San Francisco; I drive her to her apartment in a spring thunderstorm where she dreads an impending conflict with an angry landlord over her security deposit. With me, she shares her academic life, many parts of her personal life, understands my project, and cooperates in handing over any scraps of literacy information that might make my task easier — from an exam paper to an art poster she's helped with. There are no stated boundaries, no unmentionable territories, in my exploration of her thinking.

At different times during our research, Anna offers me descriptions about herself as a learner to hang onto, little clues to help me understand some of her thinking patterns. For example, when trying to select courses, she suggests that she prefers "old stuff." I place this together with the four years of Latin she has taken, a paper she's written for art history on the importance of Roman baths, and her desire to go on a "dig in Greece," and I come up with "classical" as one of her interests. But when Anna chooses to take a modern art course, I am further confused.

When asked directly to describe herself, Anna hesitates, searches for comfortable words; "I don't know, I can't say. I don't know what kind of person I am." She discusses her different names as "only labels" yet somehow representative of the multiple roles she plays: to those at work she's "A.L." — a bright, polite, and helpful bookstore clerk; to old friends who know her from her New Hampshire hometown, she's "Annie" — the rebel, the oddball; to those in her modern dance class, she's "Anna" — the empathic dance partner; and to acquaintances at the university, she's "Anna Lynn," art history major, who in her junior year is elected to the university's honors program. Finally she settles on "visual" and "political" as tentative self-descriptors saying, "artistic things matter to me" and "I think it's very important to be politically aware."

For Anna, visual understanding is immediate. Like a window transmitting sunlight, it's an almost physical experience. Of artists and musicians she writes, "I let their works affect me directly." Her concern for the visual pushes me to tinker with the verbal pictures she constructs of herself. In one of her papers ("Jazz"), Anna describes herself as "easily read" because "light eyes can't hide anything." This self-portrait presents Anna as a text: open, vulnerable, easily interpreted.

But my early field notes indicate otherwise. They include a jumble of impressions over mixed strains in Anna's interests: light/dark, intuitive/analytic, subjectivity/objectivity, passion/reason, masculine/feminine. At first I miss this juggling act because I am looking for one monolithic clue, one breakthrough or key incident to wrap my study around as if that lost paper, forgotten symbol, or submerged conversation would summarize or represent all sides of Anna.

Some notes are wildly off course. For instance, knowing her commitment to political awareness, I associate a turquoise ribbon that she frequently wears around her neck with possible political affiliations, only to learn later that the ribbon holds the key to her apartment.

Only once do I hear her political voice on fire, boiling in a pot of anger over a statement in the university newspaper about Blue Jeans Day when sympathetic students such as Anna purposely wear jeans in support of the rights of gay and lesbian students. One male, when asked by the campus newspaper reporter why he had not complied said, "If God had wanted faggots, he wouldn't have made women." Anna vents her anger toward herself as well — that she could be so unaware, so naive: "I despise that kind of attitude. It doesn't make any sense, he didn't even answer the question. He has no respect for women or any minority, at least not homosexuals."

Early in the study, I write to myself, "Figure out your feelings about her tentativeness by next time" — expressing my anxiety that Anna, as her complicated self-descriptions indicate, won't be able to articulate her thinking adequately so that I can turn it into words, putting my words over hers. In part, I am correct that Anna's strongest learning modes are not discursive but more intuitive. Yet, as Langer points out, intuition is "the basic process of all understanding, just as operative in discursive thought as in clear sense perception" (1959, 29). The presentation of intuition as dichotomous with the analytic diminishes its power. Anna's imagistic, intuitive side represented by interests in studio art and dancing is girded by the analytic mode required in her art history major. I find Anna doubly expressive. Yet she insists, "I'm not that gifted."

Anna's sense of herself as "not that gifted" comes in part from the ways she—and I (culpable, culpable!)—measure what she knows. Instead of a binary opposite or polar term where the intuitive (female intuition) is always posed as a negative, powerless stance against the mastery yardsticks, I like the overlapping, circular image of learning that many educators who are now looking at the epistemologies of women have adopted (see Martin 1985; Noddings 1984; Gilligan 1982; Belenky et al. 1986). And Anna herself quotes from Cheataw and Powell; "This vertical view of reality is a lie, a construct created to justify patriarchal subordination and control. We live in a circle, not along a line" (1986, 160).

One of the artistic circles that clearly influences Anna's life is dancing. At the university, she takes modern dance classes and belongs to a dance group. When Anna talks about the power of dancing, she describes how unrestrained she feels as she works together with her dance partners: "There's so much communication without ever talking. One person dances and the partner accompanies her as an instrument." There's an energy and communication in modern dance, Anna suggests, that represents "just another way of expressing yourself," but a way that you can't really share with anyone who hasn't had that kind of experience "without them thinking you're some kind of freak." Dance as an art form is not easily turned into words and cannot be readily translated from the nonverbal into the verbal.

The illusion of dance, Susanne Langer suggests, is "virtual," not "actual"—a power that gives the appearances of influence through the gestural: "One sees the dance driving this way, drawn that way, gathering here, spreading there—fleeing, resting, rising, and so forth; and all the motion seems to spring from powers beyond the performers" (1959, 175).

Borrowing from the dance images, Anna also admits that in college, she's trying to make her own learning process more circular, less compartmentalized. She admits that in general "the world is a messy place," but she wants to try to make her education complete, saying "I want to start seeing things as a whole." Anna drives herself toward this sense of completion during her junior year when I am witness to a kind of academic dance that propels her forward and provides her the energy to grow.

Anna in Prose Writing: A Member of the Troupe

Anna confided in me that she felt Prose Writing should be a year-long course: "I wish this class were continuing into next semester because I think there's a lot in this class in terms of people. ... I put so much into it. And I've been doing a lot of meaningful writing and now I'm going to have to stop." Her reason for favoring this class over others was that "it's so personal." Personalized knowledge is valued by Anna, who contrasts prose writing with other coursework in which she's made to look at explicit knowledge rather than rely on what Polyani has identified as tacit knowing. Tacit knowing, Polyani suggests, is more fundamental than explicit knowing: "We know more than we can can tell; we can tell nothing without relying on our awareness of things we may not be able to tell (Emig 1977, 151).

In Prose Writing class, Anna is an active participant in what educators from Dewey through Rosenblatt have described as transactional learning. For Anna, this participation does not come without some effort on her part. One of my field notes refers to the tension that precedes Anna's talk in the whole-group discussions: "She always seems nervous before she talks: I can sense when she has something to say just by watching her body, particularly her hands." When she speaks, she does so quickly. Later, Anna comments on her muted speech style as she contrasts it with Carlos's: "Carlos I just wanted to hit! Because he talks so slowly, I think. Not that there's anything wrong with talking slowly. I speak so fast." Anna's evaluative response is typical: questioning—why Carlos's talk bothers her; nonjudgmental—nothing wrong with it; and somewhat self-effacing—I speak too fast.

Anna's participation in her writing class was like her membership in a dance troupe: she was prompt and prepared, she participated regularly, and she practiced on her own. She was a part of this community in the way her dance company formed a tightly knit group. Along with others in Prose Writing, Anna engaged in the many conversations that took place there. Had I never followed her into another setting, I would not have understood that for her to be an active speaker was unusual, that her usual role was silence.

The authors of *Women's Ways of Knowing* (Belenky et al. 1986) have identified the beginning stage of some women's thinking as "silence"—a description that reflects the important metaphor of "voice" in understanding women's growth as thinkers.[1] Anna explains that she found it easier to speak up in her composition course because "I could back up what I said. It all came from inside of my head." Composition courses rub against the model of the student as blank text, as unfilled bottle, by *valuing* the experiences and feelings students develop from inside of them to speak out, to read and write from the "inside out" (Atwell 1985). In a course like Donna's, students are invited to play what Peter Elbow has called "the believing game," which makes composition studies so different from other academic communities where the "doubting game" stands as the dominant epistemology (Elbow 1973).

Anna also values listening. She describes three of her female professors, including Donna, as "really knowing how to listen." Anna describes her dance teacher, in particular, as "a really *caring* person." Nel Noddings suggests that caring involves receptivity and engrossment rather than projection and analysis (1984, 30). Such empathy with others comes through listening, which for many women is a positive stance as well as an active and demanding process (Belenky et al. 1986, 37). When I suggested to Anna that she didn't talk as much as Nick and Carlos in her reading group she said, "I felt I talked a lot," and then reflected, "Maybe I just thought a lot."

Vygotsky has stressed the importance of outer speech or dialogue in the development of inner thought and cognitive growth (Vygotsky 1978). Yet listening, without the support of talk, can eliminate women from full participation in the academic conversation, affording them the spectator and outsider role, as members of the audience rather than members of the troupe.

In the following excerpt from a whole-class discussion, Anna

---

[1] Voice has become an important term for describing women in the work of different feminist thinkers. Writers Adrienne Rich (*On Lies, Secrets, and Silence*, 1979) and Tillie Olson (*Silences*, 1978) employ the metaphors of voice and silence extensively. Developmental psychologist, Carol Gilligan works with the concept of voice in her book (*In a Different Voice*, 1982) on women's moral development to show how women's growth contrasts with that of men. And Nadya Aisenberg and Mona Harrington in their recent study (*Women of Academe: Outsiders in the Sacred Grove*, 1988) created a category of "voice" to describe the theme of deflected women in academics.

earns her community membership by adding her point of view, by drawing on her own experiences. Here Donna's class is discussing the symbolic meaning of Eiseley's childhood tree in his essay "The Brown Wasps." Donna, as usual, opens with a question:

Donna: Do things change or do we just change?

Allie and others: Both.

Donna: I mean Eiseley's tree is obviously gone. There's a change there.

Randy: I think we change because things change.

Mary: Or vice versa. Things change because we change.

Randy: I still think we change.

Linda: Like you've grown up since you've been to high school and you go back and see it in a totally different way.

Donna: Your attitude toward the soccer team has changed.

Anna: I was just thinking that he has this tree in his memory and it was a comforting thing to think back to the tree when the present got harder. I found that when I'm really stressed out, I have memories to think back to or places that I think about where I want to — ...

Donna: To hold on to?

Anna: Or just to comfort me.

Tina: You have a memory of a time and place when everything was all right and it wasn't so stressful.

Donna: Maybe that's what meditation is all about. They say you go back to a place in your mind.

While there's nothing particularly remarkable about this discussion, it's a representative slice of Anna's talk in Prose Writing class. In her nervous and quick manner of speaking, she engages in the ongoing talk, drawing on her own knowledge and feelings: "'I found that when I'm really stressed out, I have memories to think back to or places that I think about ...'" She does not remain silent.

Her ability to speak out in Prose Writing can be explained by understanding such class discussions as ongoing conversations, rather than debates. Anna describes this collaborative talk: "There are some times in class when I really want to say something because I *agree* or I might find something that I feel is interesting to *add*. I get anxious to say it. ... If I say something, I want it to mean something." Anna is not intimidated in this course because she sees herself as able to contribute. Whereas Randy wants to state his point of view and win ("I still think we change"), Anna's more interested in participation.

In a journal entry on the class, Anna further describes her need to be engaged in talk, writing of how conversation supports her thinking process and gives her confidence:

When I discover concerns of my own, they usually come from dialogue with other people. .... I really value discussions and bouncing ideas off people and getting responses. Maybe I'm insecure about developing or accepting an opinion that is fresh to me without first conferring with a better informed friend.

It is interesting that Anna feels there's something almost wrong with validating her ideas with someone else, since talking with colleagues is, in fact, how most academic ideas are generated.

In our conversations together, Anna often berates herself for not knowing enough, for not having "expertise," comparing herself to her Northern Renaissance art history professor whose "mind is like some safe filled with all the myths of the world. .... She knows so many different theories." The process of how thinking develops is missing from Anna's image of the hermetically sealed mind that stores its valuables in a safe. Nondisclosure of how scholars acquire their knowledge inadvertently misrepresents the nature of collaboration and interaction in higher education. Lack of modeling robs students of insights about the incubation process and denies them access to the messy rough-draft thinking involved in making meaning — from ideas, from texts, from colleagues.

Anna as Reader: Intimacy and Response

Anna's conversation in small reading groups reveals an even more intimate style than in the whole-class discussions. In these small peer groups, narrative, spontaneous talk dominates. In many of the reading-group transcripts for this class, the reading serves primarily as a stimulus for students to reread their own lives, rather than as a context devoted soley to deconstruction of the author's intentions.

The following reading-group episode I call "The Banking Concept of Love" because it reveals some of students' culturally acquired attitudes about love, particularly Nick's concept of love as an "investment." In the transcript as a whole, Anna has a difficult time wresting the conversational floor from Nick and Carlos who take over at many points, leaving Anna and Mary as spectators in the friendly male wrangle. For women, gaining access to the dominant discourse is often problematic, particularly in public settings. In the entire transcript from which this excerpt is taken, Nick has ninety-five conversational turns to Anna's twenty-five, so that she claims the floor 76 percent less of the time than he does. These small reading groups offer women an opportunity to work within a communal circle that is familiar and appropriate for members who belong to what anthropologists Edwin Ardner and Shirley Ardner[2] and, later, feminist literary critic Elaine Showalter (1981) call the muted discourse group. The muted group belongs to, but is not always allowed full participation in the talk of, the dominant group. Ardner developed this idea to describe research claims he felt were being made about particular cultures or tribes based only on interviews with the men. Women, he said, were left out of the generation of meaning within these groups. Showalter, picking up on his metaphor, applies it to women and speech: "Thus muted groups must mediate their beliefs through the allowable forms of dominant structures. Another way of putting this would be to say that all language is the language of the dominant order, and women, if they speak at all, must speak through it" (1981, 200).

In the following frame we see that Anna *does* manage to bring in some personal responses to the group talk about Carver's story "What We Talk About When We Talk About Love." Nick is the designated leader of this group of Anna, Carlos, and Mary because he has selected the story for the group to discuss.

Anna: That's a point in the essay too. People have a need for love.

Mary: Different kinds of love.

Nick: When you invest in a relationship, you invest a part of yourself so you necessarily are giving part of yourself up. You become half a person.

Carlos: Do you think people can have a relationship without giving themselves up?

Anna: I think you are fooling yourself if you're in a relationship and don't put anything in.

Nick: Yes. You're not committed

Mary: You have to give up certain beliefs, certain prejudices. I know —my boyfriend—I've always been the type of person who says no drugs, no this, no that. He smokes pot. I say, "You shouldn't be doing that; it's wrong." He says, "I know it's wrong."

Anna: If you can accept that, that's good.

Mary: You have to accept it—you give up a lot of your own moral values, not necessarily giving them up but accepting the ones that you know are wrong. Not that you are going to go out and do them but accepting the fact that you can't always change them.

Anna: Someone I know, someone who's married and his wife doesn't let him smoke in the house, and when he's at work, he smokes like a

---

[2] The Ardners' anthropological work is cited in the Introduction to *Language, Gender, and Professional Writing: Theoretical Approaches and Guidelines for Nonsexist Usage*, edited by F. W. Frank and P. Treichler (19).

madman. His wife, if she smells beer on his breath, makes him sleep on the couch. It's ridiculous stuff. She's not accepting him as a whole person.

Mary: If you love someone you have to accept them the way they are because you can't change them. You're not really loving them.

Nick: You also need their *investment.* You need to know that they're committed. You need to know that they have *taken a piece of themselves and given it to you.*

While the women in this group explore the interpersonal aspects of forming a relationship — of accepting new values, of welcoming the whole person — the males (mainly represented by Nick here) discuss commitment as an object — an emotional investment, as an actual piece of the self. From this short snip of conversation we learn that in intimate relationships, Nick draws boundaries: half of me for you and half for me. And Nick expects his part back.

Anna later reflects on this group discussion in her journal, which represents an ongoing dialogue since she knows that Donna will respond. Donna underlines the following parts of Anna's entry as being interesting:

Then he [Nick] went on to say that after he had broken up with his girlfriend, he was left with this refound half and didn't know what to do with it. Instead of putting it into another relationship, he had to sort through it. But I'm finding that *I gave or put more than half of myself into a relationship* and I need some of it back for me to become complete.

Anna's entry indicates that while women place fewer boundaries on relationships, they also make a larger capital investment ("more than half of myself"). Anna uses her journal to work out personal responses to ideas and readings that have been discussed in small peer groups. In her last journal entry for Prose Writing, Anna returns to the issue of love and relationships, showing that she is very much tuned into these concerns. She writes: "I think about love, I know I spend an incredible amount of time trying to figure out my love, his different channels, and where I can find myself in relation to these channels."

Response Forums: Peer and Private ■ For Anna, the reading groups and teacher-student journals turned out to be her most effective learning and feedback forums in Prose Writing class. Her oral and written responses to members of her reading groups show her to be a generous reader who always offered extended comments. In an in-class essay, Anna writes that reading groups felt more like casual conversation to her, the kind of discussions she holds with friends:

Tad and I have intensely intellectual conversations in which we talk about things disturbing us in the order of the world. We sort through relationships and individual growth. Though we don't talk often, when we do, we pick up on themes and discuss how our feelings and opinions have changed ... Neither of us record these conversations. We apply them to our lives.

Anna apparently learns to apply what she reads to her life as well. When asked how she improved as a reader in Prose Writing, Anna writes: "I have become a better *connector*. A better reader for coherent ideas. A better rereader. I see things differently, pick up on ideas that I missed." One of the ways that Anna grew as a reader, she said, was through Donna's questions and responses to what was written in the journal, weaving a connective tissue between teacher and student. Connected knowing, as explained in *Women's Ways of Knowing*, may begin with understanding people but end as a procedure for understanding paintings or books as well: "Connected knowing involves feelings, because it is rooted in relationships: but it also involves thought. ... Connected knowing is just as procedural as separate knowing, although its procedures have not been as elaborately codified" (Belenky et al. 1986, 121).

In this course, reading groups and journal writing both afford a way for students to relate personally to texts as well as provide a means for making the private act of reading communal. Unlike so much college work that's based on solitary reading without any modeling or feedback, Prose Writing offers a rich web of response forums. For the female student who may not feel able or confident to speak up in a large group discussion, these classroom literacy structures allow ways of keeping women involved in the academic conversation.

The journal response in particular invites women students to draw on a whole heritage of diary and journal keeping that has historically included women. Cinthia Gannett, tracing the gender differences in the journal tradition, suggests that for women writers the journal has often afforded a voice when otherwise women might have been, indeed often were, denied voice. Gannett suggests that the journal tradition has kept women engaged in a private discourse when their voices in the arena of public discourse may have been muted: "Simply put, since women have always had fewer ways to act on, to inscribe themselves on the world at large, they found ways to inscribe themselves, to make their own unique imprint, in texts" (Gannett 1987, 161). The use of the journal in higher education, Gannett asserts, helps women "work through their public voices and gain confidence as writers" (183−84). Although not a private journal keeper herself, Anna liked the kinds of comments Donna wrote on her journal entries, liked the dialogue that it afforded about her reading and thinking, liked being connected.

Anna as Writer: The Rebel and the Scholarship Girl

Anna drafted an early series of papers in Prose Writing that reflects her intellectual autobiography. These papers document her shift from high school rebel to what Richard Hoggart[3] calls the "scholarship boy," or in Anna's case, the scholarship girl. Hoggart describes the scholarship students as being so careful to follow the teacher's instructions that they cease to think for themselves. A close reading of Anna's papers "Exploration" and "Cliffs" allows a frame for understanding the learning patterns that, Anna says, follow her around. "I have these things that I carry around with me from class to class," she shares early in our work together, but is unable to articulate what they are. Anna's writing becomes the best narrator of her own academic development.

"An Exploration of My Own Education"—Anna's first paper for Prose Writing—is triggered by an essay called "The Achievement of Desire" (Rodriguez 1982). In "Exploration," Anna paints a negative, self-defeating, and rebellious version of her earlier self: "I hated high school," "If I didn't try I couldn't fail," and a self-description as "a kind of crazy artist with an awareness beyond society." In reality, Anna survived high school with a B average and completed college preparatory coursework, including classes in four foreign languages. She reported that her high school—in a university town—was very focused on academics: "This is a snobby thing to say but there's a whole intellectual type of person

---

[3] Richard Rodriguez adopts the phrase "scholarship boy" from Hoggart's book, *The Uses of Literacy*. Rodriguez's chapter, "The Achievement of Desire," was read in Donna's class and is from his book *Hunger of Memory*. Although Anna never had an actual scholarship, she displays many of the same learning patterns that Rodriguez uses to describe himself.

who comes out of there." What Anna's paper reveals is that in high school she was playing the role of misunderstood intellectual, not really inhabiting that part.

"Exploration" describes her gradual transformation in college from that pseudointellectual high school student to a mainstream college achiever. She writes: "Beginning in my sophomore year I began to do more than one typed draft of papers . . . and I received my first A on the college level. It was a paper of visual analysis and I was praised for both my observations and my writing." This key course, taught by the art historian whose class we will consider, became the primary impetus for Anna to declare herself an art history major.

Anna also credits her changed attitude toward education to a freshman anthropology course where she learned about an "evil side to government and capitalism," and about "what was going on in Central America and who the Sandinistas are." In college Anna gradually began to take her studies more seriously: "My classes made me look at the world around me and observe, think, and wonder." By the end of her sophomore year at UNH she'd made dean's list.

Anna describes herself as turning into a college student who likes to "be on top of the information introduced in class" or otherwise begins to "feel nervous" about her academic standing: "That semester I did everything with precision, especially in my Art of the Ancient World course, which fascinated me. I memorized every monument."

Yet, in spite of her growing success with academics, Anna's paper documents her constant doubt. She worries, that like Rodriguez, she'll become a scholarship girl who can't think beyond the text, someone without her own ideas:

As I sat in my American Art class the other day, staring blankly at the slide in front of me while the other students responded with innovative ideas, I wondered if I too had become like a scholarship student. As they were trying to explain things primarily from their visual experiences, I was trying to make sense of the names, historical facts, and visual influences that I had read about in the text.

Anna's paper mirrors several epistemological moves in her learning process that are discussed in *Women's Ways of Knowing* (Belenky et al. 1986) as intellectual developments particular to women. Coming to college as a subjective knower, dependent entirely on how she felt about things, Anna then moved into a phase that Belenky and her colleagues call "procedural knowing," where the learner wants to memorize and be in charge of her learning process. This learning stage, characterized by "procedures for obtaining and communicating knowledge," requires careful observation and analysis, both important learning strategies needed for art history in particular (Belenky et al. 1986, 95).

Like any developmental stage theory, this reflection on Anna's growth in "self, voice, and mind" is only partially useful since we all have several voices working within us at the same time. While Anna's busy learning the rituals and conventions of art history, while she's engaged in being the scholarship girl, there's still enough rebel left to warn her: "If I begin to depend too much on others for my learning, whatever it was that made me challenge and think as a young rebel will be lost" ("Exploration"). In high school, that rebel had no real cause except to be different from the other stereotypical secondary school students, but in college Anna recognizes that loss of self-identity might translate into academic conformity.

With extensive feedback from Donna and some members of her writing group, Anna continues to redraft papers on the theme of education. When she's in a writing group with Nick, it is his comments that anticipate how Anna will revise: "Eliminate Rodriguez quotes from the essay entirely and refocus on your own changes, both in and out of school." Her first paper ("Exploration") serves as a finger exercise for her next piece of writing called "Cliffs," which she carries throughout the semester. In this paper, written in an entirely imagistic style, Anna's voice has switched from the past tense used in "Exploration" to present tense narrative. In "Cliffs," she's a tightrope walker, near the sea's edge where she's precariously balanced:

I feel like I'm walking on a tight rope between two cliffs four hundred feet above a beach with large pointy rocks and wet seaweed, I feel like I would topple off at any minute, with the misplacement of a toenail. I'd fall to one side racing past the cliffs and find myself face down with a pointy rock piercing my stomach . . . I'm groveling in the seaweed again.

The narrator doesn't fall but finds that her face is "ugly" with a big "scowl" and covered with the "dirty slime" from the seaweed. She's lost and has to find her way to the rope: "I'm crawling around in misery trying to find the truth." When she locates the rope, she's free and feels "like something is too good to be true" as she hoists herself up and looks back down on herself "a few years ago." Picking up themes from the earlier paper, Anna describes herself in high school as "difficult" and "cynical" and writes this reflective section:

So I'm treading here on this wire and way down below I see myself a few years ago. I was miserable, but it didn't really bother me. I kind of got off on being the one that everyone thought was off, the one with a more cynical sense of humor and difficult tendencies. The one whose anger never ceased — always brimming. Yeah, I wanted them to think that I had problems. I wandered around the halls in my high school with a glazed expression. I argued with my teachers in class while other students rolled their yes. It didn't bother me. I knew I was seeing beyond them. . . . ("Cliffs")

Later in "Cliffs" she acknowledges that her image of herself as a rebel was hard to let go of because her "depressing logic" had taken "years to mold" her. To replace this rebellious image, Anna finds a friend (Aaron) who helps her understand her self-defeating attitude. Without an "automatic rebellion," Anna learns to "think more clearly and develop rational ideas instead of ones founded with passion." She also sees this transformation as more challenging: "It is much harder to keep a positive attitude than to be angry. By focusing on the flaws of society, you can convince yourself that being a part of it is a waste of time." "Cliffs" shows Anna's changing perspective toward life.

In another section of the paper, she returns to her sea imagery. Having come down from the cliffs, she's enmeshed in seaweed:

The seaweed was cleansed from me and I moved toward an upright stance. I am challenged by a new way of thinking. Inner tranquility is the way to truly rational thinking. I'm leaving the group of conscious sufferers.

The change described in this paper, Anna tells me in our talks, represents the major learning experience of her life. In some ways, this transformation surprises her: *"I didn't have to give up my intellect*. In fact, I've become more curious and a much better learner."

But at the end of "Cliffs," just as in the earlier paper, Anna introduces her tentativeness about such change: "I'm nervous; I don't know how long that will last; I never should have found this high wire; I'm clinging to the rope but I fear my past might pull me down."

Anna's ability to perform and get good grades in college does not afford her assurance and confidence. Instead, at the same time as she becomes aware of herself as a better learner, she also becomes more hesitant about her knowing. She talks about it this way: "It just seems as if everything I know is temporary. It just comes and goes." She later comments further: "I just memorized for tests and forgot when the ideas were not in use."

Creativity and All That Jazz ■ Anna's first two papers provide insight into her thinking process, into attitudes that prevented her from being a successful learner in high school. They also partially explain her current insecurities with university work: "I have high expectations. . . . High ideals, I think, are a bad thing to get involved with."

The other writing theme that Anna pursues in Prose Writing represents her artistic side, both in subject matter and in style. "Jazz" is a major piece of writing that Anna revises throughout the term. In this instance, Anna relies on peer and instructor feedback more fully to revise the paper from its embryonic form of music criticism into a personal essay.

The membership of writing groups shifts each time they meet to provide students with an increasingly larger audience. Anna finds this feedback less satisfactory than that of reading groups in which students stayed together all term. She evaluated writing groups as being "both good and bad." The difficult part for Anna is facing the page again after a writing group meeting: "When I go back to my papers, I feel like I'm alone again and I don't know why." Writing groups, she learns, only partially diminish the isolation of writing, they cannot eliminate it.

Her first draft of "Jazz," triggered by a singer in a local jazz club, begins with sounds: "Boo dee boo da . . . boo dee boo da da da . . . boo dee ba do do do do . . . Laurie Nash sang improvised melodies in a wonderfully deep full voice." Anna's paper tries to accomplish a number of different things: describe Laurie Nash's singing, discuss the nature of jazz, and relate her feelings about the singer to Anna's own life. The parts about Laurie Nash are mainly descriptive:

She held her head down with the microphone tight against her lips like a horn. . . . Laurie Nash looked striking wearing a short-sleeved black top and jet black hair cut in a flapper style with thick bangs and blunt sides making a rectangular frame for her face.

The more discursive sections of her paper attempt to explicate the nature of jazz:

Jazz has been described by some who have played it as a conversation; everyone staying pretty much around a subject but all adding ideas and feelings of their own. . . . When musicians work together and are feeling the same thing, great passion can be felt by both the players and observers. In this way, they extend their conversation to us.

Then there's a shift to personal images evoked by hearing the singer and her jazz group, which include Anna's responses to the music, her feeling "drained, and awed by their creativity." In this section Anna says she fades away, "feeling a world away from school." It's in this section where she loses her audience as she drifts into highly personal memories:

Some songs I associate very strongly with my dad's playing the piano and they make me feel sentimental about time passing and human existence: its brevity and the inevitable pain of losing those you love.

I thought of a TV movie my boyfriend and I tuned into one night about a scientist who had a machine that could tap into other people's experience by measuring neuron transmitters or something like that.

I envisioned a day of end for everyone and me hanging onto my boyfriend's white shirt with red and black pinstripes ascending into eternity. I held on as tightly as I could but we were separated and I slipped into nothingness without him.

Rather abruptly "Jazz" ends, with a few lines from a childhood song:

Inchworm Inchworm, inchworm measuring the marigold/
You and your arithmetic will get you very far/
Inchworm/Inchworm measuring the marigold/
It seems to me you'd stop and see/
How beautiful they are.

Because of its many writing styles, its bizarre mixture of images, and the intense personal emotions conveyed, the paper is a mass of unrealized potential. Students in her peer writing group help show Anna that her real subject is not jazz. Jazz triggers the topic of an inner experience that is very personal. In the writing group Anna begins by talking about her paper:

Anna: I guess I was going for images. I wasn't going for focus. I wanted the readers to share some of those images with me. . . . It didn't have a focus. It made me think about a lot of different things.

Sue: And is that what jazz is to you too?

Anna: That's what that performance was to me. When I listen to jazz. . . . It's not really about jazz. It's about my experiences.

David: Jazz is the triggering subject.

Sue: Yes. Jazz is the trigger.

David interprets the paper as a "kind of collage" but he and Sue both ask Anna what she wants the reader to get out of the text, indicating that its dependence upon images is not always effective: "I didn't know what you wanted me to think." David picks up on the song lyrics and inquires, "Did you want us to think that we should stop measuring our lives so that we could enjoy them?" When Anna asks the group if they think the paper is "too crowded," their responses show that they think the paper's unfocused. Sue says, "You could make a whole other paper on that movie and stuff." David suggests that he got lost: "There's a lot in there in that paragraph about losing your grip and separating and slipping into nothingness. You read it and think, 'What did I just read?'" Randy is the most directive and says flat out, "I think you should stick to one thing and focus it."

Although the paper presents the experiences of a jazz performance, it does so in a mixture of auditory and visual images but it is verbal language that her peers must contend with.

In conference, Donna supports what Anna's trying out, giving her an essay by William Zinsser on jazz:

Anna: I had problems ... I had questions with what belonged and what flowed. I kind of like the way I go from one thing to another.

Donna: I do too.

Anna: Because that was my thought pattern when I was watching the performance. I wanted to stick to that performance because that's what evoked all these feelings in me.

Donna: And that's an anchoring device that allows you to move back and forth. It's like the "triggering town." If you're nowhere at all, how can you go anyplace else? It anchors you, it gives the reader a base and then you can go wherever you want from it. It's a good technique to use.

Anna: People in the group had problems with it because I tied the paper to Laurie Nash. Maybe I should start out with the atmosphere and then focus it on her and go to the jazz group and then into my own experiences. Something like that ...

In the intermediate draft, Anna follows her own advice, reinforced by Donna, and anchors her paper at the Half Note where she's listening to the jazz concert but drifting in and out of the concert, juxtaposing her personal responses to Laurie Nash against her own inner experiences: "When Laurie Nash sang it seemed she was opening to me through her music and I answered by intensely relating her experiences to my own." In this way she's able to retain much of the imagery of the first draft but makes it clear that the songs evoke these feelings and memories. She ends this draft:

I thought that because her performance had made me so introspective she would know somehow how she made me feel. I felt as if I had gotten closer to her in the hour performance. After the concert we passed her table on our way out and I wanted to tell her what a strong effect her music had on me. But she was with a group of people having a verbal conversation, one that I could not share. I didn't want to. I knew it was through her music that I knew her.

Anna's final folder includes still another revision of "Jazz," which is much tighter structurally than her middle draft. The paper has been cut from six pages to three. She retains the movement back and forth between the jazz concert and her own responses but she also inserts much more analysis about the medium of jazz itself, partially borrowed from draft one. In this polished version, Anna has conceptualized the images that drove her first draft. She has also tackled the focus problem—now the paper is about her, not Laurie Nash, the jazz singer. And she's analyzed jazz as a form as well as the particular concert she's attending. The final draft works to combine image and analysis.

Jazz

I'm not in Portsmouth anymore. I leave my physical location behind while the jazz of Laurie Nash and the Joy Quartet manipulates my moods and thoughts with each piece they play. Their music is so intense that it stuffs the room, cottoning my thoughts and movements.

Jazz has been described by some who play it as a conversation. Each piece is gradually developed as each musician adds his own ideas and follows it till its conclusion. Jazz gathers energy from the spontaneity and imagination of those playing and through the communications between the musicians. The more comfortable the musicians feel with each other the freer they are to experiment both during their solos and as a group. When musicians are moving together and "feeling" the same energy, excitement lifts both players and observers.

I love the building energy in a piece that gets louder and more complex as different instruments contribute. First the solo bass player creates anticipation by laying down the Latin rhythm that the others are expected to join. In jazz the number of measures that he will play is improvised, not set. He will play until the impulse that creates those opening phrases has passed and he is ready to be joined. I am thrilled both by his creativity then by the addition of the drummer's slight tapping to accentuate the beat. Then by the piano player who first plays chords matching the accents of the rhythm, then gradually comes into her own. Together they are building something. They are working through their impulses while sharing the foundation of a set chord pattern. The music is so exciting because all the musicians are audibly fused.

Over the top of this foundation comes the high voice of Laurie Nash. She is a whistle, a flute, not singing words but sounds which tell me her feelings without telling me a story. I can understand her better this way. She uses her voice as a noise instead of a means to communication so she directly translates her feelings. I relate to her instead of words that might have different meanings for me. I am excited.

This bossanova rhythm, like others, has an exotic feel to it and I picture Spanish dancers with castanets in full red skirts with small yellow and green stripes. Their dark hair is pulled away from their faces and their mysterious eyes lead them back off. I lack the Spanish mystery that has always attracted me. I could never feel at home in a bossonova rhythm because of my blonde hair and English background. It makes me insecure and I feel easily read. Light eyes can't hide anything. I am envious. The music leaves me breathless but my place is unfulfilled.

Anna said that she enjoyed doing this revision, enjoyed working with the words and images. Donna found this Anna's most successful paper for the semester and copied it for her files of effective student writing.

Anna as Collaborator

"The Loss of Individualism and the Gain of the Individual" ■ Anna likes group work. She compared collaborative writing to creating a modern dance, equating the freewheeling conversation of group writing with the improvisational aspects of dancing. Communication, she suggests, is the primary focus of both types of group work. When Connie, David, and she are actually engaged in talk about their project, Anna feels the collaboration to be the most exciting. All three of them report in their journals about how easily they worked together. "Being sensitive to everyone's ideas, that's what collaboration is all about," Anna writes. Yet she also acknowledges that, to make the collaboration work, the individual members must sometimes compromise for the group: "Sometimes I felt like I was trying to make every one of my ideas happen. And I didn't like that. I'm conscious of making this a group effort."

One of the ways they achieve the group effort is to borrow ideas from each member's individual readings to pull a thread for weaving a paper together. For their initial reading Connie and Anna both picked short stories from literary magazines while David contributed an article about the music industry called "And the Beat Goes On." David reports that in the first two-hour collaborative meeting the group focused on making personal connections between the readings and their own lives: "We discussed the various windows that were presented by different authors and how we linked experiences in our lives to their proposed windows." Connie also writes about this stage of collaboration: "It was interesting to see how each of us presented our reasons for choosing the articles we did. Even though they were all distinctly different, we found something similar in all of them." In an attempt to find a common theme the group "made a list of speculations about each other's articles," which includes the following themes recorded in Anna's journal: "dehumanization, loss in the world, how we have to try to break down society's barriers."

The group also tries to decide early on about the form that the paper will take. Anna reports that it was her idea to do "character studies," but she then worries over whether that was a group consensus or not: "I hope I didn't push the idea too far," which indicates her fear of being "pushy." David suggests in his journal that this idea was, in fact, a group decision, that they "tentatively decided to write a short story . . . about three characters trapped or placed in a new environment in which they were presented with a problem." David's anxious over whose ideas will dominate: "Should one of my ideas be discounted for one of Anna's or Connie's? It's a struggle to keep personalities, persuasions, frames/windows, and styles on an even keel. The question I find myself asking: should we even try?" The struggle of this group, consistently documented in all three journals, is to create a context in which all members participate equally. David recounts that by working together they developed a "delicate understanding of our responsibilities as writers."

Once the group decides on its theme and genre, the members feel that they have to stick with these ideas. It is at this stage that Anna feels that the group becomes "stunted" and that the progress is no longer "organic". "It was like we can't grow anymore because if we did, the project would go off in different ways." Since the impetus is to produce a paper, the group loses its initial surge of energy, or what Anna describes as "the intense creative spark" of their earlier exploratory conversations. The necessity of getting this paper done shortchanges what Anna feels might haven been a more extended and creative incubation period.

The compensation for this loss of oral dialogue is that Anna experiences a new way of writing as she works on fiction with David and Connie: "It was interesting for me to write fiction within the framework of David and Connie." Anna is enthusiastic about narration; she writes, "Our paper grew as a story, not as a thinking process." She welcomes learning a new writing form: "And it didn't feel odd. I was comfortable with it. In that way the group gave me a sort of strength. We supported each other without being conscious of it." The gain in collaboration for her as an individual turns out to be this journey into form, or what Anna calls "an adventure in language."

During this adventure Anna learns that she and Connie have different ideas about how to develop the individual characters. Whereas Anna pictures the "androgynous young man" as being intelligent but unaware, Connie sees him as "trendy." Anna had even visualized this character as wearing "a grey down jacket" and having "brown hair and eyes." What emerges in their group effort is an entirely different description:

His appearance is a new androgynous fashion. He wears a long black overcoat covered with pockets and buttons. His black leather boots, midcalf length, hide the bottom of his tattered jeans, making them seem like knickers. His dark hair is gelled straight up above his head, exposing a gold hoop earring in his left ear. Wires hanging from his headphones connect him to his trendy world of pop music.

David, who has written fiction before, reflects in his journal that Mr. Androgynous was overdeveloped as a character with "his walkman and his hair" compared to the other two key characters they created. Anna is also dissatisfied with the final depiction of this male: "The androgynous character becomes somewhat problematic as I reflect." Connie is critical too, mainly of the professional woman, commenting in her journal that the "whole thing seems too contrived—the professional woman seems too inhumane." Anna feels that the characters failed to develop because "we stopped growing with them. In fact, we created characters so distant from us and each other, they had no room to grow."

No one in the group, Anna included, is entirely satisfied with the results. Anna describes the characters as "symbols for the increased lack of the human in this cold world," and she worries about this kind of detachment. The separation of writer and character feels foreign to Anna; so what she dislikes most in this collaborative experience is the sense that the characters become "fixed" and do not evolve: "We were afraid to change them." David comments, too, that after writing the paper together, the group lost its ability to be objective: "Our group became such a solidified mass of writers that we were only seeing the story through a single set of eyes."

Even if she is somewhat unhappy with the product, Anna found that the collaboration process gave her a close look at the writing processes of others. She writes that their group picked the "slowest method imaginable" for actually writing the paper, drafting the whole story together in front of a word processor. While that writing process was tedious, it was also filled with camaraderie. Anna reports that they "giggled" at their mistakes, "clapped" when something clicked, and pushed together to make "clear writing that will say what we want it to say."

For this type of project, Anna suggests that using the computer has a distinct advantage because it makes the process "visible" and also "involves" everyone. Connie agreed: "Anna typed the stuff in and David and I sat on either side of her while we all discussed what we wanted to say. This process in itself was interesting. We each had to communicate to one another what we visualized in our minds about the scene" (Connie's journal). This laborious writing process also revealed each student's individual strengths as a writer: Anna describes Connie, the outdoor education major, as a "problem solver"; and David, the only English major in the class, as a "language-lover." Compared to the others in her group, Anna discovers that her own power in writing is not so much in "technique" but in her ideas. The group work externalizes for Anna what she unconsciously knew about her strength as an essay writer. Anna summarizes: "It brought out different ideas and strengths to form one project."

What Anna initially identifies as the theme of the paper — "the gain of the individual and the loss of individualism" — becomes a metaphor for her collaborative writing process. In a final evaluation of the group effort Anna writes, "You gain and lose from any method." What is given up in an individual effort, usually accomplished in universities in a competitive situation, is "the chance to work out a problem with a group," which Anna decides is "valuable." The idea that group work can help students to feel less isolated, less lonely in their intellectual growth, is echoed in her collaborative journal: "Everyone's had millions of ideas and connections that start in a mind and stay there." Collaboration helps make these singular ideas emerge and connect, and ultimately, even if imperfectly, communicate with others. Here is an excerpt from their three page short story called "The Elevator":

"Let's be patient and stay calm. I'm sure someone will help us soon." The young woman assures. "By the way, my name is Ophry."
"If the elevator is delinquent I'm sure the maintenance people are too." The professional woman interjects. This is followed by a long silence metered by the impatient tapping of the professional woman's foot. She looks to the back of the elevator at the figure standing there. She assumes he is male by the tone of his voice, however his appearance is a new androgynous fashion. He wears a long black overcoat covered with pockets and buttons. His black leather boots, midcalf length, hide the bottom of his tattered jeans making them seem like knickers. His dark hair is gelled straight up above his head exposing a gold hoop earing in his left ear. Wires hanging from his headphones connect him to his trendy world of pop music. He focuses his glance on the professional woman. She turns away not caring enough to acknowledge him.
Ophry produces a white collapsible walking stick from her coat pocket. She opens it and begins a tapping search for the perimeter of the

elevator and a railing to hold on to. Accidently she bumps the young man's boot.

"Oh, I'm sorry, I didn't see you there," Ophry apologizes.

"I didn't know you were blind, "he shouts over his walkman assuming that she can't hear him very well.

"I'm not blind, I just have a different way of seeing things. My hearing is excellent so you don't need to speak up." Ophry finds the rail then steadies herself. She is able to relax, having found a secure space.

Anna's Evaluation

Anna ends English 501 with positive feelings about the collaborative project and the whole course, which she says, "opens you up to being more personal in your other courses" and overall "makes you more active in your education." One very specific skill that Anna gains from Prose Writing and that she attributes to Donna is a growing ability to edit the tentativeness and qualification out of her prose. In conference, Donna tells her, "You don't have to say 'I think,' because it's obvious that you're the one who's doing the writing. Just come right out and say what you have to say."

At the end of the term Anna drafts an essay in class evaluating her progress in Prose Writing by comparing it with her art history coursework. When I read her final essay, I recall an earlier interview during which she voiced some of her misgivings about art history: "In the middle of the semester, I became really confused about why I am doing art history. Why should I tear apart this person's painting just so I can get some meaning out of it? It's just there. Why can't I just look at it and get something from it. Why do I have to prove something?"

In this final essay for Prose Writing, Anna critiques the methodology and thinking process of art history, discussing the tension in her academic life between fields that require distance, detachment, and objectivity and those that welcome intimacy, engagement, and subjectivity:

I've learned that my learning in 501 is very unrelated to the learning in my other classes. . . . In 501 I develop theories. I think more about life. My life. I write about my life. I think about my place in the universe. In other classes, I learn about other people's lives, that aren't even in this time period. They're mostly dead. And I'm interpreting their lives and beliefs and influences. Trying to make sense of them. They don't even care. If they're up there looking down at me and scholars, they'd probably die three times over laughing at this folly. Midway through this semester, I realized I wasn't sure about the principles of Art History. How dare we study people who are dead? Where is their proof, their treatment of line? I thought I'd love to write essays for the rest of my life: they involve me directly. And what a better subject to study.

Let's say that I become a famous artist. And my works are flashed up on a screen in a college auditorium. Five major ones in a half an hour. All reduced. Simplified to the rawest, most basic terms. "See this influence, and that. . . . See the changes in her treatment of color . . . compare the palettes. . . . She did this after her brother tried to kill himself, that's why it's so dark. This was when she studied with a sculptor, see the differences? This month is her centennial and there is a major debate going on about the meaning in her works. She claimed to her death that this wasn't about suicide, but how can anyone deny that? Next slide please . . ."

In her major field of study — art history — there's an undercurrent of resistance; the rebel is fighting the scholarship accommodator in an academic dance of virtual energies. As we go into her art class the following semester, we will remember this rebellious voice that is warning Anna of the dangers of the distanced stance toward art. Next frame please.

Anna in Avant-Garde Art Class

I am early for art history class, which begins at four in the afternoon in Paul Arts, the building that houses the music, theater, and art departments. Waiting by the wooden weaving looms outside the lecture room, I observe the students milling around before class, some of them drinking coffee and tea purchased down the hall in the convenient art supply store. Eventually I join them with a cup of hot chocolate. Several students cluster together chatting softly, and although I cannot hear them I see by their dress that they are different: one bearded man in his late twenties has a scarf of a rough South American fabric tied around his neck, a style that is seldom imitated on campus; another woman is wearing heavy work boots, splattered with paint, and olive clothing, which seems like a kind of military uniform. I glance down at someone's hands to see two-inch fingernails painted jet black, accompanied by an arm adorned with lovely clanging silver bracelets; when I look up I find hair that's partially dyed pink, gelled straight up from her head.

When the door opens to let out the flood from the previous class, I follow students into the room and, noting insecurely that Anna's not there yet, I select a seat near Professor Hall's lectern, organize my new art history notebook, and eavesdrop on a lively conversation:

"My sculpture's finally coming together. I worked on it all afternoon."
"Great. Aren't you doing something with sand painting and cheesecloth?"
"Yes, and I'm using thorns and have marks all over my hand from them."
"What is your impetus? Is it religious?"
"No, it's not, in spite of the thorns."

Hall enters wearing a lavender-checked top over loose slacks. Thin and middle-aged, her grey hair is clipped back from her neck and she is carrying a stack of notes and art books. At this point early in the semester, I know very little about her. She earned her doctorate in 1974, lectures frequently in the university's Humanities Series, and serves on many university committees. She briefly consults with the projectionist who is sitting behind a stand in the center of the room with trays of slides. Hall makes several announcements before Anna slips in, waves to me, and takes a seat on the other side of the room. Most of the announcements refer to cultural events: "There's a well-known violin quartet that will be playing for free tomorrow evening if the snow lets up. The student art show opens this week and we need volunteers to help with posters — see Amy if you have time. There will be a 'happening' at the MUB, and for those of you who haven't seen this kind of artistic statement, this will be your chance."

After a few wry comments on her announcements, the weather, or the course material — "There are lots of dear old ladies with galoshes and umbrellas who hate Pollock but we won't listen to them" — Hall begins her lecture, which goes for an hour and a half. She seldom looks down at her notes, although she sometimes reads from books, either works of art criticism, letters and biographies, or accounts by artists themselves. She doesn't waste a beat of time as she presents the day's materials, fully illustrated with her slides. The projectionist is so perfectly attuned to her lecture that she talks to him infrequently, only occasionally asking for a refocusing.

Adopting the perspective of a student, uninitiated into art history, I wildly write my field notes in the semidarkness. The noise of the slide machine weighs on the afternoon air, not enough to interfere with Hall's voice but obvious enough to indicate there is a mechanical accompaniment to her talk. Sometimes Hall moves from her lectern to the projected images, pointing out visual details related to the artists we're considering: space, line, shape, color, light, shade, arrangement, brush strokes, even the framing is sometimes discussed. We are on Jackson Pollock, an abstract expressionist of enormous influence, whose work I've always been attracted to but don't understand. Anna later admits that she had never heard of Pollock before the course.

Hall explains that she'll do a developmental overview of Pollock's work. She intersperses her talk with comments about his life: his fragile personality, his battles with substance abuse, his various attempts at psychoanalysis, his complicated personal relationships with other contemporary artists. Usually she presents two pictures, side by side, illustrating, for example, that Pollock was influenced by American Indian art such as sand paintings and Navaho masks. From such comparisons, Hall draws generalized statements about modern art, about the principles that a particular modern artist advances. Professor Hall suggests that Pollock's return to the art of native Americans reveals an artist questioning the manufactured production of art against the natural artistic statements of the Indians. This kind of debate over what constitutes a work of art is a thread that's woven through all of modern art, she points out.

At various junctures in her lecture, Hall stops to explicate a term. She asks, "Does everyone understand what the word 'discursive' means?" and then goes on to offer both a definition and example. The discursive mind, she says, takes material such as what she is presenting and orders it. It is that verbal part of our minds that goes on talking to us and may even prevent us from seeing things in a piece of art. Unfortunately for us all, she says, art history is a very discursive field of study. Meditation, she offers, sometimes helps us stop all that jabber inside of us. Pollock, she suggests, found his own way to quiet this discursiveness through painting.

When Hall shows the famous Pollock "poured works," she explains that they were executed like a dance—the unstretched canvas on the floor, Pollock moving in and out of the paintings with the rhythm of a dancer. This creative process produced, she says, "great skeins of color woven over one another, a network of lines and splatters," suggesting a new way of representing pictorial space. This scattered effect of Pollock's drip painting is not to be confused with randomness, not to be considered haphazard, she warns, because Pollock did not always accept his results. However, the element of the accidental becomes a deliberate statement, a principle of abstract expressionists. She reads from Pollock's own writing: "When I am in my painting, I am not aware of what I'm doing. The painting has a life of its own."

Hall often displays dissatisfaction with the slides, which cannot begin, she says, to do justice to the size or texture of the originals: "Oh nuts. This is a huge painting," she comments on Pollock's famous *Autumn Rhythm*: "Try to imagine this as filling up an entire wall of this room." The large scale of these works, she suggests, marks the final break of painting as being detached from the painter. In modern art, painting requires the viewer to be absorbed in pictorial space, the environment of the work encloses the spectator on all sides. As she moves closer to the slide, she suggests to students that they need to see the originals so that they can feel "the texture of the paint and allow themselves to float around in the painting." This kind of abstract art, Hall says, "requires you to enter into a dialogue with the painting itself." Again, generalizing from Pollock to an important concept of modernist work, she says that the abstract expressionist painters were "engaged in an argument between the literal surface and virtual space in painting." They were forging a new vocabulary for modern artists.

The class continues in this way for ninety minutes. Only one student raises her hand to ask the name of a painting which Hall identifies as *Number 11*; she advises students not to bother with titles like these, but to be aware of more general dates and periods. After class, Hall lingers for a while near her desk to answer questions. Anna and I head downtown for tea and muffins to talk about the course.

Anna as Guide ■ Anna explains to me that the class is made up of two types of students: studio people who sat mainly seated on the side where I was, and art history majors who sat on the other side of the room. Studio people often hang around together, she says, based on her own experiences of taking a few studio courses. And studio people, Anna suggests, "loathe" courses in art history because "it's too detached" and usually they can't "apply it to their own work." Anna feels the conflict between these two fields herself: "It puts me in a weird position because I'm on both sides. Sometimes I'm getting more into the art history theories and other times I'm thinking that it's more pure to actually do art and then develop a theory about it." The analytic side wins this war, but Anna is also experienced in creating art herself. She has taken studio courses in both high school and college and has done some "ink washes and charcoals" and has spent "hours on her ceramics course." This split between studio artists and art historians reminds me of the composition/literature split in my own English department.

Anna knows the names of a few of the art history majors, but doesn't have much contact with them outside of her classes. "I don't talk to anyone much about art," she confides in me. When I ask her how affiliated she feels with being an art history major she says, "Not that much." I inquire about who her audience is when she writes for these courses and, unsurprisingly, she says, "My professors." Interestingly, all three of her art history professors have been women, and, according to Anna, they are very serious scholars. I later learn that Hall doesn't even realize that Anna is an art history major, although she does remember from an introductory Visual Studies class that she is a good writer.

Since there are multiple layers of information to absorb in this course, I probe to find out how Anna prepares and studies for modern art. First, there's the actual painting, drawing, sculpture, architecture, found object, or college that she has to know and identify: these serve as the primary text of the course, requiring a special language of interpretation. Then, there is Hall's commentary about this art that needs to be overlaid and connected to the works. Finally, there are five textbooks as well as numerous chapters and articles on reserve at the library that students are required to read; these deal with the social, political, and economic implications of the works. For example, in the two-week period covering the topic of "abstract expressionism," the required reading included eleven chapters from books and shorter articles from ten other books. In addition, there was also a list of recommended readings for this topic, again some complete book chapters as well as other shorter articles. Students also have access to the slide library where, at specific times and days, they may view slides on their own

Reading in Art History: The Twin Texts ■ Anna says she doesn't have much of a method for reading art history texts, that she just goes through and underlines what she thinks is important and tries to keep up with the material—not an easy task, I soon learn. Last semester when she was "required" to do a journal entry from a textbook for her Prose Writing class, Anna found it difficult to make any personal connections to the textbooks. Selecting an article on Bosch's "images of poverty" from her Northern Renaissance course, she began her journal entry by writing:

I have tried before to write reactions to some of my art history readings and barely filled half a page. It seems I read for facts and when I tried to make connections, I couldn't because it was so cut and dry. *Facty.*

facty facty. It's hard to have other insights, except into the works themselves.

Yet when Anna continues to force herself to write a journal response, she is able to relate Bosch's images of the peasant to the greed of modern society: "More and more we think only in terms of ourselves ... This Ship of Fools is going straight to hell." At another point, Anna related an aborted attempt at doing journal entries on her art texts on her own, saying that just getting the material down is difficult enough without trying to make any personal connections.

When I suggest that journal entries or some type of note-taking device for this course might be helpful because the material seems pretty abstract, Anna says that she doesn't think about it as much as I do: "We just learn it. I mean, we see a painting and she'll describe it and it'll make sense, and you'll remember some of the things she says and some of what you read." Anna says that she allows both art and music to affect her directly. Bestowed with a kind of visual learning, she describes it like remembering a "song or a particular view": when you look at a painting, she says, you get certain feelings and when you see that work again, "you return to those feelings." Anna quotes Professor Hall as saying, "You have to understand the language before the paintings will speak to you." In her study of types of creative thinking, Vera John-Steiner suggests that the power of visual thought is the ability to conceptualize our experiences as structures in motion, as relationships" (1985, 106).

The paradox of the art history major seems to be that this visual response finally must be translated into the verbal. An art history student cannot survive without solid writing abilities. As the course syllabus states, avant-garde art demands that students "observe keenly, take comprehensive notes, and organize a large amount of material coherently. Verbal and analytic skills are important."

But for Hall, there *is* a definite way to read art history. At the beginning of one class meeting, she reviews the syllabus and suggests to students that the arrangement of the course material is deliberate: "I had hoped that the order of the materials would be apparent." She then explains just how the reading should be accomplished. The first set of readings under abstract expressionism, she says, provides a global overview of this problematic period, followed by materials that support the New York art world-view—written by critics such as Clement Greenberg and Harold

Rosenberg; and finally there are statements and writings by individual artists. "You need a medium-sized box, a construct, in which to put some very individualistic painters in order to understand what the New York School is all about," Hall instructs.

I find as the semester goes on that the paintings *do* begin to speak to me, but without any feedback through class or peer discussion or written responses, I wonder just how this material is being organized in my mind. I rely on Anna to share her analysis of paintings with me, to show me how she reads a work of art. I compare my notes on Motherwell with hers and find that I have written more but Anna's notes mean more. In one of our meetings Anna explains her notes on Motherwell as she points to the painting:

This is what she [Hall] means by playing with virtual space on a flat canvas. Motherwell wants these paintings read as both open and closed. There are many different ways you can look at this painting: the inside becomes enclosed but then you are drawn to the outside because the lines form a U shape. The painting moves. When you step back, you realize that it's just a blue canvas with black lines. Finally you relate this to the artist's philosophy and all the stuff from the readings and it all makes sense.

The class spends a great amount of time on abstract expressionism but it also covers postpainterly abstraction, constructions, pop and op art, happenings, minimalist works, superrealism, gestural and photo art, idea art, performance, and postmodernism. Hall shows us how to view junk assemblages and sculptures, found objects, collages, and large installations that cover entire rooms of museums; we learn how to analyze everything from Oldenburg's vinyl toilet to the Independence Mall in Philadelphia. Hall is an expert as well at reading the political subtext in art. She brings to the surface much of what seems hidden—an artist's statements about the Vietnam war, for example. And she offers new ways of reading familiar images, suggesting that Warhol's silk screens of Marilyn Monroe—his saturated images—are both "formal" and "haunting." She draws extensively from the artists' personal lives and often recommends books; *The Legacy of Mark Rothko* by Sedes is described as a "shrill, muckraking biography that describes the scandalous behavior of his gallery after his death." She can even critique the official museum catalogs as being slanted. She reads from Rothko's Guggenheim catalog and comments: "This idea of Rothko's obtaining a harmonious transcendence is garbage. Rothko was a deeply troubled man who went to several different shrinks at the same time and got enough medication for him to commit suicide."

The complexity of reading, connecting, and interpreting the various modern art movements dazzles me; there are artistic responses, reactions, and statements against the establishment, against other artists, and sometimes against an artist's earlier work. There is autobiographical information, visual information, and sociopolitical information, which are woven into a rather rough texture of modern art in my mind. As I struggle with this sorting process, I wonder how Anna is doing. She is the expert and I am the novice, but I have no tangible things to work with, no learning structures have been provided to guide me through this journey.

Anna claims that the intertwining of biographical information with the paintings makes the canvas easier to interpret: "It's easy for me to remember his paintings because I remember his life ... I thought it was interesting, Rothko's gradual losing of sanity and how that was shown in his works, all that social consciousness and torment about his social position and all that." To see the canvas as life and the artist's life as canvas reinforces the connection for her.

Talk in Art History: Anna as Listener ■ The discourse in this class is a one-way communication system; Hall lectures brilliantly and we listen in fascinated silence. A short snip of her taped lecture on *Womanhouse* and performance art follows; we can see how packed her talk is with the visual, the autobiographical, and the political:

What we are looking at is a work called *Womanhouse* which was organized in Los Angeles in 1971 to 1972 by Judy Chicago and Miriam Shapiro and a group of their students and other women artists in the area. It was a work that was intended, as Miriam Shapiro said, to convert psychological rage into artistic energy. And what they were converting was the rage of exclusion; that is, women artists in the '60s and '70s were not part of the whole educational cycle. And at that point Judy Chicago and Miriam Shapiro were teaching at the California Institute of the Arts and had come through the regular art school thing and one of the things they had felt about this was that they were more or less always being treated as peripheral to the main functions of the art school. I have heard male instructors in this school say of women artists, "Oh don't give them a fellowship—they'll just go out and get married. It would be a waste of money." It's that kind of thing that fueled the rage that led to *Womanhouse*. *Womanhouse* was, in a sense, a performance place. It was an old house that had been abandoned, and it was taken over by Chicago and Shapiro and women artists. It was repainted, jacked up, rewired, and it became the first all-female aesthetic environment. So the whole house became environmental art work and there were spaces in which performances would go on. You're looking, now, at two of the performances.

As absorbing as her lectures were, I found myself longing to hear what other students in the course had to say, to hear what was going on in their minds. On March 3, nearly six weeks into the course, it happens. But the talk is not initiated by a student. We're learning about Louise Nevelson's work, the first major woman artist we've discussed, when five minutes before the class ends, someone asks a personal question. The speaker, a professor who is also auditing the course, says that he is "deeply troubled" by Nevelson's sculpture ending up on Wall Street in New York and asks Hall how she feels about it. Hall responds that it bothers her too but that no matter what artists feel or do, their work always ends up being "owned, transformed into artifact." The private, individualistic artistic statement in this way becomes public and political. Wall Street buys the art to display how broad-minded they are, Professor Hall says.

The class has officially ended but students linger to talk about the political implications of art, about what happens when the artistic opposition is finally folded into the establishment. This is the first time in the semester that I've heard any of these students' voices: they sound intense, concerned. One student says that artists have the choice to either "oppose the system and live on air and peanut butter" or actively seek commissions and sell their art, but that "it's a matter of how you conduct yourself in the system." Another student disagrees, saying that art is not owned by any artist. "A piece of art acquires a life of its own once it becomes public. Art doesn't belong to one person but takes on the world around it."

Hall ends the fifteen-minute overtime discussion by reaching consensus with all these points of view, suggesting, "A work of art means different things to different people in different contexts. You never can tell what will happen on the art scene, who or what movements will reemerge. There is in this field a large element of chance."

Anna later shares with me that this class discussion was an anomaly, that in most art history courses students don't talk much. When I asked why she didn't enter the discussion, Anna said, "I haven't tried to talk about it yet because I haven't gotten a grip on it yet." Since midterms were coming up, I wondered when she would begin to grasp these many artists and their movements. Anna seemed to understand well her task for art history as "learning how to think about modern art in a certain way, developing theories about modern art." Anna welcomed the test in some ways because, she says, "if you're a good writer and have read a certain amount of stuff you can get by with just going to class and knowing a selected amount of the material." The system for doing well in art history is "to remember what the teacher says about the paintings and make those connections on your test."

Writing in Art History: "We Will Write Some Essays" ■ For Anna these connections did not happen. She reviewed all the slides for modern art and even sought out some clarification from Hall personally about the difference between "gestural" and "color-field" painters. Yet her midterm exam earned her only a C, a very low grade for Anna who was used to getting A's on essay exams. When I looked at the exam, I realized that it wasn't "tricky," but just as Hall had described it. Each question was a compare/contrast between two artists and two artistic movements, exactly what my class notes before the exam suggested: "I will show a slide comparison and ask you to locate the issues within the tangled skein of art history. I'm interested in philosophical issues rather than a visual or aesthetic approach. If you begin with the color-field artists and the abstract expressionists and think what happened next, you will probably come up with the format of the exam."

The first question asks for a comparison between a gestural painter, de Kooning, and a color-field painter, Mark Rothko. After identifying and placing their work between 1950 and 1955, Anna writes:

Here we have a comparison between the two main divisions of the Abstract Expressionist movement, the Gestural abstractionist (de Kooning) and Color-field abstractionist (Rothko). Both of these artists were involved in the New York School at its beginnings, and were involved with the social economic issues concerning members of that school. They were involved with the WPA (de Kooning was kicked out and had to support himself as a house painter) and both worked in the hard financial struggle that was uniting the group, and achieved recognition as the public grew to appreciate the modern movement. Rothko had a particularly hard time adjusting to fame and financial security. When he found that when he had earned money and was elevated to a higher financial status, he had difficulty knowing how to be of the class that he and his friends had resented for so long. He had been a dishwasher at Yale while the rich cruised in their flagrant wealth. This work was done at a point in his career when his palette was beginning to darken. It would eventually become black and grey as he literally could not cope with this earth and society and his place in it.

In the margin of Anna's opening paragraph Hall indicates that Anna has let the personal life of the artist overwhelm the historical focus that is needed for her answer: "This is all good information but do you want it to take over an essay that should focus on the historic significance of the larger group?"

In the last essay, where students are asked to contrast two sculptures, Anna goes into great detail about the materials used and the overall effect of the constructions as she describes Nevelson's *Sky Cathedral*:

In this work she has used materials found in abandoned buildings, a wide variety, not simply constructed. It is collage-like, tying in old pieces from banisters and perhaps a fence, making them part of the same world – her world. The images come to me of the showing of the *Sky Cathedral* in Lower Manhattan in an old space, dimly lit with the sculptures appearing in midnight blue, like a moon glow, and later in Mrs. Nevelson's Palace, her house existing in the 4th dimension. These are two worlds, experiences that we walk into. They seem like altars.

Hall's response to this paragraph indicates that it is in this answer that Anna had gone into too much visual detail and not formed a generalization from it: "Instead of all this detail, which you don't have time to write down, you need to discuss the development of the sculptured environment."

In her exam, Anna leaned on two previously reliable learning strategies – connecting the artist's work with the artist's life and extensive visual analysis. Neither response was appropriate for an exam that demanded that students use the visual analysis of the paintings and personal details about the artists' life to form generalizations about these painters' contributions to the movement of abstract expressionism (see Hatch 1988 for a discussion of students' writing problems in art history). The many critical, visual, and autobiographical details that Anna had gathered now needed to be synthesized into a particular "theory" about artistic innovations and movements.

But it wasn't only Anna who did poorly and it wasn't only me who was confused about how one learned all this material other than the old-fashioned method of pouring it into the brain. For even when all the detail is rehearsed, it must be stirred together so that it can be articulated in a very specific way. Hall herself was disappointed in the kind of exam papers that were written, although there was one forceful essay that she read aloud to the class to serve as a model. She prefaced her reading of this exam by saying that "it's a very general little essay" but, in fact, the essay was tightly written and "generalized" from an enormous amount of material. In two long introductory paragraphs, the student explicates the paradox of the abstract expressionist movement and then with real authority seldom shown in student writing, goes on to disagree with the opinion of well-known art critics: "In fact, I would disagree to some extent with Ashton's depiction of the cohesiveness of the New York School. Indeed many of the strong founders of Abstract Expressionism developed schools of second-generation followers, whose stylistic borrowing in many cases bogged down into academicism." There were two other A exams but overall the results were not satisfactory to Hall, who characterized the midrange papers as representing a kind of "cuisinart" writing with no main focus but a forced jumble of facts and ideas.

My analysis of the student exam papers Hall shared with me concurred with the problems she had already identified: an inability to name the general trends and abstract concepts of modern art, offering instead a list of very specific but sometimes unrelated details. Anna's own comments about the exam indicated that she felt a lack of "control" over the material, that she hadn't "organized" her writing well, and that the subject matter seemed "all grey" to her: "My essays were all bad in their own ways," she admitted.

Dialogue Across the Curriculum

Shortly after midterms, Hall and I began a dialogue about how students might learn and write for art history more easily. At first I found Hall resistant to introducing new learning structures into her classroom. She was "put off," she said, by having to teach writing. Her job was to teach her subject: "My major concern is art, not students." And while she agreed that the reading was very dense and demanding, many students, she felt, weren't really "up to it" intellectually: "There's such a range of students in this course — studio art majors and art history majors — who are very different types." Finally, there was just so much material to cover, and so little time that Hall regretted there was no time left for class discussion. Just when these kinds of statements made me skeptical of the possible changes that I might offer to improve the students' writing, Professor Hall suggested before class one day that while her main concern was with art, with her subject, she also wanted to make this subject accessible to her students.

In informal talks before and after class, I began to prod Hall to think about her own writing, about how she had learned to write for art history. She confessed that she wasn't "conscious" of how she'd learned to become a writer in her field—she just did it. She also gave me some of the articles she had written—from the more informal critiques of local art exhibits to the formal journal articles—and it was clear to me that she was an accomplished and successful writer of art history. When we discussed these articles, Hall was eager to point out that she disliked her earlier writing because of what she now characterizes as its very "male, Panofsky" style.

Although Hall had no conscious plan or method for showing students how to write exams or term papers, she pointed out that on her syllabus she had suggested a paperback on writing, Sylvan Barnet's *A Short Guide to Writing about Art*, and that the assigned reading included many fine examples and models of good writing. The major learning strategy being offered for writing in this course was imitation. Paradoxically, for someone who felt that students learn to write through models, Hall said she disliked putting sample exam papers (or term papers) on file for students because they parodied them in "the most grotesque ways."

My position was that Hall didn't need to teach writing, but to disclose a way of thinking about art history that many students weren't understanding, to share with her students her own eyes and mind for analyzing and synthesizing the materials in her course. Poor writing for the novice in the field, I suggested, is often not the result of deficient skills but rather the result of the new context and language in the field that students are working within. Since Anna wasn't a poor writer in her Prose Writing class or in other art courses for that matter, I couldn't accept that she hadn't studied or wrestled sufficiently with the material for Hall's course.

Together Hall and I addressed two problem areas that I felt influenced the poor quality of writing in her classrooms: lack of class discussions and lack of models for reading. In order to show students how to write their final papers on contemporary artists, students needed to be engaged in the thinking process that the paper would require. To improve the quality of the final exam papers, I felt it would be useful for Hall to explicate an art history text so that students would understand how she read. Hall herself realized that we were talking about making explicit the kinds of things that she intrinsically knew—what Polyani (1958), whose work she had read, has called the "tacit" traditions of her field.

(See also Emig's essay on the tacit tradition in composition studies in *The Web of Meaning* 1983.)

Within weeks Hall moved from resistance to enthusiasm about trying out new ideas in her course. She reflected on her own development as a writer and told me that when she compared articles she had written much earlier with more recent writing she was doing on the same artist, she saw some real changes in her own style. If professional writers of art history go through a period of apprenticeship then surely students need practice in how to write and think about the discipline as well.

The plan for providing practice for her students was entirely Professor Hall's own idea and anticipates the final paper students would write. She first located four original works in different media (collage, print collage, silk screen, and oil on textured cardboard) and hung them around the room for students to view. When students come to class one afternoon, she asks them to take time to look at the works and make some mental notes about them, based on some of the questions she had jotted on the board to focus their thoughts: "What have you seen that is like these works? What are some questions you might ask these artists?"

The students spend about twenty minutes studying the works and talking about them, an entirely new structure for this class which they readily accepted. Some students take notes on the art, others talk, some just look. At first, when the class was reseated, they were reluctant to talk. After all, they were used to having Professor Hall lecture, but she displayed an amazing capacity to be playful, to invite students to be inquisitive and childlike in approaching the works and asking basic questions about them.

First, she suggests that they will have to "locate" the work of the artist within the modern art context. Starting with the first picture, students suggest that it seems neodadaist, echoing the experimentation with mechanical objects found in the work of Duchamp. Having named the style, they proceed to talk about what is actually in the Jim Dine collage. In the print, ordinary hardware-store objects are part of a kind of pulley system with a bright red collage signature stuck onto the surface, giving an overall effect that is difficult to read. Students quickly enter into the conversation, sometimes with encouragement from Professor Hall and sometimes not. The classroom feels more intimate now that Hall is no longer positioned at the lectern but is moving around the room by the pictures. This intimacy is reinforced by viewing works directly instead of through slides.

In the following portion of a taped transcript, Professor Hall tries to get students to talk about the concept of internal scale, of how the artist makes the viewer feel with respect to the size of the picture. One of the speakers, Amy, is a studio art major and the other, Bob, is an art history major who wrote the fine midterm exam. What interests me in this snippet is that Anna unexpectedly enters the conversation. Professor Hall proves herself to be extraordinarily adept at leading this kind of discussion, pulling the best parts from students' contributions, building a working paradigm for the class to use in critiquing an art work.

Professor Hall: Okay, tell me about that big space up there because that was an interesting remark, Amy.

Amy: He obviously chose not to fill it. We don't have any visual clues as to whether this is suspended by a crane in a junkyard.

Hall: We don't see anything holding this up do we? What do we associate a big space up in the air with?

Students: Heaven. [*Students laugh*]

Hall: Okay, that's a neat idea and I'll tell you why. What kind of comparisons was Rosenblum making in his article,[4] between color-field painters like Rothko and German romantics like Friedrich?

Bob: Comparisons about the whole death and birth idea about the sublime. The sublime was on this vast scale and was this transcendent response, the feeling of awe that you get looking at something larger, more powerful. The idea of deity, the feeling of vastness and power.

Hall: Do you know how big you are in relation to this picture? Supposing this were a slide and we projected it on the screen. Would we know?

Bob: You do, you have a referential object. You have the handle of the crank to grasp onto literally and say, "This is how big I am. I am no longer than this thing."

Hall: Supposing this thing were projected so that it was about six feet high. Would the handle of the crank tell us our scale in relation to it?

Bob: I think then we would read the crank in quite a different manner. Then it's consciously overblown and we would be responding to why the artist blew this image up well beyond life-size and what kind of responses he wants to elicit by taking that action. Lichtenstein would blow up images way beyond life-size.

Hall: What I'm trying to get people to see is that we can't tell the scale of this object internally.

---

[4] Rosenblum, R., "The Abstract Sublime," in *New York Painting and Sculpture 1940–1970*, ed. H. Geldzahlen. New York: Dutton, 350–59.

Amy: Especially since it's been ... if it was an object that we can grab, since it's been reduced, therefore we can view it. It could be a size expansion.

Bob: I would disagree with that. I think obviously the thing is being presented irrationally so that you could form a contention that the relationship to the length of the handle or the size of the crank isn't important because it has been taken out of the field of rationality. But I still don't see this taking on scale factors. I find myself prevented by the size of that handle from imagining it as a huge overblown thing.

Amy: I think the whole fact of the whole picture is a kind of study in irrationality. And that he's obviously purposely left out many objects that could be supporting his actual object that he's chosen to depict. I think it is a good point that since he's chosen to shrink the object, that it's irrelevant whether you can grab onto that handle or not. That's not his purpose in this work that you walk up and say, "Oh that could be my size so I could grab onto the handle." I think that that's totally irrelevant. If it were on the screen, it would look like something you were looking up at. Especially with that red popping out with his name. He's just elevating it to be a huge monumental crank.

Hall: Okay. That's interesting. Tell me about the space. I'm interested in your considering both sides.

Bob: If you consider this as a study for something larger, I could see you making those extrapolations, but, as it is, why would you even want to imagine it projected on the screen? Why would you as a viewer sit there and say, "I wonder what the effect would be if it were five times larger?" because it's not.

Amy: I didn't say that.

Hall: I did. I'll tell you why I said that. I want you to see that there is no internal scaling in this work.

Anna: Because if it were big on the screen it would be ... the crank would be more life-sized, and so I'd think that I would be able to grab onto it. But here, it gives me a completely ... I was thinking when I looked at it that the crank should pull the black part up into space and reveal something underneath. It gives the impression of wanting to move up in space but it can't because it's the whole — I don't know — the mechanics of it is too much.

Hall: No, but that's interesting. You're going in a direction where you would find some very interesting things out about the implications of this work.

When students end this segment of discussion, Professor Hall draws a generalization just as she does in her lectures, but in her summary remarks on Dine's work, Hall uses Bob and Amy's argument to frame her observations and conclusions. By drawing on the actual remarks of students and engaging them actively in the issues, the position that Professor Hall takes becomes one of consensus with both sides:

I think that one of the things that's going on here in this argument between Bob and Amy is that they are both telling us important things to understand about the work. The artist has quite deliberately situated the work in this huge expanse of space and then he has also deliberately not allowed us to read this space as transcendent. Would you buy that?

In this discussion, the *students themselves* have helped construct the reading of this painting; they have received this understanding not from or through Hall but *with* her and the peers that support the dialogue. The entire transcript is a testimony to how Professor Hall is able to achieve the same kind of understanding of modern art from her students' using the discussion style.

In our subsequent meeting, Anna is pleased but somewhat surprised by the change in Hall's course. She said that she found it "different" and that if Hall continued to have class discussions, Anna would be "open to it." Anna does not like to speak out in art classes because she would rather listen to what others say: "I'm not that analytical and I wouldn't want to be." Anna suggested that some of the talk by the art history students (Bob) sounded "dry and memorized."

Reading Demonstrations

Professor Hall confides that she finds the discussion style of teaching "exhausting" and returns to lecturing for the rest of the course. Next year, she reports, she anticipates building more discussions into her courses earlier on. The other learning strategy that Professor Hall experiments with involves how to interpret an art history text; she devotes part of two class periods to an analysis of an essay on Postmodernism. To prepare for this explication, Hall first elicits from the class the canons of high modernism in art, which she writes on the board. Together they fiddle with the wording and order of critical terms such as "appropriation," "critical intervention," and "deconstruction." She says, "You have to have words to think about something new." She then relates a story about how she went to the computer center to learn about word processing; when the word "menu" was introduced, she said, "What the hell do you mean by 'menu'?" This preparation affords students a review of the terminology that has been used all semester before they consider the breaking away of artists from modernism, which the essay describes.

As she reads the essay and explains terms, Hall chooses appropriate slides to illustrate the principles discussed in the introductory essay. For the first time in the course, she has merged the text of the readings with that of the slides, a technique that reinforces the concepts being covered. Postmodernist artists, for example, comment on the ambiguity of language by combining words and other media to produce a work that must be read like a text: "With this textual model, art is read as a kind of discourse rather than an aesthetic experience," Hall says.

After her demonstrations, Hall apologizes that she has not been well trained in "explication of texts" but states that that is no reason for her not to try to share her reading process with the class: "I go at a text with a real vengeance," she says, and after listening to her analysis of this essay, I believe her.

Research for Art History: Ecofeminism

Anna, along with other students in the course, is not only struggling with *mastery* of the course material and terminology, she is also concerned with her research for the term project. The final project involves a ten-page paper that requires students to investigate a contemporary but comparatively unknown artist who has a developed body of work but is considered "local, regional, or emergent"; the students must then link that artist to some aspect of modern art. A statement of intent is required from each student after midterms and they are encouraged to hold conferences with Professor Hall. The final paper, Hall says, demands that students "place a contemporary artist's work within the context of the avant-garde movements".

From the beginning Anna views the assignment as a good one, because "it requires original thinking." Enthusiastically, she locates a woman artist—Keita Metz—near her hometown and arranges an interview with her during spring break. When I try to get Anna to talk about what she is discovering about the artist's works, she is somewhat reluctant and says it is too "frustrating" to discuss. This incubation phase, or silent preparation period, of Anna's writing process I remember from last term, when she was working on two art history projects and didn't want to talk about them until they were finished. Noddings describes this phase as "receptive-intuitive" or as an "unconscious openness" (1984,168), which often accompanies some intense topic of investigation and precedes the final step when all the parts fall into place.

Not until I convince her that I'm more intrigued with her process of writing her paper than with the final product does Anna begin to disclose some information that she feels might possibly be worked into her final project. Her major job, she says, is to "locate" and "fit" her artist into some aspect of the contemporary art movement: "For every artist it will be different; each one will relate to a different thesis," she says. Through talking with her artist, a woman who paints landscapes and animals, Anna senses that the artist is making a statement about nature, about preservation of the landscape and wildlife. Metz tells Anna that she has donated a percentage of the proceeds from her exhibitions to the Greenpeace organization. Anna says of Metz, "She's very conscious" of getting people to look at things in a way that they ordinarily wouldn't." Anna claims she doesn't have a thesis about the artist. Yet from much of our discussions, it is clear that she is following a fertile lead.

In our continued talks, Anna discusses with real concern the idea of "caring for the earth," something that she says has been on her mind a lot lately. "She has always been concerned with ecological issues, which "worried me as a child," she adds. Her family moved away from California when she was young, she says, because the suburban community her family lived in grew from 7,000 to more than 36,000 in a twenty-year span, during which builders and inhabitants showed a "total unconcern for the land." More recently she and her boyfriend stopped to look at the stars on a drive home from nearby Portsmouth, partly because she is taking an astronomy course. It was then that she thought again about "how finely tuned the earth is and that because of man's abuse we will not be able to support it some day."

Anna reads two books related to her emerging topic before holding a conference with Professor Hall: Lucy Lippard's *Overlay*, which considers female images in the art of different societies, and Wendell Berry's *The Unsettling of America*. Professor Hall, putting these two threads together, suggests that Anna pursue the heading of "ecofeminism" to look for further materials and directs her specifically to a recent article in *Nation* on the topic. Anna is amazed at how quickly Hall could "locate" this artist within all the strands of contemporary art. Ecofeminism is defined as a hybrid subdiscipline that combines political interests from both feminism and political ecology. Watching Anna work on her paper helps me understand one seemingly unimportant fragment about her personal life that wouldn't fall into place for me—her objection to ear piercing.

Although Anna's interest in ecology doesn't surprise me, it reframes the issue of ear piercing around a respect for the body in relation to a respect for the land, even though Anna later claims that her rejection of piercing ears is mainly aesthetic. Ecofeminism is also a political movement and thus fits well into Anna's personal need to be politically aware of current issues. In writing under the rubric of "ecofeminism," Anna unconsciously allies herself with a group of art historians who have begun to adjust or correct some issues in art history that are related to women. Introducing the concept of feminism into the field of art, two art historians write: "Recognition of the ways in which peculiary masculine interests have often been mistaken in our culture for universal concerns has prompted us as art historians to reexamine some of the basic premises of our discipline" (Broude and Garrard 1982, 15). Once the ecological issue feels right, the feminist part is the one that nags at me.

In Prose Writing, Anna displayed some ambivalent feelings about the term *feminism*, particularly when a class discussion centered on it. When the class read Adrienne's Rich's essay, "When We Dead Awaken: Writing As Revision" (1979), for example, Anna felt everyone in the class should "just think whatever they want to think" because the discussion was "futile." Anna admitted that she could relate to Rich's idea of "having a woman's identity" and that she wanted to respond to Nick when he asked, "What's this new female way of thinking?" But she didn't respond to Nick because she couldn't articulate it: "I thought about what he said and I thought, well, I *know* what it is but I couldn't explain it, so I didn't say anything."

Anna said that some of her thinking about women's roles was influenced by a women's studies course taken the previous year. In this course she had grown tired of the women either "whining" about not being able to have everything or "shouting" about feminist issues: "You can't have it all, and I think you have to make choices. If you want to have a really good family you have to give up a lot of things; you have to weigh things out." When asked point-blank if she's a feminist, Anna says that in the sense of equal pay and rights, she is, but she adds: "I don't feel strongly enough about these other issues to consider myself a feminist ... I haven't thought about other women's issues. Maybe I will some day."

Tying her paper to ecofeminism represents a comfortable position for Anna, however, because it is a continuum of issues that has bothered her for a long time. "Ecofeminism" she explains, "is a different thing. It's taking this sensitivity and applying it to the land. And it's not exclusive to women. It's a way men are thinking about ecology as well." For students who have heard only strident feminist voices, this weaving in of feminist issues with other concerns may excite them to reconsider some of the movement's intellectual and political ideas—rather than only its sociological ones.

Anna shares an early draft of her paper with me; we talk it through with her extensively developed outline. I can sense that her commitment and excitement with the issues of ecofeminism in art have spread to many other areas. In particular, I sense some intrusions from Anna's anthropology course in a long section about the beginning of the earth and man's initial respect for the land, a section that we decide to eliminate from her draft. I feel that Anna is not just writing a paper; in some ways, she is connecting a part of her personal and political beliefs to a topic in art history. Women who take on intensive writing projects, such as a senior thesis, often become so connected to a project that, as Mary Cayton director of a university honors program, puts it, they [become] their projects (Cayton 1988).

When I inquire about what problems Anna faced in writing the paper, she says it was "sticking to one side of the issues." For example, in her paper she makes references to animals being abused in laboratory experiments but acknowledges that she's "torn" over the antivivisection stance, because her boyfriend's father does medical research on diseases such as cancer and Alzheimer's using rats, which he feels is necessary in some research situations. She says that she won't show her paper to her boyfriend because she knows it will make him mad. Anna recognizes that the use of animals in laboratory research, their advantages over computer simulations, presents a complicated issue, but she still maintains a pro-animal rights position in the paper. Some research on gender and discourse suggests that women often suffer from having to make such arguments in writing, because their expressive mode of thinking reflects a perception of the world that sees "ambiguities, pluralities, processes, continuities," rather than the thought patterns of "categories, dichotomies, roles, stasis, and causation" (Penelope and Wolfe 1983, 126).

Anna's paper uncovers a fascinating mixture of ecological and political issues that emerge "behind the canvases" of this artist. The introductory paragraph is somewhat distanced and academic: "Her detailed descriptions of the natural world make viewers look more closely at the intricacies of nature and reassess the current economic and political relationships to the Earth through ecology, feminism, and activism, and examine our roles as individuals." For the remainder of the paper, Anna personalizes the topic, switching from "the viewer" to include the reader as the "we" who share the concerns of the "I" narrator:

Her paintings invoke feelings of being in unfamiliar but intriguing places. Nature is a wondrous place from Metz's perspective and as an artist she asks that we share this curiosity with her.

The attraction to her work is that it offers an Eden that we subconsciously want to return to. Once captured we want to preserve the landscape. By bringing out the beauty in the natural world Metz makes us want to examine it more closely and subsequently see differently and with greater respect for the environment.

Metz wants to get away from the notion of human supremacy that has been developed over the years, and have viewers look onto her animals and landscapes with respect. The monkey perched on a tree branch in one of her animal portraits stares directly out of the canvas at the viewer. When I saw this piece I was forced to look back timidly. This is the response Metz wanted.

There are feminist themes in Anna's paper that she doesn't label but that are easily identified. Anna writes of an attitude of "caring" toward both animals and the landscape, which should replace our current "separateness" that has developed, says Anna, "between humans and animals, landscape, and each other." Noddings (1984) suggests that children caring for pets in cooperation with a caring adult serves as an ethical ideal and that our obligation to both plants and animals is mainly to understand how others feel about them and listen to their concerns. Anna asks just that of her reader in this paper.

Metz addresses the selfish attitude humans have towards nature by making us see a personality behind the animals she portrays which are mostly wild animals in their territory. She instills a caring attitude which must replace the separateness which has developed between humans and animals, landscapes and each other.

Anna says in her paper that "women's ways of thinking" about the world have been quieted, but that this artist's work "bonds viewers to her landscapes" with a "connective" approach. The approach of ecofeminism, Anna writes, "examines women's connections to the Earth historically and the similarities between oppression of women and the oppression of nature." The strongest parts of her eight-page paper are her political and theoretical ties to a contemporary feminist movement.

Once we are aware of the natural world we see the "tremendous beauty of ecological thought is that it shows us an understanding of and an appreciation for, life itself—an understanding and appreciation that is imperative to the continuance of life" (Greenpeace). Once this is realized, the next step is action. She addresses these concerns through her painting and through donations to Greenpeace, a 'direct action' environmental group. Metz has an annual show at her home to benefit Greenpeace. She gives them the percentage of the proceeds that a gallery would take. Greenpeace is her choice over other environmental groups because the money will go directly into doing things. .... It is young and full of enthusiasm whereas Sierra Club she suggests has become too government connected.

Professor Hall writes Anna a two-page response, starting with the paper's strengths and then commenting:

However, I am puzzled by the lack of connection between her views and her style. That an artist with a "message" would use recognizable subject matter is one thing, but the way that subject matter is translated into paint on a surface is something else. How is paint handled? Does the artist paint outdoors, directly from the motifs, or indoors from sketches or from photographs? What group of contemporary figurative painters have styles that resemble the style of this artist?

For Professor Hall, the major weakness in this paper is a lack of visual analysis, affording it only a B plus grade.

Anna had eliminated a long personalized beginning to the paper and avoided any extended visual analysis because she felt from the midterm exam that Hall wasn't interested in this. In this paper where such material would strengthen her thesis, Anna has shied away. But she is able to create and retain a voice in this paper that is more related to Anna than to the art history texts she reads, a paper that personalizes and invites the reader in — not always an easy task in academic writing. Here is a short section in which Anna discusses more closely the context of ecofeminism:

Many artists are trying to re-establish lost ties with the earth through 'primitivism.' These are being examined by women who are finding a long history of myths connecting them to the Earth, and by men suggesting a need to 'reevaluate the socio-esthetic structures and values of the society in which we live' (Lippard, p. 45). This has manifested itself in performances, making physical contact with the earth, large scale sculpture called Earthworks, as well as in sculpture and two dimensional work. Metz is established in her connections to the Earth. Her work is trying to make connections to the viewers and the Earth beginning with a curiosity.

And in her ending, Anna makes a strong political statement:

Protection of the environment Metz believes should be an important consideration of people. She addresses this through her art. Metz' work implies a return to nature, increased awareness of political/ environmental issues, and calls viewers to action by presenting a consciousness of the harmed. Through her paintings we realize how deeply connected to the Earth we are and our choice becomes to understand our relationship to the Earth as individuals and learn what we can do to prevent its widespread destruction.

Anna commented that she felt good about her paper, that it was one writing project in college that she did mainly for herself. Anna had learned about art criticism by writing and being engaged in the critical thinking process of the discipline.

Anna goes off to San Francisco for the summer for an internship in an art gallery. She is anxious to get away from New Hampshire, from academics, from all that has become so familiar. She evaluates Professor Hall's course as being one of the best she has ever taken, because she learned about the art world and how political it is, not just how to analyze paintings, and because she can apply what she is learning to her future work. "I've been able to apply things in modern art to other issues instead of just keeping them in art history. And I was having problems with just keeping things in art history. Just analyzing someone's work seemed so silly."

From San Francisco Anna writes that what she misses most about UNH is her dance company, because "freedom of expression through dance is very important and unique compared with other college work."

My relationship with Professor Hall ends on a collegial note. I'm on my way out the door to visit the Ramses art exhibition in Boston with my family when Hall calls. It is hot, I'm rushed, but her words invite me to listen. We chat briefly about how both her exams and her final papers were much more satisfactory. In some cases, the finals were so much improved that she discounted the midterm exam. "Thank you for letting me see that the students' problems were not conceptual. It was really a problem of language," she concludes.

Nick's Literacy Role Playing 3

M y researcher journal entries raise endless questions about Nick: Why the single earring and the bandanna wrapped around his head? Why a fountain pen for his personal writing? Why the torn jeans and boots held together with tape? My notes also indicate my hesitation, perhaps even resistance, to working with a man as complicated as Nick. I fear being snarled and knotted in language—his words and mine interwoven to portray Nick. As much of a stereotype—almost a braggadocio—as Nick sometimes seems. I do not want to paint him as a flat character, playing to the groundlings. For beneath the mask of the angry, bored student is the half-smile of a young man who loves words and sees the world through an artist's eyes.

Researcher Journal Entries

Between Nick and me, there's a sense of boundary, territory, and distance. I feel intensely involved but very unconnected with Nick. I find him articulate, interested, and responsible about his end of our association: he always shows up for our meetings, saves all his papers, and has much to talk about with me. On the other hand, he pushes me away. If I invite him for a beer or offer to loan him one of my old typewriters, he refuses.

My worries about using Nick as a case study are endless: he's adopted, has experienced multiple divorces, has a mother who's recently become a minister. Yet what Nick says about his personal history I think is true; that if you scrape the surface of anyone's life, they all will have these "harsh" things in their background. As a researcher I have to own up that no student who agrees to talk with me once a week about their reading and writing processes could be considered *typical*. And then I ask myself, what kinds of people do we learn from anyway?

Each morning in the summer, I get up early and creep down into in my basement office by 5:30 A.M. before the heat and the noise of the day. I feel as if I'm in a tomb, sealed away with all these secret notes to decipher. How silly it all seems on the one hand and yet how important it becomes to me. One day after spending a long morning writing about Nick, I drive my children to the local swimming pool and encounter him on the way. Suddenly Nick appears like a ghost. So much did I believe that I was him; he had to be someone else.

His intense anger can storm me by surprise. At the end of May when classes are over, Nick and I meet in my office to talk. As dramatic thunder booms outside and spring hail hits against the roof on the third floor, I position a swivel chair near the entrance way for Nick to occupy. He arrives wearing a brown plastic garbage bag for protection against the weather. As Nick begins to talk, I discover through the loud squeaking of the swivel chair, that he's agitated. He's just learned that he has to share his room for the summer with a new housemate that he dislikes. Nick says that he took a yardstick and "measured the room exactly" so that each of them would have the right amount of space. The housemate, however, ignores this division and shoves Nick's things out of his way. Anticipating an eventual confrontation, Nick says, "The only way to remove him from my room is to fight him and beat him. I can't be held responsible for what happens between us this summer."

Strong words and unfamiliar strains of violence that stir in Nick almost push me away from understanding. Nick explains that he uses his anger to accomplish just that: "My anger keeps me comfortable and safe somehow," he says.

These issues tug at me today as I write. I try to piece together where I am now, as I reflect on our relationship. I am not saying that Nick remains a stranger—in fact, he reveals far more intimate things about himself than Anna does—but that he seems foreign at times, dark. Physically, Nick *is* dark with brown hair, steel blue-grey eyes, chiseled fine features—very handsome, and thin. His small gold earring adds a bit of mystery and his red and blue bandannas become his dress signature. I learn that he had his ear pierced on a dare from a woman friend and that it bears no particular significance, except that when he returned home from college in his freshman year, his older sister chided, "Nick went away to college and learned to smoke cigarettes and wear an earring."

When I ask Nick to describe himself, he emphasizes his tempestuous, almost Byronic side, saying that other people sometimes think of him as "arrogant, somber, brooding, cold." As an example, he talks about his part-time job as a cook, in which, he says, he sometimes gets a little self-righteous:

Like at work sometimes I get arrogant. I start telling people what to do. The waitresses will come up and ask me to do an order and I'll say, "Don't talk to me, get away. Get out of my kitchen." Generally I don't mean to be serious about it. But there's that little flash of cathartic relief in being able to snap at someone and maybe watch them scamper away ... Managers come in and say, "Do this, do this, can I have this?" The food is saying, "Cook me, cook me."

Activities that do give Nick satisfaction outside of school are sketching and writing. Since childhood, he has kept a personal journal and he has always loved to draw. Sometimes he combines these two activities, as in the calendars that organize his college activities. (See Figures 3–1 and 3–2 for comparison of two calendars, one from October, which shows his tidy life at the beginning of the year, and the other from April, when he's "wiggin' out," to borrow his own expression.) His journal and his sketchbook can be flipped over and the previous page left unfinished, so they

Figure 3–1 ■ Nick's October Calendar

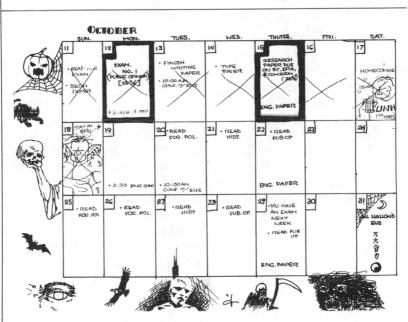

Figure 3–2 ■ *Nick's April Calendar*

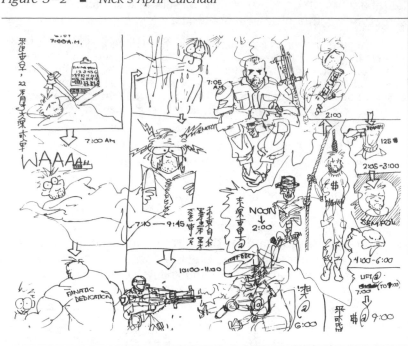

represent no threat to Nick, who uses both for release: "If the page is a failure, I go on to the next day, fresh start. No revising." This dabbling he contrasts with *real* artistic involvement: "An art object is something you labor over. Something you go back to time and time again to question your ideas for doing things."

Nick, in fact, entered college as a studio art major and stuck with this for about a semester. The obstacle to being an art major, as he saw it, stemmed from his not having prepared an art portfolio from his high school. Perhaps an even larger issue was that of competition. Nick had always been good at art: "I used to be the best artist—always. As long as I've lived, I've always been the best artist of everyone who has known me and now I can't do it anymore." Both time and energy account for Nick's leaving art as a major: "I'd try to do other things, and I'd let art slip, and then I'd try to do art and everything else would slip." And failure to be the best, failure to complete art projects such as a huge sculpture that he attempted, eventually contribute to his giving up art as his major: "Failing at art, or doing badly at art, really upsets me."

Lack of success with art is intensely personal for Nick because "with art, the problem is if I fail, I fail myself."

Nick described his hours in the art studio chipping away at a big slab of plaster that he couldn't master and couldn't shape into anything meaningful for himself. Finally he managed to create a very abstracted head, a project that took him so long that he didn't finish enough other portfolio work to pass the course. Nick's relationship to art was so intense that he abandoned it for fields where he might achieve more control, where he did not need to be quite so immersed.

When I met Nick in Prose Writing class, he had declared political science as a major and was toying with journalism as a minor; Prose Writing is a prerequisite for the journalism sequence. Nick believed that the writing course would allow him to pick up on a latent talent: "I was always a good writer, always. . . . I had a certain fascination with words."

Nick's academic career has been anything but comfortable or safe. He's changed majors three times: first from studio art to psychology, and finally to political science. These different disciplines don't seem related and probably shouldn't be, since Nick believes that the real purpose of a liberal arts education is for "poking around," for "flirting" with different disciplines. He is more concerned with exploring academic territories than with connecting them to one another. When I ask him how he goes about relating the information from one class to another, he says that there is "no exchange," that in his school career "there's only been a couple of times that one class has related to another class." Nick's advice to students who have problems declaring a major is not to get too "nervous" and to "take your time and experiment" because, if you find a major that doesn't fit you, "you will hate it and you will fail. You might even flunk out of school." Nick speaks from experience.

Second semester of his freshman year, Nick failed his sculpture course and barely squeaked by in Japanese. He finished the sequence of language courses and repeated Sculpture 1, so he never left school entirely, but his academic career has been enough of a seesaw to extend his education for an additional semester to make up credits. His present grade-point average is 2.4, but it has been as high as 2.8. Most of Nick's friends graduated in May and, because he wishes himself out of college life as well, this was a difficult period for him. Nick said that he worked out some of this conflict in his mind previous to graduation, but he knew he hadn't really resolved the issue.

Things I think I have worked out in my *head*, but I'll find that when I get into the situation, my *heart* says something else, and I can't convince it otherwise. ... In fact, I worked graduation night and I got depressed because that was my class—all my friends. People I had seen and known for four years were all out in the dining room drinking with their friends and seeing each other for the last time and it was all very cathartic for them. And I had this immense feeling of being left out. Here I am cooking their food for them.

Yet Nick is in no rush to graduate because of particular career aspirations. He has no professional or personal goals, as he jokingly indicates: "I don't want the $30,000-a-year job, the red car, the dog named Spot, wife named Mary, whatever. I don't want these things ... And that's what really horrifies people, when I say I don't want this."

When I ask the inevitable question about what he *does* want, Nick, who is truly appalled by consumerism, responds that he doesn't want to be a "professional," who he claims to be "narrow thinking, confined, orderly, and subjugated people mainly characterized by "jargon," which indicates how things are "slotted and arranged so that the professional becomes the authority and has to take on that role regardless of whether he's prepared for it." Nick suggests that his goal is to remain "woven into the fabric of ordinary, regular people, into humanity." An interesting goal for Nick, which may represent a conflict between head and heart.

Education has become a difficult experience for Nick, as he is hurled toward the last semester of his senior year: "It's emotional pain. Trauma. Learning eats up my time and makes my neurons knot. Learning is busy work. Not fun anymore."

Let's rewind by one semester to see if Nick's educational malaise can be unknotted by understanding his academic demands, by looking at the strands of literacy that are woven into Prose Writing and his political science coursework. As we go into Prose Writing class, we need to hold in mind some of Nick's words that describe his various sides. First his *yin* words, which show flux and process:

All I know about myself in any given moment is a handful out of the sea. That's all that I can grasp about myself at any one point. And then ten minutes later, the handful has changed and it's a different one, and I try to go with that.

And then his *yang* words, which reveal solidity and mastery:

All information is important. I think what gives college-educated people their advantage over the masses is that they know that all information is important.

Nick in Prose Writing: Top Billing

Nick finds his Prose Writing class somewhat of a "relief" from his other coursework where he characterizes himself as "struggling through all the assignments." His writing course offers him "a little creativity" and allows him "to relax and carry through some thoughts, instead of the abbreviated thinking I do in every other sector" of academic life. Both Nick and Anna describe Prose Writing as "very personalized" in comparison with most of their other coursework, which emphasizes segmented learning.

Initially, Nick was among the most talented writers and articulate class members, and he is not reluctant to say so: "They were good classes. A release, amusing. I was also one of the better ones in there so it was an ego trip." But Nick's skills are not so much better that the course isn't challenging to him. In one of his early peer-group responses, Nick compares Prose Writing course to Drawing II, a studio art course:

There are shades here of Drawing Two: another place in which I found a challenging multitude. I suspect I am among many talented others where (arrogantly perhaps) I expected only a few. Now again I find myself among peers, rather than inferiors as far as this medium will take us. It is a tantalizing situation: the potential returns for me to be alternately challenged and inspired. They have the ability to untangle my creative inertia.

For Nick—confident and assured of his talent—his peers in Prose Writing offer the stimulation of the competitive context that Nick once met in studio art, minus fear of failure.

Nick sees Prose Writing as a place where talk was always encouraged: "The English department, I've found, is always more open" (Nick will change his mind about this statement). He goes on: "Donna's class was very relaxed; if somebody had something to say, they'd just go ahead and say it. Everybody just sat around and talked all the time." Certainly Nick has no problem contributing to the ongoing conversations in Prose Writing class: his speech style is expressive, polished, and assured. He reflects at the end of second semester that he feels he "was almost a better speaker than writer," which seems "weird" to him. It is this oral ability, I later discover, that will serve him well in political science.

Often Nick's oral responses reflect his interest in the political. In particular, when the class discusses Adrienne Rich's essay "Writing as Revision," Nick takes on the instructor's role by defending Rich's militant language, reminding the class that the piece was originally written as an address, that it's been tailored for a specific audience: "Remember," he says "that this was a speech given to get women to accept political positions." Nick understands well the implications of public rhetoric.

In the whole-class discussions, Nick is an active participant, often serving as the leader. We have already considered Nick's leadership role in the class discussion on Freire (see chapter 1), which is not an isolated example of his taking over the conversational floor. Sometimes he poses a question in a group discussion and then answers it as well. When the class compares Freire and Hirsch's ideas, for instance, Nick gets so excited over the issue of cultural literacy that he argues: "How can you define cultural literacy? How can there be one culture in America? We don't share the same culture." Nick displays a variety of different discourse styles in Prose Writing: he is a leader and a follower; he raises questions and answers them; and he offers considered response.

In the following classroom exchange, Nick, along with others, follows the receptive discussion mode that has been modeled for peer response groups. Here Donna offers her own writing for the scrutiny of the class, starting with a little history of the paper. Her draft—"A Rock by Any Other Name"—tells about her exploration in a New Hampshire woods, where she stumbles upon a boulder of granite. This experience, as I discussed earlier, takes her back to Australia, where the aborigines have rocks called *narguns*:

Rock is rock and stone is stone.
Or is it?
This rock triggered memory. I was not the only stranger to this place. Here was a rock from the legends of a land 10,000 miles away. Here was rock out of place, out of time. Here was Nargun.

Donna gives the class some specific questions to guide their reading of her four-page draft and she then opens the discussion:

Donna: When I'm working on a draft of what I want to say, I let everything else go to hell. I purposely gave you a draft. I started this paper with myth-making and added the idea of the "story-telling animal" when I read the article [by Kathryn Morton] last year. And then I come back to the idea of leaving home. Should I just work on one of these ideas?

Allie: One thing I like is on the third page, the line "Why does anything have to leave its home?" Maybe you could relate this to why you come to New Hampshire. *I liked* how you put yourself into your environment at the beginning. *Maybe you should connect* your Australian experience earlier in the piece.

Nick: For me, Australia popped out of nowhere. *I think we need* to be
more involved in the part where you come across the rock.

Carlos: I liked the elements of mythology on the second page and the
whole paragraph on the Nargun worked for me. *Maybe I'm more
receptive* because right now I'm reading about mythology.

Anna: The part that worked best for me was how you didn't have to come
out and make a connection but do it through descriptions.

Sue: I'd like to know more about your experiences in Australia.

Donna: Where should I put that?

Sue: Before you get to the rock.

Nick: First you are in the woods and then you're in front of a rock. *Why is
this rock such a strong power for you?* (emphasis added)

This exchange is a model of effective peer response, what Donna
had intended for Carlos's "Oblomov" paper. In the italicized
phrases above, students show Donna how they *received* the
paper. Donna gets supportive feedback and genuine questions
from her students, not negative criticism. And Nick is an
exemplary critic.

In the whole-class discussions Nick shows an ability to shift
in and out of different discourse styles: one is aggressive and
dominant, saying, "This is how it is"; the other is receptive and
cooperative, saying, "This holds true for *me*." His facility with
multiple presentation modes, however, does not mean that he is
able to name or identify them. In a class discussion of *Women's
Ways of Knowing* (Belenky et al. 1986), Nick demands, "What *is*
this new women's way of knowing?" And later, in private conversation, Nick reflects the same frustration over the distinction between connected and separate thinking: "Why is it that I can't
figure out what the difference is? What the hell does it mean?
Separate from what? Connected to what?"

So facile is Nick at switching or shifting styles that he isn't
conscious of differences. Because he has his footing in the dominant discourse, because he is permitted to move freely within
modes of connection and autonomy, Nick can't hear the muted
discourse of his female peers. And in fact, when he does hear it,
he often dismisses it, as we will see. Nick has a choice of discourse
styles and such choice affords him a kind of verbal power.

Nick in Reading Group: Dominance and Difference ■ Nick liked
Donna's idea of holding an individual reading conference with
each student at the beginning of the semester: "Usually reading is
something you do yourself," he reported, "but without feedback,

reading by yourself is only so helpful." Feedback comes for Nick
through the forum of the reading groups where he is an active
and sometimes dominant influence. Here is another excerpt from
the Raymond Carver discussion with Nick, Anna, Mary, and Carlos
as participants. Notice in this excerpt how much Nick talks, how
often he interrupts speakers, who these speakers are, how and
when he changes topics, and whose topics he supports.

Anna: Laura didn't say anything, she was like ...   1

Nick: Yeah, it was funny how they covered, they did cover   2
everything you'd think of if you think about love. If you   3
were just sitting there thinking, well, what do I think   4
about love? you'd think about specific things, you   5
wouldn't think in broad abstract terms. I think they hit   6
on that really well.   7

Carlos: I liked his style of writing. What I thought was   8
weird was what I had written for this week. This is the   9
second time it's happened, I wrote what I had to write,   10
the first draft. And I go back and read this, it's exactly   11
what I want to do with my writing. And I went back and   12
read mine, and it's overbearing. This has profanity, but   13
mine's really got profanity.   14

Nick: If you're doing dialogue that's sometimes   15
necessarily the case. It's got to be realistic language ...   16

Carlos: Right ...   17

Nick: Or you're not going to believe these people are   18
talking to each other. You're not going to perceive how   19
they are towards each other. Or get the characterization   20
at all.   21

Carlos: Well, I liked it. The thing I was talking to   22
Sarah about ... I picked up on this but didn't take the   23
time to think of it but all through the story, they kept   24
referring back to the light coming through the kitchen.   25

Nick: The setting, yes.   26

Carlos: There's some significance to that and I've got to   27
try to figure out why. The author didn't just put that   28
in there for mystery.   29

Mary: It's just there to let you know that they were   30
talking for a long time ...   31

Nick: It symbolized the passage of time, I'm sure, but it   32
also sits them still. Like I read the intro and they were   33
saying ...   34

Mary: I didn't like the ending ...   35

Nick: I think that works really well.   36

Mary: The ending?   37

Nick: Yes, because Carver is—the remark about him is that   38
      he sets his characters up and then limits them, he   39
      constricts them so that they don't do much. They say   40
      what they have to say, do what they have to do, but they   41
      are realistic in that they don't try to break out of   42
      boundaries. These people are sitting in this kitchen over   43
      this table, drinking gin and that's all they're doing.   44
      They keep talking about going out but they don't go out.   45
      They stay in this room. The light fades and it gets   46
      dark and they're still sitting there and they're not   47
      going to move, not for a while anyway. I think that   48
      carries really well. I was impressed by it.   49

Carlos: Yes. I liked the style of writing. I just like   50
      this kind of writing, with dialogue.   51

Nick: It came out really well. Were you bothered at all,   52
      that he didn't seem to come up with any concrete   53
      theories? He didn't slide any theories in their dialogue   54
      about what love actually is.   55

Anna: I think that was off the subject . . .   56

Mary: Open to the reader . . .   57

Anna: Because I don't know the definition, well   58
      what do we, what is love . . .   59

Nick: I think that's the point. I think that's the whole   60
      point of the dialogue. You don't know. He's pointing   61
      out what you think of, not what you actually think   62
      of *it* and do you make any conclusions. He's just saying   63
      this is what you think of.   64

Nick is the dominant speaker not only here but throughout this entire transcript. Here he interrupts Anna and Mary twice each, disagrees with Mary at one point (line 36), and at another place expands her point in a didactic way (lines 32–34). Nick also interrupts Anna twice: at the opening when he switches the topic away from her discussion of Laura (line 1) and at the end (lines 60–64). When Anna is using talk to work something out, Nick takes the conversational floor and draws a conclusion—"that's the whole point." Interesting, too, that Nick intervenes in Carlos's talk only once and in that instance (line 17) Carlos has interrupted Nick. Nick just continues on after the break. Nick supports all of Carlos's topics (line 26, "The setting, yes.") and does not switch them to his own agenda as he does with Anna and Mary.

Nick's ability at controlling the conversation does not mean that he consistently dominates. Like other group members, Nick uses the text as a way of talking about his own life, often in a quite personal and disclosing way. Here Nick discusses divorce, an area in which he is an expert:

Nick: I don't think that's right. I think it's tough for   1
    kids to go through a divorce, yes, I went through two, but   2
    I think at the time ...   3

Mary: You're an expert ...   4

Nick: It was much wiser. Once you get to a point in a   5
    marriage where divorce is imminent, you can't have the   6
    semblance of a happy home while you're not happy.   7
    The kids will read that. It's worse for kids to wait.   8
    If you don't they'll be disillusioned; if you do, they'll   9
    be disillusioned. It's better to shoot it right in their   10
    face, "This is what we have to deal with here." I think   11
    that's much better to go through it. I've known people   12
    who have done that too, waited until their kids are in   13
    college—freshman year. As a matter of fact a lot of kids   14
    find that their parents are in trouble.   15

Mary: Doesn't that get you though? Whatever happened to   16
    forever, to commitment?   17

Nick: People grew up. People decided that if it didn't   18
    work forever, it wasn't going to work forever and you   19
    didn't have to suffer. It used to be that you had to   20
    suffer. Divorce was a dirty word, nasty, you didn't do   21
    that. Now people get sick of a marriage, they try it. I   22
    can't really put down divorce because I've seen people who   23
    really, really try to make it work. And have it just fail   24
    anyway. Because they just grew apart, they grew into two   25
    different people. There's a lot of room for it in a   26
    marriage—no one's willing to be half a person. Even if   27
    they start as unified whole, eventually they could   28
    possibly grow apart.   29

Mary: Especially if they get married young ...   30

Nick: Yes, it's just a reality.   31

Mary: Because I think about my parents. My parents have   32
    been married for twenty-two years, and they've both   33
    changed so much since I was a little kid. But they're still   34
    happily married ...   35

Nick: Not many people can do that ...   36

Mary: They can change and change with each other.   37
    They're changing differently, doing new things, but they   38
    still include new things, they still include each   39
    other.   40

Nick: That's good.   41

In this second conversational frame, in which the turn taking is even, Mary and Nick interrupt one another almost equally. Although Nick's amount of talk still dominates, he is also supportive of Mary's statements—"it's just a reality" and "that's good." Their discussion has a collaborative nature. There is a real difference between an overlapping conversation, in which all members are building on each other's contributions, and an interrupted conversation, in which one or several speakers is intent on controlling the conversational floor. Nick is good at both.

In agreement with what linguists have found about gendered aspects of mixed-sex conversations, in this small group transcript Nick mainly agrees with the males, feels freer to interrupt women, and in general, as a male, dominates the talk. Women are more silent, suggest Thorne, Kramarae, and Henley, not because they are passive, but because of "the mechanisms, such as interruption, inattention to the topics women raise, which men use to control women's silence in mixed sex talk" (1983, 17). This reading-group transcript corroborates many of these gendered discourse findings, but the most interesting finding of all is that none of this verbal behavior is conscious or intentional on Nick's part. And without an understanding of gender differences in discourse styles, linguists suggest that dominance will prevail: "Difference, however, is only part of the picture; the fact of male-dominance—built into economic, family, political, and legal structures of society—is also central to language and speech" (Thorne and Henley 1975, 15).

Nick's Dual Journals ■ Not only does Nick switch discourse style when he talks about the classroom readings, he also adopts two different voices in his journal responses—again proving his flexibility in discourse strategies as reader and writer. One voice, characterized by distanced and formalized prose, is found in his first reading response for Donna's course. He has been asked to respond to Rodriguez's essay "The Achievement of Desire" in his journal, after he has held a reading conference with Donna. Nick writes an extensive two-page journal entry, titled "Let's Think About This," but only three paragraphs of his essay relate to the actual reading:

Mr. Rodriguez has felt the draw of life's motion.

He has been sucked into the unsteady currents since an especially young age (owing to his particular history). Too young, in fact, too small to navigate the enormous ebb and flow, the huge, swirling undercurrents of time. Too young to understand his peril, but old enough to sense it.

Rodriguez watched his past sweep away from him, just as all of us have snatched ours, similarly. This past has fallen in an orderly progression (one of his choosing). Is it the "education" he has endured which has made it so?

In his own final analysis, could he see that his schooling served only as the tunnel through which his past raced by? It gave him one other thing: when it is all done, education can act for the tragic vice of hindsight. With it, he may now see clearly where the shreds have fallen.

When Nick asks Donna for a written response to his journal, she complies with an equally long reaction that reflects her sense that Nick's writing deliberately shuts readers out:

Nick, you wanted a response. My feelings as a reader are that you are trying to keep me out, keep me at a distance with bravado and flash — my terms for the "abstract" that lacks said substance to stuff buoyant. You are making the readers job overly difficult by not allowing us to see the path of your thinking. ... Had I not talked with you previously [the reading conference], I would have had a difficult time connecting to Rodriguez until the second page. On purpose?

The other voice that Nick uses in his classroom reading journal is more immediate and personal. After he reads Donna's draft of "A Rock by Any Other Name," he writes her a long reaction, titled "A Sliver of Journalizing." Here Nick comes in so close that we feel him breathing on top of Donna's prose, following each word, responding to how he feels as a reader. There is much less of the mannered prose style that characterizes Nick's Rodriguez response.

I'm drawn into the cool hush, watching you penetrate the dappled sunspots, several yards distant. I note the cypress and watch for "sleepy stone" (which I fail to see because of the sudden alliteration — it disrupts my descent with you into the woods).
Perhaps "these dense woods" wouldn't have to be were the phrases not in such proximity (editor to editor: don't shovel in too much info about granite, it could tend to bog us [the collective reader] down and, perhaps, it is more important that you wonder than know).
I am able to approach, I draw nearer and can make out more clearly the details of what you see in the disrupted effort of the ruined wall. I am very close behind you now, as you follow it deeper into the foliage.

In this response, there's no question that Nick's reading of Donna's piece is an empathic one, nor is there any sense that Nick has another agenda except to be helpful. Nick writes in the first person, "I," rather than in the more detached third person of the Rodriguez response. He could have written, "Don't use alliterations, don't be so expository, show, don't tell," but he chose engagement rather than distance, placing his directive suggestions for changes in parentheses (editor-to-editor), which protects the flow of the paper. He ends his response with "If you know what I mean," suggesting that his responses are entirely personal ones.

Nick's first journal entry may reflect his insecurity about what style (stance, pose, voice) to adopt for the course, and it most likely reflects the kind of writing he has been rewarded for in the past. Nick is equally "at home" in many voices—formal rhetorical strategies and personal literary approaches—and employs a full range within his classroom journal. By the end of the semester, his classroom journal becomes increasingly informal, as the following entry on the Carver reading group illustrates. Here Nick writes directly to Donna as his audience, addressing her in parenthetical asides. In this journal response, Nick as a reader connects personally with Carver as an author, with the setting and characters in the story, drawing it toward him, echoing the immediacy of Carver's writing in his own response. And yet there's a touch of arrogance in his response—"eloquently put, Mr. Carver"—as well as the sense of performance that dominates even his most informal prose.

Truth value in huge, fluffy abundance (please oh please don't put a question mark and an arrow pointing to fluffy, just let it go by this time). And eloquently put, Mr. Carver, with your excellent use of dialogue.

What strikes one the most is the immediacy of the setting and the situation. The shreds of descriptive prose complement the character's interplay, almost perfectly (nothing is perfect by definition) I am right there in the kitchen with the two familiar couples.

I am witness to their growing inebriation. And the fading light. They connect so closely as to be those whom I've known for years. And when they talk about love, they don't converge on a prevailing idea: they instead meander through their personal thoughts (some more in common with mine than others) concerning their own personal experiences.

This is not about what love is, as you might tend to believe if you're trying to be clever. This is what love does. 'What we Think about when we Think about love. . . .'

The Personal Journal Keeper

When Nick offers to let me read his personal journal that he has kept since childhood, I am too curious to refuse. I want to hear the tone, the voice, the style. Will it be any different from the journal he is writing for Donna's course? Will the posturing and distancing dissolve? What literary boundaries will he establish in his journal, if any?

Nick's personal journal is neatly and legibly printed in black ink with his fountain pen, the entries always dated and the time recorded both at the beginning and the ending of each entry, if even only a calculated guess: "5: something A.M." Every entry carries a title:

Time is Gonna Come Sunday

Primped and Prepped Monday

Sullen Wound Tuesday

Time as a Jockstrap Wednesday

Whiskey is Water Thursday

Running Boy Friday

High Impact Switcheroo Saturday.

Some entries also end with a yin/yang sign (☯), which, in Chinese philosophy, represents two principles—dark/light, feminine/masculine—whose interaction influences the destinies of creatures and things. When the yang is on top, Nick explains, the day has usually been a bummer. Nick says his use of the sign indicates contextual changes in his own life.

The audience for the journal is not just Nick but an implied reader as well, who is sometimes addressed as "Brother." These randomly selected lines indicate the implied (you) audience within this journal:

You will recall my dissertation on irony burns; two pages ago? Ha. That's a funny one, *you* betcha; "*Pardon* this elaborate metaphoric divergence. The appeal was compelling"; or, "Oh yeah. Got rather a lot sidetracked there. The storm, *you* see was the intended conclusion. That is: it's snowing hereabout." [emphasis added]

Or this entry:

Hello. I'm back. *You're* delighted, I know.
And no: Things are not improved in the least. In fact, they've gotten loads worse. Meanwhile: I'm sliding through the slippery streams of my blood. Deep into the abyss.

At the same time the audience is Nick, as this lyrical entry on the loss of his bandanna indicates:

7:16 pm
Aagh. Woe of woes. I've lost my blue bandanna somewhere along my meandering day's course. My trademark said Jen. Or if not so much that, then an object of warm endearment for me; the rag did, after all, accompany me in the bizarre trip to the July Fourth Dead and Dylan show. A sizeable task. It is gone. I am thus additionally despondent.

Or this short but telling entry about his desire for female companionship:

8:08 am
So where is MS. almost right?

Or this partial entry which mentions Prose Writing within the context of his other subjects:

Intended to study before sleep but looks doubtful. I still owe many hours to the academic leviathan of UNH. The monolith has trapped me in its elaborate web (bureaucracy) and lunges at me with four curbed fangs. English is the most persistent assault; but weak and defendable, easily (although I owe a make-up paper in addition to this week's five pages) For Pol [foreign policy] strikes more blows. They are less constant yet more threatening . . .

The journal style ranges from the formal —

Lue (Lucifer) unleased only blustery arctic winds, thus far. He doth me slight injury, this day so far.

— to the abstract dissertation on the soul, which shows his very writerly, self-conscious, and literary style:

The soul actually is a pretty neat idea. Especially with all the complex trappings that are draped over it through all the theorizing humans are apt to do when they'd like to cling onto a belief that makes no sense. So does the soul.

Still, I'd like to think that I've got one lurking in my rubbery life. The essence of me. Arrogantly enough, I am drawn toward the hollow promise of some life eternal. Eager to think that the most of what I am precedes me and will persevere afterward . . .

Am I so pleased with the essential me? Admittedly so. With the sanguine teen-years now three years past, and adolescence on the waning end of its tortuous circle, I have assembled a ramshackle identity, that fits just right (and right before momentous change, ironically enough). It doesn't seem to forge much of an impression on my peers (ha), but I'm relaxed with it: it is me.

Within the "rubbery" quality of Nick's life, he has built a "ramshackle" identity partially through the medium of this journal itself: writing in Nick's personal life is a way of knowing. Prose Writing class has tapped into the same challenge of constructing personal knowledge and is thereby valued by Nick over the kind of role playing that he is asked to do elsewhere in his academic life. As Nick says, "School is what I *do*, not what I *am*," which echoes Pirsig's claims (1974) in *Zen and the Art of Motorcycle Maintenance* that the "university is a state of mind."

Nick as Writer: The Ticker Tape Process

We have considered Nick as speaker, Nick as reader, and Nick as journal keeper. But what is Nick like as a writer in this writing class? He enters Prose Writing with a positive image of himself as a writer: "Somehow, I'm a good writer. That is, I haven't a clue how it came to be or from where I learned it; yet it persists" (reading journal). In fact, he is a fecund and versatile personal journal keeper who is in control in his writing, just as he was orally, of a wide range of styles: from a mannered, almost baroque tone to the inviting voice of his response to Donna's paper or his personal commiseration on the loss of his bandanna or revelations about his soul and identity. But Donna does not read Nick's personal journal; what she responds to are his formal papers and his classroom journal, both requirements for her course. Being privy to Nick's journal made me alert to whether or not Donna's course would allow him the same range of disclosure and self-understanding that his personal journal affords.

Nick's first formal paper for Prose Writing leans on an assigned essay by Edward Hoagland, "What I Think, What I Am" (1981). In this essay, Hoagland defends the flexibility of the essay form — hybridized as it has become — as imitating the "mind's natural flow" and sounding like "the human voice talking." Nick is quite conscious that Hoagland's essay encouraged him to combine narrative and essay techniques in his own paper, as indicated in his class journal: "Were you to take this first paper I've written and use it as the representative sample among essays, you would all but prove Mr. Hoagland's theory and establish it as law." The understanding that an essay captures both the mind and the autobiographical helps Nick forge a technique for drafting his first paper, "A September Evening Trip," which, according to Nick's evaluation in his class journal, represents his own "human voice talking."

Several times early in the semester Nick admits that he is almost more interested in the form of his writing than in its content, and his first paper affords a wonderful example. Written while Nick was madly researching a paper on NATO for his political science course, "September's Evening Trip" begins as follows:

There are swarms of locusts hiding somewhere in this library. No. I suppose that it is only the dull buzz of these stark, florescent lights on the morbid quiet one would find in libraries everywhere.
 Papers are rustling to either side. A sniff. And now a cough. And low voices hum from an indeterminant point among the stately rows of

unused books. Another cough and a vague tapping noise.

My vestigial will power is crumbling; my eyes look away from this page. There are shallow steady breaths and slouched bodies surrounding me. Some are corpse like: silent and limp in their plastic and aluminum chairs. Others work feverishly, bend low over a high stack of books and papers, eyes scanning crazily through the pages. Their pens are clutched fiercely between their fingers: the blunt end twitches and wiggles mere centimeters from their pursed lips.

I was one of the latter type, the mad researcher. Until a few moments ago, that is. Now I'm an observer. And this is what I see.

Libraries are places of fortitude, of diligence. They are places of absolutes. I find myself oddly compelled. I am consumed by the Puritan work ethic: I'm super-responsible. "Can" lapses into and out of "must."

The paper follows this format of alternating between what Hoagland's essay describes—"what I think" and "what I am"—for five plus pages, first presenting descriptions of what Nick is seeing:

These books and papers and pencils and plastic chairs and humming lights ... it's made us all mad. Look at the little maniac struggling to capture all the information ever written on the combined field theory. Look at the brunette in her cubicle who has suffered over the same paragraph of Hobbes's *Leviathan* for twenty-five minutes.

And what Nick is doing:

Thoughts are running together into a white noise in my head. There is no room for more thoughts, great or small. I'm banging against the steel door that locks off the unused majority of my brain. Words are pinning me to its cold surface.

And his dissertation on libraries:

Libraries are places of worry. It condenses on the brain when the effort begins to fade (condense like a neutron star): the most cruel aspect. There are clocks in all the corners, they tick loudly. Milling people become enough of an event to sap the last of your concentration. Murmured conversations leak into the text. Words begin to tremble in their neat columns. They start lurching and heaving across the page, colliding and overlapping one another.

In his self-evaluation of the essay, Nick reports that even though he had to "become Queen for a Day" by handing in his paper late, he's "delighted" with what he wrote. What he feels works best in his essay is the "flow into and out of storying and essaying, alternatively: that, and the overall rhythm thereby established." Nick is more interested in the textuality of his paper, in its movement and fabric, than in the message it conveys. He hopes the reader will follow these "changes in momentum" but concedes, parenthetically, "(*I am the primary reader*)." Nick is clearly pleased with this paper and is disappointed in Donna's response. In conference she applauds its writerly quality and careful structure but wants Nick to push on to more substance, suspecting that the paper has not challenged him as a thinker. She wants him to avoid the "bravado and flash" that she called him on in the first class journal entry.

The paper is well-written and reads wonderfully aloud, but it seems more of a performance, a spectacle, than an act of discovery or thinking. For some students, this paper could be ground breaking, but for Nick it is almost effortless, written in spurts between his intensive library research for political science. Students who come into writing courses with fairly sophisticated skills can be difficult to work with since they have long been rewarded for their first draft efforts. Such students often resist challenging subject matter and the process of revision, adhering to the forms and topics that historically they have been able to handle well (see "The Case of the Reluctant Reviser," Chiseri-Strater 1984). Donna confronts Nick directly about his attitude toward revision in a conference on another paper:

Donna: Do you ever revise?

Nick: Uh, not yet.

Donna: Do you ever feel the need to?

Nick: Not really. You see, I don't, I don't know what it is, I don't seem to write things that spark an interest in me the second time to the point that I'm going to write them again.

Donna: Or see them in a different way that would make you want to approach it . . .

Nick: Yes . . .

Donna: Differently? Or is writing a kind of catharsis for you?

Nick: Sometimes, yes. I think—mostly, in fact, it's a cathartic thing. But I don't know, I haven't done too much creative writing besides my journal.

Donna: What's *creative writing*? I thought all writing was creative.

When Nick and I talk about his writing process, I confirm his resistance to approaching difficult topics. Good paper subjects for him are limited by his sense of investment, of how much time a particular topic might take: "We're talking serious time here. I'd prefer to get these English papers down and write 'em out, something, 'hey, that's a good thing to write about'—bam! Five pages right there." Although he is willing to *think* about a topic and let his mind *wander* over an idea "while walking to class, walking home," when it comes time to write the paper, it is something to get done, bam!

Before he drafts a paper, Nick writes a short, one-paragraph to one-page "blurb" of all the mental notes he has gathered, which, he says, sometimes *eclipse* the original topic and *trigger* further ideas. Actual desk time for writing an English paper was three to ten hours, on and off, depending upon the subject of course. When I asked about the recursive nature of writing for him, Nick said that he didn't go back or reread his text when the paper was flowing; only if he felt *blocked* would he redraft. He compared the linear quality of his writing process to watching a ticker tape:

Because when you write it the first time, it's like looking at a ticker tape as it comes through the machine. You look at one section of the ticker tape at a time. You don't follow where the ticker tape is going, you just assume that it's landing.

And although Nick's writing process works well enough for initial drafting, it cannot tolerate revising, chiseling out the little parts to make the image in the stone or plaster clearer for the reader. Because Nick is the primary reader.

"Living Through": Nick's Furies

Although Nick locates his next topic fairly easily, he admits that "Living Through" is a "rush job" written on familiar issues that have been "consistent" as issues throughout his college years. The paper explores at least three potentially turbulent themes: first, career-oriented students; second, Nick's mother as role model; and third, Nick's future, Nick's fate. Unlike the last paper, Nick evaluates this effort negatively, claiming that all three themes are "underdeveloped," that the writing is not "coherent," and that he sounds as if he's "whining and bitching, making excuses and justifying" himself for "not having a handle on it all." In terms of form, Nick thinks that he should be writing "essays" and fears that the paper falls into being "just a narrative." This paper does have an entirely different tone: there's an economy to the adjectives used, a rawness in the thinking, and an honesty that is bare as well. At the same time, the issues he explores are masked by abstractions and lack of resolve in the actual writing, not just thematically. He begins "Living Through" with a description of careerists, centering the reader ("you") firmly at UNH, pitting "you" against "them":

Were you to stand almost anywhere on the UNH campus long enough, you would find yourself engulfed by mobs of career-minded students.

This is particularly the case with certain strategic areas: the engineering building, the school of business. They will not notice you however; they are consumed with their relentless climb toward riches and "success."

The careerists indulge in greedy fantasies of reaching "the top." They are lost without the hierarchy, through which they will run, walk, or crawl toward hopeful financial security. Some will attain this economic greatness, most will not: a hierarchy is a steep pyramid which narrows abruptly near the pinnacle: there is room for only a few. Still they will aspire to it.

Next Nick folds in the wonderful theme of his "durable" mother, which wanders off into abstractions before we have any concrete details:

My mother is durable. She has lived a true life. The truth is in experience and in the courage to face it. Adversity will come in a true life, and happiness too. Neither will be an enduring sensation. The true-liver will not expect it to be so, but will maintain a semblance of themselves in the uncertain face of change.

Her story is not an epic. It is not especially outstanding. One might easily overlook her. The significance lies in her method, not in her history, because her history is hardly unique.

My mother has just become a Baptist minister. A career, yes, but not for "success." A career for happiness (transient though it may be). Mom awoke one night and decided on pursuing theology, not to regain the thread of her prior education, but to move on to the next stage of living. At the age of 52, she returned to a student's life (while preserving the elemental self).

And finally the theme of Nick's conflicts are introduced in the most abstracted sections of all, describing the real position he has taken about a kind of moratorium on career choice:

I am not a career-minded student. I do not seek the confines of 'the top.' I will carve my horizontal path through life, climbing here and dipping there. My success will not be measurable by economic scales. And it will be dynamic; my security will be temporary, coming and going in the face of new circumstances.

Experience is most useful when it is lived through; it is not a by-product of living. It is a lens with which one may discover much about oneself. Experience allows us to see ourselves as we remain after the trials of pain and joy, and as we are in them.

In this paper, Nick uses some personal examples from his mother's life to begin to explore his thinking about an issue that concerns him: his lack of career choice. It is a wonderful "discovery draft" for further thinking and writing. And in spite of his equivocal feelings about the paper, Nick decides to share it in his first writing group although he has some reservations about writing groups: "Writing groups are productive but on a primitive level. I mean you can still plow a field with a stone plow." In what he calls the "pre-response, responses," Nick decribes the oral reception of the group (which includes Anna) as positive, which "surprises" him because he thought the paper "lacked cohesiveness and substance enough that it was rendered unintelligible." What interests the writing group is Nick's "role within the paper," suggesting that, as the draft stands, Nick serves only as a reflection in the descriptions of his mother. Students ask Nick to "distinguish" between his mother and himself and "show the relations" more clearly. And while everyone identified with the theme of the careermonger, students agreed he should "tone it down" a bit.

In his class journal entry, Nick describes each student's oral response and adds that "Anna didn't have much to say in the group, actually. She agreed with Tina and Neil's points. But she didn't have much in the way of fresh insight." But when Nick receives students' written responses to his paper, he has a different perspective on Anna: "Anna's conclusions were more profound than the others on the whole. She poses questions which incline me toward an (elusive) adequate central idea." Nick goes on for several paragraphs to talk about Anna's astute response and ends with a rhapsody that masks his fear about writing on this topic:

Anna dearest, you have hit the nail exactly on its puny head. This theme leaps into the spotlight of obviousness to dance a jig and taunt the audience. "Where are you going?" What a question. . . . This paper is a rationalization of my insecurity (about the future). A cover-up for the dissonance of being (apparently) unprepared. Good spotting, Anna.

The supportive feedback that Nick receives on this paper from his writing group and from Donna does not push him toward revision; rather, he backs away from this topic, and thereby from these issues: "There's no potential for the paper" he says, "It doesn't strike me as anything relevant."

In fact, the topic is *so* relevant that it strikes dissonance in him, as this statement from our interview indicates: "Will I ever have a car? Or a house? Will I ever get a job, or a career? Will I ever make anything out of my life: As soon as you say the one thing, there's the echo behind it." The echo can be heard to reverberate with Nick's current life issues. "Living Through" takes on two of these issues: it addresses Nick's quandary over career decisions and his lack of a mentor to help direct his academic life. In an interview with me, Nick questions, "To what extent am I *justifying* that I'm not seeking a career?" He realizes at the same time that all those "careerists," as he calls them, cannot possibly achieve the success that they dream of because "there isn't a piece of the pie for everybody . . . They don't understand that they have to fight tooth and nail to do it." Nick, on the other hand, will lay back and "abstain" from wearing the straightjacket, from putting on the professional mask and spouting "professional jargon." Nick's paper "Living Through" reveals his ambivalence about his commitment to noncommitment.

"Living Through" is also about the role of mentoring that his mother has played in his life, but he challenges even that: "To what extent is my mother an *excuse* rather than an *example*?" he asks. In mulling over a possible revision, Nick says that when he started to think about his mother and "why I respect her and why I have a certain feeling about my life," he decided that his mother wasn't the real theme of the paper either. In fact, he says that the part about his mother is kind of "corny." For Nick, the dream that helps shape a life is a diffuse dream: "My rainbow doesn't just arc in one direction. It sort of spreads out."

Nick's inability to revise this particular paper may be explained by the fact that the issues may be too close, too weighted, too discordant to approach any closer. Some male college students seem to prefer to write about topics that are circumscribed rather than the messy, circular subject matter that women students often choose (Chiseri-Strater 1987).

Approaching this messy draft, Nick retreats. Unlike women writers who often see life as a text to be written and who read into texts parts of their own lives (Gannett 1987), Nick separates the textuality of his life from himself. Nick's issues are separate from him, he explains to me: "This is probably a minor point, but it makes a difference to me. My life isn't my text—what I saw around me, what was happening was." For Nick there is a "self" or "series of selves" that exists autonomously from life, not within its multiple facets and complex connections.

Nick's Muses: Erica, Heidi, Peggy

Nick's next series of paper topics reveal his intense interest in forming relationships with women, if not an equally intense dread of these relationships. Two of his papers focus on encounters with women, one of which represents his only attempt at revision in the course. The first of these papers about a relationship, "Sudden

Attachment to Her," is framed as a letter beginning "Brother," an opening often used in his personal journal. Nick continues this six-page epistle about an encounter with a woman called Heidi, beginning with this opening:

Brother,
I have written to you before concerning this delicate matter and shall again, now. It is Heidi. It is my sudden realization about her. And about myself; in some ways, more than latter.

Nick goes on to describe his sexual conquest in fair detail:

Together we have had nearly flawless sex. But there has been an undercurrent I did not understand. Her lips against my stomach or chest are meaningful; her hands coursing gently through my hair are expressions of genuine fondness . . .

When he next writes about conflicted feelings over the relationship, it seems to the reader that this is the usual sort of poor timing and circumstance that happens to relationships at college:

And as I have remarked a mere 40,382 times today alone: I don't need them (girls). I can enjoy life to its minuscule fullest without the torment of small-talk, lines, the scope scene, games, tricks, ploys, pretense, facade, and the dreaded day-after awkwardness . . .

But, by the end of the paper, Nick makes a more explicit reference to his apprehension over beginning a new relationship, harking back to a previous one that ended in disaster:

I'm sure you recall, Brother, Erica, the Usurper, my ex-would-have-been wife. Thoughts of her still invoke a subdued panic in me. Our two years of committed bliss are easily overpowered by the five months of doom and catastrophe that followed. Although that small taste of hell occurred nearly a year ago, I still flinch at the phrases "commitment" and "love."

Although the paper does not detail this further, Erica, I learn, was Nick's girlfriend, with whom he had an intense and extended two-year relationship that ended in personal anguish for him: she threatened to commit suicide when Nick broke up with her. Although Nick later realized that he was not the cause of her depression, that a breakdown was inevitable for his girlfriend, he blames himself for not understanding her vulnerability:

I'd been such a complete pillow for her for so long. I had been such a complete guardian, such a complete caretaker, that when I pulled all that away, she had nothing. Nothing. No reason to live. I had to lie to her and say, yeah, you have this to live for and that . . .

Eventually Nick steered Erica into counseling (meshing with his own interest in psychology) and stayed with the relationship until she was healthier, explaining: "I wouldn't have been able to live with the fact that the woman that I loved for two years, that I loved better than anyone else, that I was the reason that she killed herself."

Donna does not probe these implied issues: she "receives" or accepts Nick's paper but does not push him to work further on the draft. In fact, they have a verbal tug of war as Donna reads the paper in conference and comments on it aloud:

Donna: This makes me question everything in relationships in general. How much, when things get started, is it a factor of need, who you are, and what you are going through at the time?

Nick: These questions are kind of steering you toward a paper on my exgirlfriend.

Donna: I'm not steering you toward anything. I'm giving you basically my reader response. I'm showing you how I respond as a reader, not so much telling you what to do . . .

Nick: And I'm telling you how I respond to your comments.

Donna: Okay . . .

Nick: The need factor was very much prevalent in that relationship.

When writing teachers invite students to choose their own topics, students often submit papers about autobiographical situations that are disturbing. Issues like rape, child abuse, suicide attempts, broken homes, and death cannot be kept outside of a writing classroom, dropped at the door. They need not become the only topics that students pursue, but often such subjects offer the strongest path to strengthening their writing skills because of the commitment invested in a personal topic. Nick lays out many possibilities for such papers, but he is so easily satisfied with his first draft efforts that he does not pursue them. Nor does Donna allow Nick to make her the cause for his writing a paper on his past relationship. The commitment must come from Nick.

Interestingly enough, Nick chooses "Sudden Attachment" to share in an all-female writing group. In an interview previous to the peer-group meeting, Nick told me he thought the paper might "shock" the women in his group because the paper was pretty "gritty," which he translates as "realistic." After the group meets Nick admits in his journal response that he'd been wrong about their reactions, and wrong about them:

I must admit here my surprise. My group consisted of Sarah, Allie, and myself. I became convinced that one or possibly both would display themselves as foo-foos. In that regard I was mistaken.

It is not a disappointment, however. My companions proved

themselves (unknowingly) to be thoughtful and more hearty than I had envisioned. Both, it turns out, have real talent, or at least substantial skill.

Donna cannot resist a marginal comment on Nick's journal: "Ohh how we make assumptions!" Nick's judgmental stance toward other students' reception of his work is consistent in this course. He is sure that students (particularly women) will be unable to understand his writing, but he is thankfully proven wrong. Their "primitive" feedback could fertilize his thinking if he would let himself revise.

Nick goes on to draft still another paper about a relationship, which he first titles "Blindness for the Madonna" but revises to "Third Time Under," about a woman named Peggy. Both drafts share an identical lead, in which Nick paints a romantic portrait:

She was always more beautiful in the pale light of the autumn moon. This night, that moon was full. Its halo diffused through the thin ripples of clouds in a circular rainbow: with no ends and no pot of gold. What does it mean, I asked aloud.

Both versions chronicle the same story, with the only minor changes being a refinement of the wording and tightening of the structure. "Third Time Under" plays with the pun of meeting this same woman in autumn (fall) and falling under her spell, coupled with the theme of drowning—three times under and you don't come up:

I wanted her, two falls ago, although I could not. She fills my ideal of woman, more closely than others. But I was deeply in love with another, not nearly so close. I could not admit that I want to love Peggy too, not even to myself.
    She in turn, did not admit her draw to me. I was her "Artman" so long ago, but I refused to see. She would smile at me and we would laugh
together. We talked openly and with sweet words; we even dared to flirt. We rarely touched, but I reached out, anyway.
    It was my first time under.

In the revision, Donna applauds Nick's ability to manipulate time, his movement between the previous falls and the current one. In this revision Nick chronicles the familiar discord between heart and mind:

It was a hard fall, my second time under. The night is crisp and cold. The moon shines on us still, but the halo has gone. Have I missed its meaning? I do not know yet.
    I look at Peggy through the steady fog of my breath. I am remembering my last two falls, but without the pain. It has dwindled in a year's time. I think of my past desires for her. How similar they seem to my present ones.

"Third Time Under," tightly woven, filled with intensity and intrigue, is a personal narrative about Nick's tangled encounters with a woman: she is the seductress and he is the victim, merely put under her spell. Nick does not attempt to reflect on the complexities of this relationship, he just narrates the story. In the final scene, it is the power of words that seduces him: "I am happy, tonight. More so than I've been in months. Just because of her words. As I stroll through the dark, I wonder if I can be her friend, her lover, or both. This fall, I am, once again, under her spell."

In the same writing conference as above, Nick asks Donna, not timorously, for an evaluation of his paper, saying, "I was actually wondering if you think this was a well-written paper."

Donna: I think so. There's a lot of things working here. Writing about these things, we all have such a capacity to be trite.

Nick: I was really impressed by this paper myself because of the content.

Nick reports to me that he wrote the paper in a kind of "explosive fit" and then worried about whether or not it was any good because he hadn't paid much attention to the form:

Like I said before, I concentrate a lot on form, about as much as substance. But in this particular paper, the substance kind of removed me from paying attention too much to the form. So I was glad I carried it off.

Nick's sense of "carrying off" a piece of writing reflects the performance aspect of his prose style; he "masters" the text. Through the powerful act of writing, he achieves the control that he cannot achieve in life.

Nick's Politics: Boom

Even though Donna hints at further revisions for "Third Time Under," Nick chooses not to revise but to draft yet another new paper, this time with political themes, "And the World Said Boom." Nick's essay voice is woven together with some narrative parts; this paper is his only attempt in Prose Writing to deal with issues outside his personal life. The paper begins at the boundaries of the universe:

From out in the swirling currents of invisible particles that drift among the giant planets (a mere four billion kilometers from the sun), the view of our world is vague: a tiny bluish splotch amidst two other similar splotches. Each whirls in a distinct eclipse about the star that obscures its image.

Three paragraphs later, the reader arrives at Earth:

Even from barely forty-million kilometers, the Earth's secret is unexposed. Among its companions, it is the largest, yet not by enough to seem, in any way, remarkable. It is still some three and a half times smaller than the smallest outer-system giant. Our world has but one claim: it holds life.

And the next section comes back to Nick:

From a yard or two, the obscure planet Earth is teeming with living matter. Which is where you would find me, were you at the appropriate point.

At 7:00 this morning my clock-radio stirs me from a shallow sleep, offering me no hints about our world, or about life. My awareness discerns my own life and that of my roommate and little more. The routine evidences of life around us make no impression on me. I lumber for the shower . . .

In the dormitory bathroom Nick discovers a pamphlet called "Beyond War," which he relates to his personal thoughts:

The pamphlet is another group's attempt to sober our view — to provoke us to glance away, even momentarily, away from the microcosmic dilemmas of our personal world to the world at large. Reluctantly, I submit that the horror of consciousness will keep man's stubborn mind asleep. Like the accident victim who cannot recall the crash, we will seek to delete the untidy fact from our discriminating recollections. We have forgotten the peril into which the Earth has been propelled.

We have forgotten about the Earth Nick suggests, because we trust our leaders to be in charge, but, as Nick warns, they are self-invested:

Security issues. Power-people; our leaders, despite their common jeopardy with us, are consumed with being overrun by someone. Man's war-like countenance is easily exposed and lined to innate territorialism, perhaps as much as our death-wish and predacious instincts.

The essay ends with Nick's guilt over his lack of responsibility, his lack of commitment toward issues of nuclear war and preservation of the Earth:

Profound helplessness. I am suspended between my neglected duties as a living being and my conclusions about the failings of our system, at the hand of power-people. An irreconcilable contradiction is burning my skin with the shower's hot water. Perhaps the steam is obscuring a conclusion.

I have a frail human psyche. I will have to abandon this line of thought or risk sinking into an irretrievable depression.

Again, there is no resolve or commitment at the end of the paper: Nick goes one giant step forward but retreats into existential despair, his sense of "profound helplessness."

Nick's Evaluation: The Fly on the Wall

Nick did not rework any of his papers for his final portfolio. He submitted his first paper, "September's Evening Trip," and the original draft of "Third Time Under" for grading. By his own criteria, "September" is a good paper because it "flows" and shows "creativity in action." "Third Time Under" Nick submits not on the basis of the form that Donna praised him for, but for its content. Nick says that during Prose Writing he changed from an initial concern with form, from having perfectly balanced papers such as his first, to an interest in content, to conveying meaning: "I started working a lot more on content than form," he tells me. When he does this he finds, "my form went all to hell." The strain of concentrating on content can cause a temporary loss of writing skills that is regained over time as development catches up with learning (Vygotsky 1978). The visible content of "Third Time Under" is a narrative account, while the hidden content is Nick's ambivalence toward forming intimate relationships.

Each paper for Nick stands as a separate assignment, a completed product, finished and then abandoned. Because he does not invest in the process of revision, Nick cannot use writing as a way of learning, as a way of achieving resolve about any of his persistent and nagging problems. What Adrienne Rich suggests about revision for women could be true for Nick as well: "Revision—the act of looking back, of seeing with fresh eyes, of entering an old text from a new critical direction—is for women more than a chapter in cultural history—it is an act of survival" (1979, 35).

Thematically, Nick explored a number of issues in his writing: his place in college and his family ("Living Through"); his intimate relationships with women ("Madonna," "Third Time Under," "Sudden Attachment") and his political awareness ("And The World Said Boom"). But churning beneath these papers are his current conflicts: outrage at the professional education he sees his peers seeking; his dance with intimacy and isolation; his consciousness and fear of the fragility of our Earth. But he does not (cannot?) resolve these issues through writing.

Nick is situated in a precarious position on William Perry's charted journey of intellectual and ethical development: he is in a stage of "temporizing," which Perry views as a "deflection from growth" (1970). Nick is postponing commitments or career choices: he says that when it bothers him to think he has "missed the boat," he just remembers "what boat it is that I'm missing." Although he writes about intimacy with women, he claims that when he is through with a phase of his life such as college, he is done with all the people associated with that period: "I'm the kind of person who will avoid getting back together ... My best friend from high school I don't call or write to. I don't want to see her again." As for his many college male friends who graduated in May, Nick has demarcated boundaries for them as well, seeing them like a "rock-and-roll band—we hung out together, got really famous, then just broke up."

So what does Nick learn as a writer in this course? He came to Prose Writing with fairly substantial writing skills and leaves the course unscathed, with those same skills intact. It is tempting to say that the course did little for him but provide additional practice in writing. And if there was not a journal in this course, which required regular self-monitoring and evaluation, there would be no way to disagree with this assessment.

It is Nick's reading and writing responses that allow Donna to understand that despite his resistance to revision in her course, Nick did change a great deal with respect to attitudes toward writing. Nick's journal responses record two major realizations that contribute to what he calls his "renaissance" in creativity: one he calls social and the other personal:

My realization is two-fold then: a view back to the personal realm and a view to the social. On the personal level, I have come to see myself as I think in my essaying; a fresher look at my writing method. Socially, I have reluctantly recognized the relevance of the reader. Whereas my previous disposition rendered me adamantly opposed to assisting the reader's understanding (that's his/her problem), was my previous self; [I now understand] that writing is for the reader's understanding.

When Nick and I discuss his changed concept of audience, he says that the classroom reading assignments helped him better understand audience expectations:

When we started doing the readings, I realized, 'all right, I'm reading these pieces as other people are going to read my pieces.' And because of that, I felt maybe, I should be concentrating on what the reader wants to hear, or what the reader is going to be most interested in.

Formerly, Nick saw the reader as the "person interceding in the communication between the writer and writer as primary reader."

Nick's concept of audience was as "secondary" and "objective," what he calls "the fly on the wall."

Nick is learning to read like a writer, calling on what Donald Murray has called the writer's "other self" to assist in exploring the meaning intended and the meaning realized (1982, 166). Nick's notion of an implied audience has been expanded through the professional readings as well as through the reality of a peer audience. And although Nick does not change that much in actual writing skills, he changes his attitudes toward writing.

Donna's comment on Nick's final folder shows her disappointment in his refusal to refine his work but acknowledges that Nick's learning in this course came through reading and group interaction:

Nick—I can't help but wonder what would have happened this semester had you chosen to push, to extend yourself. Nonetheless, I liked seeing the revelation you mention in your journals—the development of the consciousness of the social. . . . You are a good writer and now that you are aware of the reader, I expect good things have been set in motion— we can expect much in the future.

Nick as Collaborator: Collage or Portraiture?

Nick credits the collaborative project for uncovering his real strengths as a writer: "Oddly enough, the collaborative effort showed me something new about my writing: I have a greater propensity for rendering narrative than for explaining my thoughts in an essay." And although Nick ends the collaborative project positively, he begins with skepticism, with "bafflement" as he calls it. His initial collaborative journal entry indicates his quandary over how several hands in the pot will *not* spoil the brew. Drawing on art metaphors, Nick fears that a collaborative paper, which should emerge as a cohesive whole, as a portrait, may in fact end as a collage, or even pastiche:

You know. It entirely eludes me how it is that one enters into a collaborative assignment of this genre. My failing I know. Perhaps I read too much of a baroque portrait into a written work. One hand may grace the page with complexity and intricate insights. A uniformity of detail; visual course—an even flow at gradual velocities, consistent and consuming.

Many hands may not render the cohesive whole. Instead, simplicity must prevail; the insights, each emerging from a separate origin, will not adhere. They must be reduced to a common denominator and forced together. . . . A collage has assumed the position where a portrait would have been.

But he is game. In preparation for the first collaborative meeting with Neil and Tina, Nick makes notes in his collaborative journal about how group members might respond to his particular reading choices. His strong awareness of the collaborative team shapes the critiques of each reading he selects. For example, when he reads a short story by Robert Herrick, he first connects it with his own style: "It reminded me of my own prose, sort of, on my best day." He remarks condescendingly, however, that "the style of Herrick ... may not have such a fervent reaction from my fellow collaborators." After his extended and political response to the Herrick character whom he compares with Rousseau, Nick warns himself not to expect others in his group to read the story in the same way: "Obviously Tina and Neil are doubtfully going to share my enthusiasm or familiarity with dreary Renaissance psychology/sociology/political science/philosophy. But perhaps my connections will inspire a suitable topic for us, if the text will not." Does Nick feel that his reading of these texts is so much more complex that Tina and Neil will not understand or is he truly concerned with their reactions? A bit of both perhaps, hidden thickly behind his abstract prose style.

When Nick locates a short piece from *New York Magazine*, called "Love: The Fervid Quest for the 'L' Word," he recognizes its potential appeal for his group: "Thus it came to me that this piece was a sure thing to submit to the group. In fact, it's such a sure thing that it threatens to dissolve itself into mediocrity as the most vile specter: the cliche. Egad." And Nick is right, not about the mediocrity, but that his group likes the piece and plans to combine it with another article submitted by Neil on "bullshit" to produce a topic. In his journal, Nick describes the genesis achieved at their second collaborative meeting:

"This is it!" proclaimed Neil after an hour or so of deliberation on the matter. He was referring to the vestigial diagram we had assembled in our theorizing. The thing had been born of my confederates' attempts to explain the difference between "loving" and "in love" (I had got it backwards, which could well explain my frequently disastrous relationships).
... Neil has pledged to unravel the intricacies of our meager diagram. One would think he'd read a message from god in it.

This topic, however, has been constructed by totally ignoring Tina's contribution: "Well, mine was the first to get eliminated — we all seemed to enjoy it but with two much more intriguing essays to write about, we concentrated on talking about those" (Tina's journal). And while Neil produced the diagram, it was Tina's (conciliatory?) idea to combine Nick and Neil's essay into writing about love and bullshit.

Figure 3–3

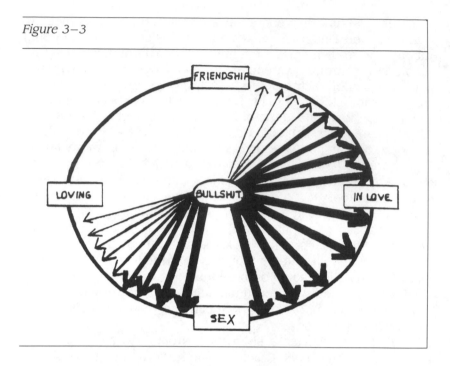

Nick, unaware that they have slighted Tina's ideas, becomes excited by the visual aid. He records how the group continued to refine the diagram before they began to write, to use it as a kind of prewriting device: "We were able to hammer out the niceties of our 'solar-system model': we defined the elliptical cycle as intrinsic to all two-party, loving situations." Their model is shown in Figure 3–3.

With this elaborate visual model, however, the group is not necessarily propelled forward as Nick had hoped: "We now have an elaborate understanding of our model. Still, we've no way to use it. So far, the apparent importance of the thing has over-shadowed a relevant application."

In this collaborative context, Nick reflects sensitivity to the group dynamics and records them in his journal. Neil, creator of the diagram, exudes, according to Nick, "a strange fervor" over his invention, a stance that Nick is well equipped to detect: "Neil's tone, though, rings oddly (for someone like him) of arrogance: his insistence, for example, that he guide the development of the model and be the responsible member regarding the written definitions." Nick recognizes Neil's influence and contribution but is puzzled in this situation by his communicative channels: "Through the lens of his fervor, he fails to *receive* while consumed in his sending." The collaborative context allows Nick to see a side of himself (arrogance, ownership) displayed in another person.

Nick's group holds its collaborative conference with Donna, having only the one-page diagram and many stunning but unrecorded ideas. Nick reports that the group was in a "rut" before the conference and that Donna, "our starboard bow," helped save the drowning writers. She simply puts them back on course by reminding them that they'd intended to incorporate the article on "bullshit" with the "mating game," but so far they'd only dealt with the love problem. As Neil notes in his collaborative journal, the conference also helped them devise a form for the paper: "The conference brought forth some options that we had never thought of. We could do some of it in the form of a narrative. In fact, we could use any form we wanted, except poetry." (The exclusion of the poetic form is entirely the students' perception, since Donna does accept a collaborative paper about the history of chocolate written entirely in poetry in another section.) The conference ends, Nick says, with "a brief brain shower and the floor was littered with ideas and examples." Tina notes in her journal that Nick was resistant throughout the collaborative conference to the idea of using a narrative introduction.

But at the next in-class meeting, no one had produced a lead. The group could look around at other collaborative group efforts being drafted and worry that they were trailing behind. Nick's analysis is that his group has "not done enough groundwork (set enough rules) through which we may each write coherently with one another." Therefore they use class time to establish the "tone" for their paper, outline and break up the sections of the paper, assigning Nick the lead even though he insists that his talents do not lie in this area: "I am apprehensive, though, about my negligible capacity for rendering a narrative which would be agreeable with two other authors to such a degree that they could pick up the threads and progress onward." Nick's journal entry shows some of the discomfort over the risks of leadership in such a project.

Collaboration challenges Nick to work in a new form; rather than strictly personal narrative, Nick must create a fictional character and situation that will provide the context for discussing their diagram. As Nick writes in his journal: "In effect, I set the tone myself, with the lead-in and definition (discussion) of bullshit." Nick recognizes that what he drafts will be subject to change: "Of course, my two pieces will not stand immutable." Here is his finished lead for the paper, a narrative written in his posturing (but amusing) style:

Sampson departed for home still dizzy from the dull euphoria of his affections for Madame X, to whom he'd just paid an unexpected but well-received visit. She had so enchanted him that it was not until his first thoughts of Delila did he feel the sharp cold of the damp autumn night.
   What if she finds out? He asked himself and faltered in his pace, nearly tripping over the curb. The truth? He puzzled for a moment. What was so terrible about a friendly visit? Sampson caught himself on this thought and stopped dead, the October winds whirling around his ears. Friendly? But not especially platonic, was it? No. The terrible offense against his long-time girlfriend Delila was simply his mood before he'd thought of her; his consequently obvious feelings for Madame X: the other woman (potentially, at least).

This lead mirrors the Peggy/Erica conflict of "Third Time Under," characters who in this context have become Delila and Madame X. But instead of being a personal narrative, this paper moves into "essaying," as this explication of the term "in love" illustrates:

Sampson was Delila's undisputed boyfriend, as she was equally his girlfriend: they were "in love." That is to say, each gained warmth and security in the presence of the other. And enjoyed it, immensely. Their love was reciprocal: in love with one another rather than loving for each other (which is actually a more altruistic affair), it was a good thing Sampson believed that. Thus it was particularly important to smooth over potentially harmful situations which might and had occurred—he didn't want to bruise his relationship with Delila: he needed her affection.

According to Nick's journal, his collaborative group worked nine hours straight on the night before the project was due, which included wasted time when Neil tripped over the computer plug. Titled "Emancipation Thursday," Nick begins his entry again with "Brother," and compares his state to that of a brook trout: "After last night's nine hours, I am left to expire in my own thoughts, like a brook trout cast onto the dry bank, to flutter and wriggle myself to death in the wake of my completed journey upstream." The collaborative paper from Nick's group was twelve pages long, the most extensive project from the class, and, in many ways, one of the most creative. The text alternates between narrative and essay, just as Nick's opening paper for the course did, but in this instance, the purpose and intent is to explain the different terms that define the orbit of love relationships shown in the diagram. One of the expository sections that Nick wrote is about bullshit, a subject that he expertly describes:

Bullshit can, therefore, protect us. Which is a fair guess why we use it so often, even in intimate settings (Sampson was, after all, still quite in love with Delila). It provides us with room to maneuver; a certain freedom from particular consequences. Bullshit can also assure us of the actions or attitudes of others; acting as either inspirations or awe-evoking propaganda. Bullshit gives us a controlled way to win friends, and influence others.

And more on bullshit from Nick, who writes not only about society but also about himself, his self-disclosure, his sense of autonomy:

Our society is rampant with bullshit. It is slung between every two people and among all conglomerations. It prevails because it is intrinsic to our external selves; the facade we display to the world and to everybody in it. We are, to each other's eyes, a baffling patchwork of sincerity and bullshit. Our core self is remote, private. Even the most open among us cannot truthfully claim to present the same self externally as internally.

In this group of two (very articulate) men and one woman, the main character of the paper is male. And somehow the bullshit section, which aptly describes the remote and private side of Nick, does not ring true for female experiences. What does Tina add to this group? According to Nick, her contribution was "typing" the paper: "I am grateful to Tina, by the way, for her volunteer effort behind the typewriter. Certainly, this is by far the most dreary responsibility involved in the whole process" (Nick's journal). Tina, like Nick, writes of the "personal interaction" of the group and reflects that it was not "superficial." Her journal also suggests that the two men are aware of their dominance: "There were times when they [Neil and Nick] asked for input or said I wasn't speaking enough—but when I thought something should be changed or added, I did; I spoke when I had something to say. Why speak when you don't?" (Tina's journal). In terms of the actual writing of the paper, it is impossible to untangle Tina's bits and pieces, since she wasn't "assigned" to write particular sections as Nick and Neil were.

For Nick the most important part of collaboration becomes communication. Nick writes in his collaborative journal: "Verbal interaction precedes all else because it is the surest facility for fusing the ideas and insights of many writers." He ends his collaborative journal entry, addressed to "Brother," by discussing the importance of talk in a very abstract way:

Speak, my boy, or you will not see to think (not in the appropriate direction, anyway). A given insight is an elaborate logic-pattern, progressing from unique schemes of association within each author's

mind. Words in exchange are the only feasible means of viewing
another's thought, however obscurely. Without our eager larynxes, we'd
have been lost—rendering a collage where a portrait should have been.

In his final evaluation essay in Prose Writing, Nick suggests
that communal support with other skilled writers has inspired
him to excel, to write well, to unleash his withered creative forces,
to find the Nick behind the words and posturing:

With a soft 'whoosh,' I've come to this renaissance: a stirring of
slumbering curiosity and creativity. I have come to it, guided by the
influence of my classmates. I was no longer alone in the labyrinth of a
solitary thought process (read: writing), but among others whose insights
drew me through the labyrinth. Alone I was the undisputed superior, cast
against the background of barely-literate masses: supreme and stagnated
with the lack of inspiration. With the return of the challenging multitude,
my creative inertia has become untangled.

Nick attributes this unraveling of creativity to the community
of students in Prose Writing class, who, like him, are dedicated
and engaged writers, interested in discovery through writing.
Nick's peers help him grow as a reader and writer who has been
used to remaining within the singular web of his own mind rather
than sharing his insights and thinking (with the uncreative multitude). William Perry points to the intellectual community as a
source of solace for the student venturing his lonely way through
the relativistic world, poised on the edge of making an affirmative
decision:

Our mentors, if they are wise and humble, can welcome us into a
community paradoxically welded by this shared realization of aloneness.
Among our peers we can be nourished with the strength and joy of
intimacy, through the perilous sharing of vulnerability. (1981, 97)

Nick's Seminar in Political Thought

Nick's crazy, radical, socialist high-school history teacher stimulated his first interest in politics. With his high-school class
Nick visited the Soviet Union for nine days and developed a
sustained interest in Soviet foreign policy. Nick admits that not
everyone is concerned with politics, but he feels that those who
are not most often are "woefully misinformed or uninformed or
both." People who watch the news and think they understand
what is going on, Nick suggests, "have no clue to what's going on
because they don't understand the news within a political context."
Nick tells me that he is attracted to political science because it

helps him understand the "big pattern" or "series of patterns" that governs our world and makes him privy to who is in control:

Politics is crap and political society ultimately is crap too, I think. But at the same time that is, de facto, what is going on and who is in control. What they do affects all of us whether we know it or not. Tax laws, for example, have affected us greatly. Every time a president takes office, that affects our lives. The way people conduct their lives very often depends upon who their leader is.

I had learned from reading Nick's personal journal that a political science class could be a fairly dreary place. He made this entry during his foreign policy class:

Dien Bien Phu Tuesday, 27 October, 1987, 2:19 P.M.
    Am sitting rigidly in Foreign Policies of Europe in an afternoon delirium. It has begun not quite as baffling as yesterday's Public Opinion class in which despondence arrived riding the back of a mysterious computer assignment (which weighs heavily, naturally enough).
Professor X. babbles ardently on about various common errors on our papers. Most of us are left unmoved in the aftermath of our tenacious effort. I, for one, was left a battered heap of fact-filled schizophrenia – dazed and unfocused in the early morning dark. I am thus unattentive to his sullen tones (as if he were Marvin, the paranoid android).
    Now he mumbles vague outlines of Norwegian foreign policy. What about the T.V. in the middle of the room, X.? 106 new states in the world (U.N.) since '45. You don't say. But what about the tube? Clips from the French Massacre at Dien Bien Phu. Hello? He's not paying any attention.

So I'm relieved second semester when Nick tells me that he is taking an advanced seminar for seniors and graduate students, in which they will be using literature to explore political issues. Shakespeare and Plato lure me toward auditing this class with Nick instead of another foreign policy course. Nick had also talked with me previously about Professor Adams, how "brilliant" he was, and how he had helped Nick become a closer reader of political texts: "I had read all the books already and I read them again. And I was surprised and impressed with my professor because he got me to think about those things in ways that never really occurred to me before." With Adams's permission and his relative amazement at my project of following student-writers into their major disciplines, I began to attend the late-afternoon seminar.

I go early to the Social Science Building, and climb the three sets of stairs to locate the seminar room. There are barely enough chairs for the eighteen students who will be seated around the large square seminar table in the small square room. I select a spot behind one of the wicker-backed chairs, wait for the course to start, and listen. I note that students call each other by their last names, a style I later learn is endorsed by Adams.

One pair of students is debating whether it is better to read Plato all the way through once, then go back and read each section more carefully, or whether it is better just to go through the text slowly and think about each part, without worrying about the overall picture.

Another conversation is taking place about jobs. A dark-haired female student—Miss Manning—who is perusing the want ads, talks about getting a job in Japan. She says that the *Wall Street Journal* has an ad for training in Japanese. Mr. Sweet asks in a nonplussed tone of voice: "Why would you want to live on an island with those creeps?"

Miss Manning, taken aback, replies, "I take offense to what you have just said, Mr. Sweet."

Mr. Herald, the graduate assistant, saves the day by interjecting, "Mr. Sweet, have you ever known anyone from the Far East, I mean actually *known* them?"

Mr. Sweet backs down and apologizes and immediately afterward asks how to spell a word. When Mr. Reed suggests that he look it up in the department's dictionary, Mr. Sweet declines. Then Mr. Reed, picking up on the conversation, asks Mr. Sweet what he wants to do after graduation. Sweet replies that he wants to be a senator from the Granite State. Eyes roll to the ceiling as other students begin to trickle into class. One young man I recognize announces that he has heard that law schools and other professional schools are accepting video-taped applications instead of written ones. "Far out" is the consensus.

Professor Adams enters. He's tall and balding. After he places his tea mug at the head of the table to mark his place, he then leaves. All I originally know of Adams comes from the university catalog: he graduated in 1962, went on to earn his master's degree in the Midwest, and finally took his Ph.D. at a prestigious West Coast university before coming to UNH. What I come to learn about Adams is that he is trained in a very specific school of political philosophy, known as the Straussian interpretation of classical works: Allan Bloom is one of Strauss's newly famous followers. The Straussian approach to old texts embodies a kind of "reverence for its author" and an attempt to "suspend modern thought," to "suspend one's own judgement," so that the reader can "understand the author as 'he understood himself.'" (Burnyeat 1985, 30). Strauss's own textual interpretations heavily influence those who have studied with him or with one of his students: "A

Straussian ... is someone who reads secular books religiously" (Dannhauser quoted in Burnyeat 1985, 33).

When Adams reenters, I note that he is meticulously dressed in a navy blue blazer, yellow and blue tie, and red suspenders, fairly formal attire for UNH. I begin to realize that other students are also more "dressed up" than in art history or Prose Writing class. Some female students have on skirts and wear jewelry. None of the men have on jackets or ties but some wear button-down shirts and slacks instead of the more casual attire. Nick and his friend, Eric, however, both arrive in tattered jeans.

Had I not traveled with Nick into this new territory, I would not have really understood this side of Nick, one quite different from his engaging, collaborative, if sometimes dominant, behavior in Prose Writing. Political science class helps me reinterpret Nick's speech and his abstracted formal writing style as well.

Talk in Political Science: "Dish of Blood" ■ Adams starts the class: "Pretend that I am Moses and you are the Red Sea," he indicates with his hands as students scrape their chairs back from the table. Adams discourages note taking in his class because he wants full participation in the discussion. He then returns the weekly papers, and, in a formal manner, calls students by their last names. Adams makes comments as he is passing back the papers: "You will get back from me more than you give," he says. His grading policy is made up of a complex system of stars and checks: "To get an A in this course, you will need sixty-eight stars or sixty-eight thousand dollars." A student jokingly inquires if he is accepting foreign currency this week. Adams likens his grading system to double jeopardy: "I might go beyond two stars for a weekly paper. If the light goes on, you can give the question a try. Because the world is not necessarily rational, you have to earn your stars."

Adams discusses the misspellings on the weekly papers, saying that students are only allowed two per paper and then points are deducted. The major problem with the papers that week, he says, is that students "soared": "I want you to taxi with sufficient speed before you take off in the air. Don't talk as though Aristotle alone could understand you."

He says that in this course: "I will teach you how to read a book. I am of the opinion that if it takes a writer a year to complete a book, perhaps it should take us a year to read it. There are not many books that have lasted as long as *The Republic*. We are like grasshoppers looking at an elephant. I want you to make connections. And I'm not opposed to speculations." Then he hands out the questions for the next week, which follow in descending order in terms of possible points to accumulate.

Adams explains the duties of the weekly discussion leaders: "You are responsible for my job," he says. "You may ask questions. You can make points. I reserve the right to bring it back into the ballpark and I define what the ballpark is. Don't get too anxious about your presentations," he adds. Adams also explains that the role of the graduate students in the course is to "facilitate talk" and to "assure that the conversation doesn't flag." Mr. Sweet asks if the graduate students get course credit for this role. "Credit?" Adams feigns astonishment. "We're paying them."

When Nick suggests to me later that Adams likes his little "guidelines," his observation is confirmed as the rules and regulations for behavior are spelled out and as power and hierarchies are carefully mapped out. All this banter occurs in a humorous, fatherly, but authoritative, manner. It is clear who is in charge in this course. But talk is encouraged; coleaders are assigned to lead one of two weekly class discussions and the total credit for these presentations is listed on the syllabus as 20 percent of the final grade.

Nick and Eric lead off as coleaders of the first student-led discussion focused on education and the building of the *polis* in *The Republic*. Nick, who didn't have money enough to buy the book, borrows mine, which is one of at least four different translations of the text being used in this class, including Allan Bloom's. Nick and Eric, seated next to one another, have consulted with the graduate student, Mr. Reed, for several hours in preparation for their discussion and have made a wad of notes. Eric begins the presentation by reminding students that in *The Republic* Socrates is talking about building a *polis* from scratch. Nick joins him, explicating Socrates' discussion on education, on how the guardians have to begin with a particular basis of philosophy.

Within five minutes, however, Adams interrupts them: "Did it strike you as strange that Socrates and Glacon agree that we have to build a city? If you guys were building a city, what would you do?" From my field notes, the conversation goes:

Student: Get together and rebel.

Adams: Rebellion is successful.

Student: We would go through a purge. We'd promise to fight for the cause.

Adams: Would you state the principles of rebellion?

Nick: It has to be a stable kind of government.

Adams: Let's assume we are successful.

Student: We'd have to get them to work.

Student: We'd have to write the rules.

Adams: The constitution, what does that establish? What does "we the people" mean?

Student: Equality.

Adams: What does a government establish?

Student: Offices of the executive, judicial, and legislative bodies.

Adams: And do you anticipate what they would say about education? Can you find any discussion of education in the constitution?

Student: It's up to the states.

Adams: Yes, it's left to the states. What strikes me is that, in *The Republic*, they don't set up a government.

Nick: They become the rulers by virtue of being the founders.

Adams: Yes. What you say about the government is absolutely right. But it doesn't tell us about their society, not that they create a government but that they worry about education.

Nick: They are concerned with longevity, that the revolution they pull off will succeed so education is important.

Adams: Perpetuity. You are right in a way, Mr. Wilson, but did you see something beyond that?

Not only does Adams interrupt them before they have really "taxied" off the ground, but he has an obvious agenda for how each point should be covered and is the implied leader for the entire discussion. Nick, undaunted by being interrupted, poses questions himself to Adams in the ensuing discussion: "Could we have a modern example please?" To which Adams replies, "Alexander North, the Red Guard, the Soviet Youth Organization." And Nick feels confident enough to disagree with Adams: "Impossible. You can't assume that the guardians won't grow up and figure it all out. There's a difference between what you believe and what you think" (An echo of his mind and heart conflict?). As Nick shares with me later, "I love to start sentences in that class with 'Not necessarily.'" Gone is the "narrative conversation" of Prose Writing class: enter the pugnacious, interruptive style of politics, of the debate.

At one moment in the discussion Adams encourages Nick to engage in a verbal duel: "I glean that Socratic censorship doesn't sit well with you, Mr. Wilson." But Nick, having abdicated his role as leader, is busy drawing sketches of Adams and only swings in and out of the discussion with other students. Adams's final point in this discussion is that censorship of literature is important in the *polis* because poets write about fear of death, and if the *polis* is to be defended, the guardians must not fear death. Their identity must be wedded to the state.

Most of the students (with some notable exceptions—a couple of women and men remain silent) bravely enter the discussion arena at various points during the two hours, courageously toss in their ideas, and then back away and listen. Few exchanges are sustained beyond several turns and few exchanges attempt to build on what has gone before; yet students do not entirely dismiss or argue another student's point. Students are in the debate for themselves to display what they know to the professor. Adams, polished as a performer, leads and the students attempt to follow him. When they get off course, as Mr. Sweet frequently does, their answers are sometimes not recognized, as in this exchange: "Rest your arm for a minute, Mr. Sweet." By the end of the discussion, there is some sense that the class has "covered" a particular territory in the text, but there is no summary or wrap-up. What students take away from this discussion depends entirely on how deeply they processed and understood the verbal exchanges. Nick says that "you have to really think, and plug in" during the class or you'll be lost.

When Nick and Eric linger after class on their presentation day, Adams admits that he talked too much during their discussion, that he had hired Reed and Herald to make him silent. When Adams unexpectedly asks for my opinion, I suggest that students submit an outline of points they intend to cover, so that they'll have an opportunity to present them before Adams chimes in. He acknowledges that it is difficult for him to resist controlling the discussions.

After class, I expect Nick to feel frustrated—thwarted, foiled—over his presentation, but instead he is relieved that he was spared, as his personal journal entry indicates:

Dish of Blood Tuesday
16 Feb. 1988
4: something p.m.

Yesterday's encounter with seminar in politics left me somehow unscathed. He just wasn't into the assault. He battered me a bit and clutched my throat. And while he could have brought me to my knees, his grip slackened and I struck and ducked away. Not as though Eric and I didn't talk our meager insights into the ground; but Adams and his grad-student hunchmen [sic], weary editor of our clumsy analysis, swarmed the discussion and usurped it. We sat, stumped and silent. Appreciating the cool air out of the spotlight.

Nick's words do better than mine at showing the combative, "bloody" style of this class discussion, which humiliates the uninitiated into silence.

Nick as Guardian: Educating Elizabeth ■ Nick describes his political science class not as a farce or an act, but more like a dramatic presentation. Nick says the class could be "a Shakespeare drama, with one dominating role. The various other roles are important or not, depending upon screen time." When I ask him how he feels about playing this role, Nick says that, for him, "my roles are real" and they are sustaining because "they are even real when I'm not in them. They're still there."

When Nick and I talk about this course, about his presentation, I probe him to describe the discourse style of the classroom. He calls it a "dialectic between him and us," with "us" being all the members of the class: "It's sort of a chance event. Seems to happen with one person on one day when suddenly Adams says something that blossoms the room with light ... and then we start forging along." Nick suggests that the discourse doesn't have any particular "direction," that there's "no order" and "no system" for the discussion because it is a seminar class. Students just try to "say something that matters." And, if that doesn't work, "try again later." Gone is the rough-draft thinking of Prose Writing class: no dress rehearsals allowed, performances only. Overall, the ongoing discussion style is to "catch enough pieces of something, of people's arguments, so that you realize that you've realized something." Of his own presentation, Nick suggests that he was "just poking around" and Adams sensed it: "So that when I said something that really wasn't leading me anywhere, except into confusion, he would slap one on the wrist and say, 'You can think of it that way, but think of it this way.' It's a very 'yangy' class," he concludes.

When I inquire as to how one boards this risky dialectical merry-go-round, Nick says: "It's not a support thing. You open your mouth and your neck is on the chopping block. ... But you don't take it personally if no one will believe or take as credible what you say." And, later in our conversation, Nick reflects further on the discourse style in what he admits is a very sexist way: "You have to have some balls to stand up in that class and say something. You have to have some guts to say something." And some students, Nick suggests, aren't prepared for this in their academic careers: "Some people are not ready to go into this little room, sit down with this professor, who is obviously a very

smart man, has a great background in the material we're discussing. They're afraid to sit down and shoot the shit with him.
But that's what you have to do."

When I suggest that this classroom style may privilege men,
Nick points out that there are men who don't speak up in class
either, or that when they do talk, "their voices are kind of hoarse
or their hands shake." Nick remembers his own "terror" when he
first spoke in one of Adams's classes. Now he has accepted that
his responsibility as a student in a seminar is to "make a showing,"
because the class is "very competitive."

Nick later concedes that the class may not be all that welcoming
to women students and recounts that, one evening when I wasn't
there, a woman burst into tears in the hallway after class. She
was walking with Eric and Nick, crying and berating Mr. Herald,
the graduate student: "I can't believe him, I can't believe he's
such a jerk." When Nick and Eric tried to calm her down, they
were amazed that she was "seriously crying her eyes out." Apparently Mr. Herald had cut down one of her arguments in the
discussion and the woman held off until after class to express her
feelings about that exchange.

I pointed out as well that Adams frequently uses sports metaphors and violent movie characters to explain things, that references to football and figures like Rambo are very exclusionary.
Nick is dismayed by this information: "Really? Does that really
exclude you? I think that most people follow that, the women
included." Later in a discussion with me, he reflects on the similarities between sports and politics:

Last time I was talking about Socrates, about how our guardians can't be
afraid of death or lament or cry, I was thinking that is so much like the
football mentality. ... I think, for some people anyway, that it's a very
apropos sort of analogy. It works so well because nothing is like sports;
sports makes it easier to display, because nothing natural is like sports.
Sports is totally bizarre behavior.

Although Nick showed some empathy toward the female student
in his seminar, he was merciless toward Mr. Sweet. When I first
joined the class, I sympathized with Mr. Sweet, because, as an
outsider to this class and to the discipline of political science, I
identified with him. Even when he raised his hand, using the
appropriate oral petitions—"Excuse me, sir, but could you
please show me where you see that?"—his inquires often went
unrecognized.

Or the responses to him might take on a more sarcastic note,
as in this exchange:

Adams: Repression, neurosis are examples of man's being at war with himself. Do you ever repress anything, Mr. Sweet?

Sweet: Once.

Adams: I practice every week from four to six. Freud would say that I'm at war with myself.

Nick tried to explain to me that Mr. Sweet didn't go by the "rules" for the class, that he "wastes class time on irrelevant remarks." Nick said that the class opinion on Mr. Sweet was that "we've all seen and heard the same thing out of Mr. Sweet and none of us has any sympathy for him. He tied his own noose, he held it above his own head and hung himself with it." Nick accused me of being mistaken about Mr. Sweet. It took some time before Nick finally disclosed that Mr. Sweet had been part of the class presentation with himself and Eric. I express amazement at this information and madly check my field notes to find that Mr. Sweet, who was sitting on the opposite side of the table, had fumbled over one point during the entire session and was shot down by Adams. Nick reveals that Mr. Sweet didn't show up for any of the preparatory meetings: "And you had sympathy for him. That guy was supposed to do the presentation with Eric and me and he didn't even attempt it. He never even talked with us—nothing."

I lose all feelings for Mr. Sweet on the day he made an outrageous sexist remark. Nick tells me later that he was "horrified and amazed, even disappointed, that not one of the women in the room reacted" (nor the men). The question before the class was whether or not a political society can treat the sexes as equal. From my field notes, here is the exchange:

Adams: Do you think men or women are more important to the *polis*?

Sweet: If women are more important, then tell me why at the aquarium male fish sell for three dollars more than females?

Adams: We are talking about humans, not fish, Mr. Sweet. Are women as tough as men? Yes. You can't explain that men fight wars by saying they are stronger.

Student: Couldn't you just cull from the women a few of them to fight?

Adams: If you could afford to risk some of your women. It only takes one bull but a lot of cows to perpetuate cows. If you can afford these women in terms of your population. This is a practical matter, though, not a matter of principle.

Eric: I'd like to take the conversation away from war. Are we creating a patriarchal society where women must stay at home?

Sweet: I'd just like to point out that it's fun to domesticate women though.

Instead of helping a student like Mr. Sweet along in learning the rules and rituals of the course, as happened with Carlos in Prose Writing, Mr. Sweet becomes the class scapegoat.

Reading the Texts: "To Be or Not to Be" ■ Nick assures me that Adams's interpretations of the texts they are reading are "pretty solid and immutable." When thinking about the readings, Nick says that he sticks "close to Adams's ideas" because "he has obviously the most informed ideas" and his thoughts will "guide you where you are going." Adams announced early on in class: "I am trying to get you to see what I see." Nick intends to do just that.

When I ask Nick how he feels about this model of reading to discover the teacher's interpretation, Nick says he thinks it is "an intelligent thing to do," because it allows Adams to do what he does best: "I take Adams in a very classical sense. The classical idea is of the teacher teaching the art he is best at. Adams knows what he knows, and he knows even more than he's telling."

Nick describes his own reading process for this course as one that centers heavily on the questions handed out each week: "You keep the questions in mind, and you carefully go through the text piece by piece and try to look for details, try to look for things that are omitted, for pauses, for shifts in the conversation, for things that strike you as peculiar." Nick suggests that Adams is "trying to teach us how to go about finding that stuff by a procedure so that we can bring it to another work, or class, whatever."

I inquire about what Nick is able to get from the text on his own. In his reading, Nick finds many "mirror images" in *The Republic* to other material he has read—Marxism, Freud, and commentaries on the classics. He sometimes copies quotations from the reading into his private journal. When I asked what would happen if he responded to those other ideas that he is uncovering in his readings, Nick says that his personal connections to the texts are irrelevant: "Then it wouldn't be an *analysis* of *The Republic*. It would just be my reaction to it. We are doing an *analysis*."

All of this close reading must relate carefully to the political outline that Adams has provided on the syllabus. The readings are grouped under two headings: "Socratic Politics" and "Shakespearean Politics." Under "Shakespearean Politics," the readings are arranged from the Pagan prince—Coriolanus—to the tyrannical prince—Macbeth—to the model Christian prince—Hamlet—and so forth. The literary aspects of the text, Nick says, "don't mean doggie doo, don't mean squat" unless they relate in some way to the political slant. And the political explication used is ahistorical and decontextualized. When I comment favorably on one of Nick's class remarks, he disregards it as unimportant:

The problem with that kind of analysis and exchange in class is that you're taking your modern interpretation and applying it to a classical work. You can't bring your own context into this. You're not a classical thinker, you're not from Athens, Rome, or Greece. You don't think like they do. So when I come up with something about the arbitrary nature of society, that it depends upon the culture, well, that's a nice fine point but it doesn't relate to the text. Socrates wasn't saying that.

When I ask Nick for an example of how the class discussion *does* help him better understand the text, he uses the example of the "the noble lie" passage, talking at length about his misreading:

I missed that case entirely, because I was thinking of it as a *brand* or *kind of lie*. I thought it was characterized as *noble* because it had a certain *intent*. And surely that's the case, but the noble lie is a specific thing. And he [Socrates] states it and I missed it entirely. The lie is that, on the one hand, mother is the whole earth and hence everyone is brothers; and, on the other hand, the state is the mother. It seems so obvious now. It's a complete conflict in two sentences and I read right over it.

I wonder if Nick will ever face any tension between his own responses to the text and those of Adams. Nick is assigned to lead the discussion of *Hamlet*, under the syllabus heading of "The Christian Prince." Having never considered *Hamlet* in any political paradigm, I am curious how the class talk will go and ask permission to tape the discussion. The questions that frame the discussion are: (1) Would Hamlet have made a good king? Use the definition of king extracted from *The Republic*. (2) Analyze the "To Be or Not To Be Speech." (3) Discuss why Hamlet neglects the ghost as a sign.

At the beginning of the discussion, Nick keeps up a good match with Adams, who earlier on has interrupted the presentation and turned it into a dialogue with Nick over the issue of Hamlet as the Christian prince. From the recorded transcript, here is their exchange:

Adams: You've asserted a tension between reason and passion. Is that the tension, do you think, the tension between a passionate, unreasonable, erotic son and a calculating side, or a more theoretical side? The view of Hamlet, the normal view of Hamlet, is that Hamlet is rent with indecision because of the war within his soul. Is the war in Hamlet's soul the war of reason and passion?

Nick: The passion—eros—isn't a game. It seems to be for honor, his sense of loyalty. That seems to be what he's motivated about. In terms of Christianity, I don't think that's necessarily the case. Vengeance is not a purely Christian virtue.

Adams: What's the Christian response? If we were good, God-fearing Christians and someone spoke to us of vengeance, how would we respond? What's the example of say, Jesus? Christian vengeance seems to be a cheap thing . . .

Nick: That was one of the things that actually indicated to us that Hamlet was not the ultimate Christian. Because, on the one hand, he seemed to believe that Christian story his father told, [but] his actual behavior was not guided by Christianity at all.

But later in the discussion, when Nick is being led by Adams to interpret Hamlet within a strictly political frame, he ultimately resists:

Adams: Think in political terms. The Norwegians and the Danes are not friends. Hamlet's dad seems to have taken the wind out of the Norwegian sails, who then go beat up on the Poles instead of the Danes by killing Fortinbras's father. Yet Fortinbras has what you folks mention Hamlet doesn't: he's decisive. But his goals would not be similar to Danish goals. Think of Hamlet's choice of Fortinbras. What does this tell you about Hamlet?

Nick: His nationality, he's much more atuned with honor, someone who'd respect . . .

Adams: Could you afford a president as cosmopolitan as Hamlet? Would you guys want a president as cosmopolitan as Hamlet? What's the problem with a political leader who's cosmopolitan?

Nick: Loyalty.

Adams: What's the key, the key to political life?

Students: Stability . . .

Adams: Stability, in part, but the key distinction everyone in politics must make . . .

Nick: Us and them.

Adams: We Americans, those Chinese. We Soviets, those Afghans. And Hamlet is seemingly indifferent to those distinctions . . .

Nick: That make the noble lie.

Adams: You guys, I didn't want to direct this though. I'm getting at the cosmopolitan. I would say that Hamlet is a citizen literally speaking of the cosmos. That, by the way, might be the key to unraveling him. What does he think of Denmark?

Students: It's a prison.

Adams: Twice he says it's a prison. By the way, that's a nice thing to have a prince say, isn't it? (*He reads from the text, ending with "There is nothing good nor bad, but thinking makes it so."*)

Not only does he give the kingdom over to the avowed enemy of Denmark, but his view of Denmark—think of the scenes from Shakespeare's history plays, "this England, this sceptered isle."

Nick: You can contrast that with Corilanus pretty well, with Rome being such a prominent theme all through. Hamlet is by himself—Corilanus tries to be a solitary character, but Rome is always there—but with Hamlet, you don't really get a feeling that the country is really important. *The whole play is about Hamlet, from his point of view, his internal turmoil, what he's going through, and it's very focused on him alone.* And that indicates that he's removed from that political environment. [Emphasis added.]

While Nick stands outside after class smoking his unfiltered cigarette, he admits that Adams had just pushed him too far away from his personal interpretation of the play. "It's about suicide, that's what that play means to me," he says firmly, in a merging of his heart and head.

Nick as Writer: Bilateral Exchange ■ During the first semester Nick had remarked in passing on the discourse strategies of political science classes. In one of his conferences with Donna, Nick explained that, in writing for his political science classes, his main concern is to "display information." The professors, he says, are not interested in "personal opinion," and the writing is mainly "analytical, not interpretive." By the end of the first semester, Nick concedes that he has "lost his tolerance for the formality of political science writing."

Much of the writing Nick did for other political science courses involved a rescarch paper, but in the Political Thought seminar, regular writing is built into the course. There are twelve weekly papers (35 percent) and a final term project (35 percent). Adams talks a great deal about evaluation of writing when he hands back the weekly papers. Even though the intention of the star/check system, he tells me later, is to take the focus off grades, it doesn't come across this way to me: "No three star papers this week," he comments. "Nothing knocked my socks off." Such comments set up a competitive situation—grades, stars, whatever. Before midterm, Adams hands out little slips of papers with numbers on them and then explains that the highest possible score is twenty. Adams announces that there are fifty-four possible stars left for the course and that "it's conceivable that someone could get seventy-four stars, but no one will." Out of the twelve papers listed on the syllabus, the class only completes six, never really getting through the assigned writing.

Nick comments on his fourteen accumulated points (of a possible twenty) in his personal journal:

How I long for civilian life, with all its anonymity. 17 bloody years of school. Come on; enough is too much. Let me fade into mediocrity, already. Critical Analysis may slaughter me, in the end. It has smote me furiously already.
And. I've got 14 out of 20 stars in Seminar. Yip- f——king Yah. My enthusiasm has slithered thither.

When Adams makes comments about the actual writing of the occasional papers, he compares them to students expectations for their future professions: "The next thing you'll be writing will be law briefs. How many of you are going to law school?" He suggests that students should spend more time on their introductions: "'Well begun is half done,'" said Aristotle. "The trick is in the beginning." "Support your interpretations," he asserts. "Don't just restate facts" and "Get your facts straight." Don't just "assert" your point: "argue it, defend it." Each week he complains about the grammatical abuse in their papers, spelling and syntax errors. He often refers to the overly "abstract" quality of their writing. Once he even jokingly asks, "Do you have brain parasites?"

Nick describes the writing for political science as a bilateral process: "It's just you and Adams, that's it." "Writing is more telling," says Nick, comparing the papers with the class discussions. Adams wants "a very clean procedure" in the papers and "no fiddling around before you get to your point." Nick finds the questions valuable, both for focusing his reading and his written responses. When he receives his first paper back, I meet with Nick who judges that his first paper "is not a satisfactory piece of work at all. I was reaching. It was a total reach." I read the comment on his paper—"Be more careful in your writing"—and ask Nick how he interprets that. "I never read his comments," Nick admits.

Nick submits five two-page papers for evaluation to Adams in response to the questions that are handed out for each section of the text. All Nick's papers share similar features: they all have terse introductions—sometimes as short as one sentence; they are all written in formal and abstract language—they have no personal, and very few concrete, examples to back up the statements; most of the papers reach an insight or make a point only in the last two lines. The middle sections of these papers could be characterized as a kind of verbal thrashing around, or what Nick calls "a reach." Nick's papers remind me of what Anna said about her midterm exam essays in art history: "They are all bad in their own ways."

Of the five, one is my personal favorite, as well as the paper that received the most points (three checks and one star) from Adams. In this essay, Nick is more concrete than in any of his others and shows some creativity as well as a strain of his sarcasm. The essay is titled "You've Got Your Democracy in My Oligarchy; You've Got Your Drones in My Democracy: Introducing Tyranny." It is written in response to this question: "Discuss the oligarchic vs. the democratic regimes. What is their essential character?" The paper begins in Nick's mannered, distanced style:

Tyrannical society is the most imperfect of Socrates' four societies because it is the most thorough embodiment of unrestrained eros. It is the most erotically inclined, and thus the one in which reason is most rarely employed.
    The nature of tyranny follows from the nature of the tyrant as he has, in effect, been given a mandate by the masses (supreme when assembled) that his nature is best to lead. His rise to power was in response to the inevitable conflicts that democracy creates. Fundamental among these errors of democracy are the thirst for no master, the decay of traditional and natural hierarchies, and the unswerving insistence that he be allowed complete freedom.

A few paragraphs on, Nick offers a concrete example, based on his own political interests:

Without naming names, Socrates has profiled one Joseph Stalin, former tyrant of the USSR. His support came from the party members he placed in positions of authority, rather than the masses at the outset. It was still internal conflict, however, an ideological squaring-off in the face of the succession after Lenin.
    Stalin, though, was quite the popular leader, nonetheless much as Socrates describes. His leadership shone most brightly in the time of war. And like him (the Socratic tyrant), Stalin was consumed by his fear and ruthlessness in restraining his power. Stalin originally formed a triumvirate to curtail Leon Trotsky, the apparent successor to Lenin. Just as a democracy may not act in time, neither did Trotsky. He was defeated, and so were each of the other triumvirate members in turn.

Nick ends the paper two paragraphs later:

Therefore, he must eradicate the intellectuals, and with them goes intellect and reason. Jealousy and suspicion, coupled with the craving for power are these tyrants' purest expressions of eros in control of his nature and, thus, of the *polis*. Reason has been finally subjected.

Adams circles four spelling errors in Nick's paper, some which are the result of his typewriter's missing *L*, others of careless typing and negligent proofreading ("fo" instead of "of"). Adams corrects Nick's grammar, substituting "between" for "among" and suggests "forecast" over Nick's word "profiled." His final comments ask Nick to "Connect war and tyranny. What relationship does

Socrates see?" He also suggests that Nick's "writing lapses hurt a bit" and that he "leaps too far, too fast."

Nick shares with me that he knows his papers aren't that good but that he has "no clue" how to make them better.

The Final Paper: Combining the Personal and the Political ■
When Adams suggests that I might like to look at the work of one of the better writers in the course, Mr. Hemple allows me to read and copy his three-star paper. This student is able to accomplish the following in his paper: to set up more tension and argument at the beginning; to give more textual citation, which is appropriately underlined and explicated; and to provide a more developed ending than in Nick's papers. Whereas Mr. Hemple's papers conclude, Nick's build in a crescendo and fade out. Overall, there would be much to be learned in this course by exchanging papers, and modeling more concretely what kinds of examples are appropriate, instead of the continual admonishment for students not to be so "abstract" and to "watch their spelling."

When Adams and I finally sit down to talk, it is almost the end of the term and I am mainly thanking him for allowing me to attend his course. When he asks me for suggestions about the course, I have many but offer only two. One, I tell Adams that I think he is doing too much correcting and editing of student writing. Rather than waste his time hunting and circling errors, I suggest that he just make a note to a student that he or she has overstepped the allotted number and force the student to find the writing errors and revise. It is after all, an upper-level seminar. Such a policy would more likely eliminate the carelessness that pervaded the papers I had seen (even in Mr. Hemple's paper). Revision, I thought, could probably fit in well with Adams's "star" system.

Second, I share my feeling that the two-page format itself might be reconsidered. I encourage him to experiment with another form, to see if students could tap into other resources in their writing. Adams is amenable to altering the final term paper since he suspects (and he is correct) that few students have actually started it. Toward the end of the course (mid-April), Adams polls students on two issues: (1) whether they want him to continue to interrupt them during their final presentations or to let them first present what they had to say. Students vote to be interrupted; (2) how many hours they have already spent on their final projects. Most of them have not begun. Mr. Hemple is, in fact, the only student who has invested any time on it beyond a perusal of possible sources in the library. Students vote in favor of Adams's final writing assignment, which they, in part, helped design.

He asks these political science majors, who are mainly graduating seniors, to "think of this paper as the capstone of your careers." He calls for legibly written (not typed), grammatically correct, coherent, and *thoughtful* essays, drafted within a two-hour time limit on "The Value of Political Science as a Career." He gives many suggestions about the form that the paper might take: "It might be in response to the favorite old question: You meet a derelict standing around after graduation and he asks, 'What do you have in your hand.' You answer, 'A diploma.' 'What's that?' he asks you. Write an essay responding to what it means to go to college, perhaps a letter to a brother, undergraduate, or offspring about what you learned as a political science major. "Dartmouth, he says, has a whole course devoted to answering the question "What is political science?" Adams says that he wants students to "make sense of your education and account for yourself, because taking four years out of your life to study is a rare opportunity." In keeping with the content of the course, he suggests that students may decide to write a dialogue or play. Certainly he describes many options. I thought I heard a sigh of relief from around the seminar room until Mr. Hemple inquired if he could still write a traditional research paper.

Students respond well to Adams's invitation to write from personal experiences. Eric, Nick's housemate, drafts a play in the form of the dialogue between himself and Nick, which begins, "Well, Nick, what is political science?" Interestingly enough, Eric writes stage directions such as "(*with a smirk*)" and he also advises the appropriate behavior in his stage directions: "(*interrupting*)." The play ends with "Reader: take care." Overall the frame of the paper is better than its content, but what the reader knows from the paper is that Eric has understood the literary conventions of the material he has been reading. Another woman student who aspires to be a teacher herself reviews all her mentors at the university, including Adams, and compliments him on his "patience" in dealing with Mr. Sweet. Finally she notes that she has had "painfully few women professors at UNH," that all her best professors were male.

Nick's paper is hastily drafted during a battle with ear infections and the crunch of his other final work. He believes that if Adams wants a quality end product, he should provide more time for it, like Donna had with the collaborative projects. Students do have three weeks to turn in their papers. Not surprisingly, Nick adopts the journal form for his final paper in this course. In the first paragraph, he speaks of the freedom of being released from a rigid format:

Expiration Date Wednesday, 18 May, 1988
1:40 P.M.
Brother,

This that I now write to you is the last gesture my expiring political science career may manage. This paper, that is the capstone of my educated pillar, I have labored over these last 17 years or so, has a merciful format. It has been (at last) freed from the suit and tie analysis regime and left to our anarchistic pleasure. And I now brother, have got the home court advantage.

Mixing an informal tone with reverberations from Shakespeare now and then, Nick speaks of this paper as a "salvation from the manicured clutches of political seminar" — a fairly bold statement given his audience — and then reflects on how this came to be: "Luck you say? Perchance to dream? Aye, there's the rub." The major section of this very short, three-page paper reveals to Adams that Nick has had a bad semester and is in doubt over his future:

The reflection requires a mirror: To know who and what we've been is to gaze back in time through the lens of who I am now. A tricky question.
    Who's there?
    'Tis me: The student, pausing on my way down the short-lived lines of the dead. As I am still the student, so am I also worse at it than ever. Things that smell of academia have, this year, made me wince and grit my teeth in the doing of them (I've been doing them poorly too).
    My recent problem is that I've been unable to leap back into ponderous study. Blindly and nimbly opaque to the light of the obvious. That being that the pillar I've built is all but done and yet does naught for me but engulf me with its cold shadow: I am already beyond my poor contribution to this academic monolith.
    School is of very little consequence to me now. My major is done, my gen-eds done; I am now merely playing out my time left, awaiting inglorious civilianhood.
    That being as it is (the gospel), I've had to ignore it utterly. I've tried to convince myself that the ferocious assignments racing past me down the lines of the dead were of the sincerest emergency. To bolster myself against the screeching truth proved just barely too formidable. I tried in earnest to scale the towering pile of post-midnight hours and mine the riches of intellect, but only reached it halfway.
    And now, brother, at the end of this year (but woefully not the entirety of my academic career), I'm convinced of two things: school and school work are contrived and, overall inconsequential.

Adams interprets Nick's paper as a case of "senioritis," which he says usually occurs two semesters before graduation. This may be true, but there is more trouble rumbling beneath this paper than Nick reveals. He hints at it in this passage of the essay: "This is where I find my brain now, in this cynical garb. The minor (school, finance, health etc.) has distracted me from the whole picture."

Nick has had a very bad semester: although he is doing just enough work to make a showing in Adams's course (he gets a grade of B–) and is sailing smoothly in Foreign Policy (his only A), he is completely drowning in two courses in the English department. Because he failed to meet his first deadlines in his journalism class, he was dropped from the course. When we talk about this, Nick rationalizes that "more than anything, journalism contributes to the amount of bullshit that's floating around the world, contributes to deluding people and biasing opinions." He finally drops out with a failing grade, refusing to join "that wad of crap" because he realizes that in the course he had been "writing nothing for no reason."

Nick is also bored in his other English course and speaks scathingly of the paper requirements for Critical Analysis, which he seldom attends. "Busy work" he calls the writing, "suck it up and spit it back out." But his regurgitation only earns him C– and D grades on his papers. Finally he solves his problem by following verbatim a paper suggestion on the syllabus and writes about "bird imagery in *Macbeth*." In this paper Nick actually counts all the birds in the play and explicates the meaning of each: "In all there are seventeen bird allusions throughout *Macbeth*. Most of these are metaphorical, drawing parallels between bird characters and behavior." This paper earns him a B. After these two English course experiences, Nick has changed his mind about declaring an English minor: "I hate even coming into this building," he tells me when we meet there.

And he has been sick several times, the last flu coming during exam week when everything is due for everybody. He has tried to work thirty hours a week to pay for his apartment and his accumulated bills. But there is no place for any of this personal turmoil in his academic coursework, no place to write about the fading student, except in this final paper for Political Thought. Nick outlines his "abandoned" art career for Adams and then his flight from psychology as a major, in which "theory after plausible theory, all of which contradicted each other" pushed him away:

Finally I came to political science.
And stayed.
Political science is the guts of all social interaction, and will be as long as man understands "power" in this world. As best as I can make it

out to be (Descartes has forever thrown doubt into my apparent head), political power acts as gravity—not always the strongest of forces, but everywhere present. At last I found a body of interrelated information that I could use to divine the truth (if only that of the evening news).

In this paper, Nick writes of "education" as limiting, rather than expanding, his growth: "Education serves to set the individual to a pattern—the higher the level of education, the more specific the pattern. Education will channel one's aptitudes into neatly trimmed categories and enforce particular definitions upon them." And he is sure that money is the evil force, for it is money that Nick hears fellow students talk about: "As I gaze around at my fellow seniors, all cheerily desperate to leave, I hear talk of money. 'Do you have a job yet? is the urgent and trembling question.' 'How will you get to the top? How close to it are you starting out?'"

Nick ends his essay for Political Thought by saying that he wants not even a "taste" of this monied life because, idealist that he is, "What I want lies within me, not without."

Overall Adams is pleased by the altered final assignment, which he says "beats the hell out of reading term papers." He feels that by and large what he got from the class are "intellectual biographies" and "reflections on their own educations." Although he learns some things from reading these papers, they were, he suggests the "things I wish I didn't know necessarily." Adams reports that his students discussed personal tragedies, such as giving up a musical career, experiencing the death of a parent, living in an apartment house where someone was murdered. Overall Adams also learns that these students are "very young" and that "they don't have enough conversations with one another outside their classes." Adams likes the assignment enough to redesign it for future classes, requiring as well a rough draft. This addition comes, he said, because of one student—a senior—who wrote that this was the first paper in her entire college career for which she had ever written more than one draft.

A colleague who helped transcribe Nick's tapes becomes so involved with listening to his voice and his problems that she asks if she can add her voice to his and mine and all the others. In a long essay, which I give to Nick, she shares with him how much she has identified with his stream of issues about money and professionals and that she too once felt like Nick.

In transcribing the interviews on Nick, more than once I have heard echoes ... some thunderous repetitions of words I vividly remember saying (I won't become one of Them in their suits and ties and empty, futile lives—I won't, I won't), wincing at the proclamations that I too thought were absolute truths to an honorable life (possession of money equals loss of integrity, self-respect only comes from going it alone), that I am sure will be brought quietly to rubble by the passage of years in Nick's life as they were in mine.

Nick and I compare the two courses that I attended with him: seminar in Political Thought and Prose Writing, two small snips of his seventeen-year academic career, but courses that present very different vignettes of Nick. Of these two styles of learning— combative, competitive, and argumentative against cooperative, collaborative, and consensual, Nick prefers the latter: "I'm a happier person, I'm a nicer person, and I'm someone I can respect more when I don't have to fight tooth and nail for everything."

I look at Nick, his hair grown long for the summer; I see the jean jacket plastered with IBM buttons and a silver cross for effect. Then I close my eyes for a second and listen to his voice and Adams takes his place. Which discourse style will shape Nick's life after college—that of his personal journal or of political gamesmanship?

The Discourse of Discourse Communities

"Ways of Being in the World"

The various disciplines (or disciplinary matrices), humanistic, natural scientific, social scientific alike, that make up the scattered discourse of modern scholarship are more than just intellectual coigns of vantage but are ways of being in the world.

Clifford Geertz
Local Knowledge

D isciplines such as art history, political science, and composition studies represent more than fields of knowledge, more than content areas. As Clifford Geertz suggests, they embrace methods for understanding and interacting with the world, "ways of being in the world" (1983, 155). The past chapters have been devoted to my visits across the university curriculum where I cast scenes that consider the students' perspective on various discourse communities. In peering through these windows into the minds of two state university humanities majors, I found culturally and multiply literate students in place of the hollow "impoverished souls" projected by contemporary literacy critics. From these very close accounts of what has been described as "the ethnographic present" (Heath 1983), I will step back and consider what I have experienced through our informants about the discourse of these very different academic settings, in which the routines and rituals for literacy are sufficiently disparate as to constitute separate cultures. I hope to share what I now understand from watching Anna and Nick read, write, talk, and think in these disciplines, as well as what I felt about "being there" with them. First, I would like to review some of the larger contextual factors that surround this study, issues that were raised in the introduction but may have since faded in the reader's mind.

During the period that this study was conducted (1987–88) and for some time afterwards, the cultural literacy debate engaged the attention not only of the public, but of many college educators, whose student bodies served as the main targets of these attacks. Some educational critics enlisted as advocates of our post-secondary schooling reminded us that our national educational system is anchored in our distinctive American heritage of skepticism, pluralism, and relativism, not in the Eurocentric tradition of exclusion and elitism (see for example the interesting collection of essays on Bloom's book edited by Robert Stone). The University of New Hampshire, busy building its own identity under a presidential invitation to "create a community of scholars," formed no particular institutional response to this cultural literacy argument. Yet, as I negotiated entrance to my settings, the ongoing debate sparked conversations between myself and the professors whose classrooms I wanted to study, yoking my research to higher education's global concern with standards of cultural literacy.

At the outset, I suggested that the University of New Hampshire faces an increase in liberal arts graduates over previously favored majors such as computer science, business, engineering, or even the more agriculturally oriented majors such as forestry. Graduates in the hotel administration program, for example, have decreased by one-third, while the number of students declaring communication as a major has almost tripled. Nick's field—Political Science—has doubled its graduates in the past decade, but, according to the university's Office of Institutional Research, the major no longer attracts the political activist but has become the spawning ground for future attorneys (much to Nick's disgust and dismay). Anna's major—art history—has retained a small but steady number of graduates in this field while the number of studio art, dance, and theater graduates have declined. This short summary reminds us that, like any institution, this university is a modern and complex context, always undergoing considerable change in response to economic and social influences, which in turn are linked to the institution's history and ideology. In this instance, a relatively stable economy, along with a slight shift in values away from materialism, is allowing more state university students to return to the traditional liberal arts as majors rather than being pressured into purely professional or technical training.

Another context-specific issue that this study addresses is how students perceived their university's institutional challenge to build a "community of scholars." For in addition to this being the university's stated goal, the idea of disciplines themselves as constituting discourse communities has entered professional conversations within several fields, including composition studies. Building on the work of Raymond Williams (1976), who warns against evoking unexamined "keywords," some critics suggest that serious consideration should be given to how the term *community* is being used (see Harris 1989).

The concept of the university as "a discourse community" implies either that there is one unified shared set of academic language norms that encompasses the entire university, or that each discipline or department itself displays internal agreement with respect to literacy codes and conventions. Yet, as Nick's experiences within the English department alone reveal, Journalism, Prose Writing, and Critical Analysis courses all had very different demands, not only in terms of writing style but of classroom discourse styles as well. When I reflect on Anna and Nick's experiences at this institution in their chosen majors, aside from their commonality as university students, there is no doubt that they felt little affiliation with the university or with other students in their majors. Instead of the university or its departments mentoring either of these students, it merely held them while they nourished themselves on their own. In fact, Anna and Nick can be considered as literate in spite of, not because of, their contact with the academy.

There is, I think, a paradox in positing college classrooms as a spiral or nest of neatly linked "discourse communities" when the student's perspective is weighed. Community should imply a place where the norms of behavior and rituals and routines of language are implicit to all its members, not just to those in control. Unless the concept of community is consciously built into a course, as it was in Prose Writing, the idea of discourse community(ies) refers mainly to professional scholars' circles, which are primarily linked through a complex mesh of writing and educational contacts, not within any given institution, any department, or necessarily any classroom. Anthropologist Paul Diesing describes this type of community as a group that shares behaviors and standards toward its work: "A community is located by finding people who interact regularly with one another and in their work. They read and use each other's ideas, discuss each other's work and sometimes collaborate. They have common friends, acquaintances, intellectual ancestors" (1972, 17). Rather than having *community* serve as a default term, I think it should be reserved for places that make an effort to initiate students into their institutions, disciplines, or classrooms. From the students' perspective, the literacy norms within most fields—the reading, writing, talking and thinking patterns of the discipline—most often remain powerfully invisible, not offering ready access for them to earn membership in any discourse community.

Through the experiences, then, of two students who temporarily made camp in the university fortress, I will consider the literacy practices of three academic cultures, drawing on the types of talk, textual analysis, and written discourse that were valorized in these classrooms. I would characterize Anna and Nick's experiences in their liberal arts courses as those of silence and emptiness with respect to literacy and learning. Why did this loss occur? How did the educational system fail them? In analyzing the overlapping spheres of academic discourse, I will look at three areas: (1) the discourse of the institution, (2) the discourse of the selves, and (3) the discourse of Composition Studies. I will discuss "what went on" in these academic settings, keeping in mind that any conclusions I draw belong to the complex, real world described in this ethnography.

The Discourse(s) of the Institution: Gender, Language, and Pedagogy

The differences that mark us as male and female and shape our consciousness are patterns extended through our perceptions of the phenomenal world and inscribed in the philosophies, ideologies, and pedagogies that constitute our culture.

Madeleine Grumet
Bitter Milk

Anna and Nick's experiences in the academy have been shaped in the ways that Madeline Grumet suggests we are all "engendered." Yet, as college students, Anna and Nick share the same tangle of young adult issues and feelings, as expressed in their worry over education, career choices, and human relationships. Nick, in particular, repelled by professional training, fears that he may have no work niche when he graduates; he is also frightened of personal intimacy. When Anna's relationship with her scientist boyfriend crumbles in the second half of my study, I am witness to her ambivalence and insecurity about new choices of friends and conflict over her career options. As narratives depicting the intellectual journeys of two college students poised at the end of their undergraduate careers, Nick and Anna's stories resonate with the strains of myriad other students who have also wrestled with these familiar life decisions.

Anna and Nick provide descriptions of one another that seem like gender stereotypes. Nick refers to Anna as "vulnerable" and much like his ex-girlfriend: 'There's a vulnerability about her [Anna] that's appealing, not naive, but vulnerable and open." Anna, on the other hand, associates Nick with men who are "nice to women when they want to be and then with their own friends, they are all macho." To Anna, Nick represents "a double role." Are Anna and Nick themselves doubles? Light and dark; vulnerable and guarded; open and closed; stasis and change; collaborative and individualistic each searching for that missing part of themselves, the male or female counterpart?

As alike as Anna and Nick are in their life issues and their passionate rejection of mainstream politics and economics, they are vastly divergent as learners. Nick rests assured of his multiple talents, his *mastery* over words, over information, sometimes over people. Anna's literacy presents itself in a more subtle way, which might be called *ms.tery*, an approach to learning that affirms the importance of connection, collaboration, and caring. When Nick temporarily welcomes these interactive, "feminine" pedagogies into his Prose Writing course, he considers them as yet one more style to add to his impressive repertoire of academic roles. Anna is more at home with feminist pedagogies and uses this mode of knowing frequently to pull her coursework together from the isolated disciplines within the university curriculum, and to integrate her public and private selves.

When gender issues emerged as central to this study, I was not surprised since I had made a conscious effort to include both female and male college students. As a researcher, though, I discovered the importance of gender-related issues through the eyes of my informants, by watching subtle behaviors like Nick's dominating and Anna's muted speech patterns. After choosing to work with Anna, I originally speculated that she would be the student who would suffer most from the mastery model of teaching that is most often endorsed in higher education. But Anna proved me wrong by working against the dominant discourse style and creating her own mode of learning. One clue to her transformation of mastery learning is mirrored in a quotation she used in a paper for art history. The quote, taken from a feminist critique of women's values, attacks the pyramid model of life where men are placed at the top under god, with nature at the bottom: "This vertical view of reality is a lie, a construct created to justify patri- archal subordination and control. We live in a circle, not along a line" (Cheatam and Powell 1986, 160). While Anna uses this quotation in her art history paper to discuss the kind of caring for the land that ecofeminism endorses, it also describes the recursive and circular pattern of learning that women students often bring to educational settings. In the end, Anna becomes a successful learner, not because she adapts to the mastery model but because she makes a conscious effort to "connect" her course work, an approach documented by feminist scholars looking at the different learning styles of women students. Nick, however, remains the separate knower within the academic setting, compartmental- izing and isolating his coursework.

Although it is easy to accept that male and female students might display different learning styles, it is less comfortable to admit that the university as an institution primarily rewards mas- tery or what Nick calls "abbreviated learning." "Mastery" was the preferred pedagogical model rewarded in both political science and art history, as exhibited in the presentational styles of the lecture and the debate.

The lecture/recitation format, represented by Anna's art history course, Walter Ong (1978) suggests, derives from the man-made university system without contributions from the dis- cursive, epistemic, and intellectual traditions of women. Lecturing involves the student in a passive style of learning and encourages what Gilligan (1982) and her colleague Nona Lyons (1983) have called "separate knowing," an epistemology that rests upon im- personal authority and rule systems for establishing truth — William Perry's "dualistic" stage of thinking (1970). What seems potentially abusive about the lecture format is the exclusion of how the knowledge within the discipline comes to be; knowledge is invisibly constructed and presented as absolute. Listening to the mega- scholar's mind at work is like being part of an appreciative but nonparticipatory audience.

Certainly the lecture format serves some useful pedagogical purposes in higher education, but we might question its privileged position in so many university courses. When Mary Hall, the "reflective practitioner" (Schön 1983), turned her classroom over to her students, engaging them as novice art-critics, they joined her as exploring, involved learners, forging their understanding of works of art together, even taking risks in their responses. After this class discussion, one student in the class told me, "Getting through all this material is her agenda, not ours."[1] Rather, the student's agenda is to learn how to "do" this mental activity called critiquing art. If we accept learning as a "process" and not mere transmission, a class discussion—aside from involving students as learners—prepares for the critical thinking they will later use in writing for the discipline and presumably in all their courses.

Classroom discourse style revealed itself as the most gender-sensitive feature of the settings under consideration in this study. Linguist James Gee suggests that discourse can be thought of as a kind of "identity kit," which comes "complete with the appropriate costume and instructions on how to act and talk so as to take on a particular role that others will recognize" (1987, 1). The way that talk in particular was used in courses corresponded to the pedagogical model for learning encouraged there. Considerable feminist scholarship suggests that it is through oral language use as well as written discourse conventions that patriarchal institutions such as the university have sustained their powers. Many women academics themselves have expressed their discomfort over the combative and argumentative model that pervades the profession, wherein women are expected to be publicly assertive authorities who challenge the intellectual views of others in their fields.[2]

Nick's Seminar in Political Thought demonstrates another primarily male discourse style—the combative model of the debate. Even though the class is billed as a seminar, in which discussions should ostensibly take place, all of the verbal interactions flowed through the professor, as each student worked alone to "master" the material under consideration. The only access to the political

---

[1] It is important to admit that many students grow to like the impersonal mastery style of learning, which allows them to remain unconnected to their instructors and coursework. In fact, some college students resent classes in which they are required to prepare and to participate.

[2] See *Women of Academe: Outsiders in the Sacred Grove* by Nadya Aisenberg and Mona Harrington, an entire book devoted to the common problems and professional patterns of women in the academy based on extensive interviews with women scholars, many of whom have experienced aborted careers in higher education.

meanings of the texts in this great books curriculum is through the professor, who serves as censor for all alternative interpretations. The seminar emphasizes a hierarchical and unbalanced power structure, wherein the professor and his graduate students both control and interrupt the stream of talk. Rather than building on individual student contributions, each student engages in separate "bilateral" exchanges with the professor. Although students learn to be verbally aggressive, the class members do not become intellectually aggressive and language serves as a weapon rather than a tool for constructing understandings. This kind of seminar model may be, in fact, more deceptive than the strict lecture format because it masquerades as an egalitarian forum in which each voice counts.

It has clearly seemed easier for educators to understand and accept the language differences found among other cultures, such as native American Indians (Philips 1972), Hawaiians (Au 1980), urban blacks (Baugh 1983), and rural blacks (Heath 1983), than to acknowledge the differences in how men and women use language within that microcosm of society we call academic life. The continued exploration in the ways classroom discourse encourages — or, in the case of gender issues, perhaps discourages—learning offers one of the most exciting research areas available, one that has been better mined at the early childhood and elementary level (Barnes 1976; Wells 1986; Cazden 1980; Bruner 1983), but that needs further research in higher education. The growing number of scholarly articles and books devoted to gender differences in language use (see the 150-page annotated bibliography in Thorne et al., 1983, as well as the extensive sources in Frank and Treichler 1989) point to one critical issue: that we need to provide opportunities for students, male and female, in our classrooms to have experiences shaping ideas through collaborative talk, rather than monologic discourse. The more collaborative style of Prose Writing courses encouraged a shared discursive floor as well as listening to others, a way of knowing often attributed to and valued by women. This discourse style needs to play to a larger audience in our college classrooms, beginning with professors listening to the wide range of voices of our students, rather than only to themselves talking. Male student need to listen and hear what their female classmates have to say rather than interrupt and dominate discussions. Women students need to hear their own voices raising questions and confronting issues. And women's silences need not always be interpreted as unarticulated knowing but as thoughtful reflection and productive meditation. Language should be used to transform experiences rather than simply to transmit knowledge.

Ironically, while Anna succeeds within the male-dominated university setting, Nick is left unsatisfied in spite of his familiarity with mastery learning. Ultimately, I think, Nick will remain adversarial, distanced, and possibly alienated from his learning if he is not invited to participate in more conversations and fewer debates. A feminist pedagogy is required in higher education, not just for women, who need their learning style reaffirmed, but for male students as well, whose educations will be shortchanged if they are channeled through coursework without being asked to reflect on, revise, rethink, and personally construct what they are learning in one course and connect it to other courses and finally to themselves.

Educational practices should not be adjusted to make the classroom climate a warmer place for women so that they can then adopt the traditional, accepted, and patriarchal modes of discourse. Instead, feminist teaching practices can also empower the male student who is too often allowed to march through his coursework without exposure to alternative ways of learning and knowing. Constructed knowing, as it has been renamed by feminist thinkers, benefits both males and females in the academy by switching the emphasis away from agonistic discourse toward dialogue, exploration, and sharing.

Educational philosopher Jane Roland Martin (1985) asserts that bringing women more fully into the academic conversation changes our "vision" of higher education and "transforms" the education of both males and females. All educators, Martin says, need to become more "gender sensitive" to the pedagogical approaches that pervade our classrooms:

In a society in which traits are genderized and socialization according to sex is commonplace, an educational philosophy that tries to ignore gender in the name of equality is self-defeating. Implicitly reinforcing the very sterotypes and unequal practices it claims to abhor, it makes invisible the very problems it should be addressing. So long as sex and gender are fundamental aspects of our personal experience, so long as they are deeply rooted features of our society, educational theory—and educational practice, too—must be gender sensitive. This does not mean that we must ... hold up different ideals for the two sexes. It does mean that we should agree ... that sex is the difference that makes all the difference. What it does mean is that we must be constantly aware of the workings of sex and gender because in this historical and cultural moment, paradoxically they sometimes make a big difference even if they sometimes make no difference at all. (1985, 195)

The Discourse of the Selves: Aesthetic Understanding and Curriculum Development

The absence of attention to the aesthetic in the school curriculum is an absence of opportunities to cultivate the sensibilities. It is an absence of the refinement of our consciousness, for it is through our sensibilities that our consciousness is secured. If our educational program put a premium on the aesthetic as well as on the instrumental features of what is taught, students would have an opportunity to develop mental skills that for most students now lie fallow. Attention to the aesthetic aspects of the subjects taught would remind students that the ideas within subject areas, disciplines, and fields of study are human constructions, shaped by craft, employing technique, and mediated through some material.

Elliot Eisner,
"Aesthetic Modes of Knowing"

Just as issues of gender informed my understanding of the discourse of the academy, feminist theory helped reassemble some thoughts about aesthetics and curriculum. The feminist critique in its challenge to notions of literary canonicity and male standards of discourse also challenges male aesthetics: "The feminist restructing of cultural models urges the same subsuming of exclusive masculinist aesthetics into larger conceptual frameworks that can include the full range of all human experience" (Caywood and Overing 1987, xiii). Watching Anna and Nick both inside and outside their classrooms unexpectedly forced me to rethink the narrow way that literacy is defined in higher education. The ability of both students to respond to their worlds in terms of art, music, and dance as well as in writing made me challenge the verbo-centric and propositional knowledge that dominates our classrooms. As a composition teacher, I wonder just how much we are missing when we ask that all knowing be translated into writing. Are there perhaps other ways of tapping students' responses to course content that do not rely exclusively on the written word? Isadora Duncan once displayed her artistic need for nonverbal channels of expression with this remark: "If I could tell you what it is, I would not have danced it" (Gardner 1983, 224).

Anna and Nick's multiple literacies—what Maxine Greene describes as "multilinguality," and Howard Gardner as "multiple intelligences"—were difficult to uncover, because so much of their visible energy was devoted to the public rendering of ideas, which in the university setting usually translates into "doing papers." Both students were capable of producing and displaying the traditional discourse of their chosen discipline but neither found this kind of writing very meaningful. It was not until Anna attempted to integrate her own personal perspective into her paper on ecofeminism that she discovered a new voice for writing art history, a voice that emerged partially because of her aesthetic responses to the living artist whose works she studied. Nick, however, never invests himself into developing a personalized style for writing in Political Science, posing instead behind his many verbal disguises and wasting his flexible talent drafting academic essays that primarily display knowledge.

For these two students, then, it was their private literacies that kept them afloat during their academic terms. They had both developed literacies for survival, which were crucial for retaining some personalization within the impersonal context of the state university. Both are highly visual students, using a learning style that is often rewarded in elementary schooling but is sharply severed in higher education. What literacy educator Ruth Hubbard says about the visual learning of elementary students holds true for all learners as well: "Pictures as well as words are important to human beings in their communication; we need to expand our narrow definition of literacy to include visual dimensions" (1989, 150).

Nick and Anna's ability to respond in images, through sketches, photographs, sculpture, or painting remained latent talents, unmined resources. Anna did include photographs in her paper on ecofeminism and Nick did generate a computer drawing for his collaborative paper for Prose Writing, but such visual responses are marginalized in most college classrooms. And in another course not discussed here, when Anna had the option of creating a program for a play instead of writing a paper, her instructor graded her down because she didn't include sufficient verbal explanation. Thus even when other forms of response are invited into our classrooms, we expect the written counterpart as well. Nick's intricate sketches—some that actually provided political commentary on course material—were never seen by any of his professors. Yet his jottings and drawings often had more to say than any of his written responses to the assigned materials (see Figures 4–1, 4–2, and 4–3).

Anna's participation in contemporary dance and Nick's habit of keeping a personal journal represent alternative private liter-

Figure 4–1

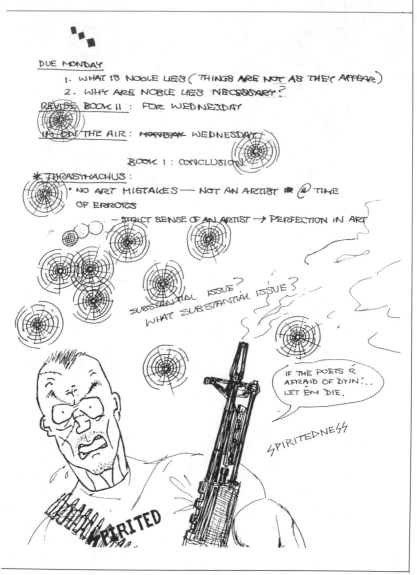

acies, which were seldom reflected in their academic work. For Anna, dance afforded another language to express herself without the verbal emphasis that dominates academic literacy. Dance, as Mikhail Baryshnikov suggests, may be linked to Anna's facility with foreign languages: "Dancing is like many new languages, all of which expand one's flexibility and range. The dancer, just like the language scholar, needs as many as possible; there are never

Figure 4–2

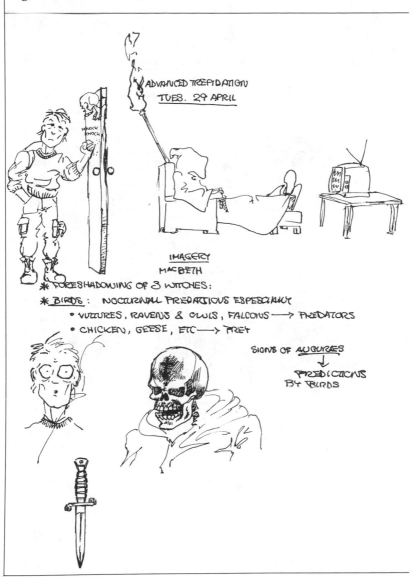

enough" (Gardner 1983, 226). Through working with the pattern and structure of dance, Anna could communicate through her body and her emotions. When she moved to San Francisco, she told me that it was her dance company that she missed most, both for its sense of "community" and its "freedom of expression."

Nick's private journal, which draws on some of his many *153*

Figure 4–3

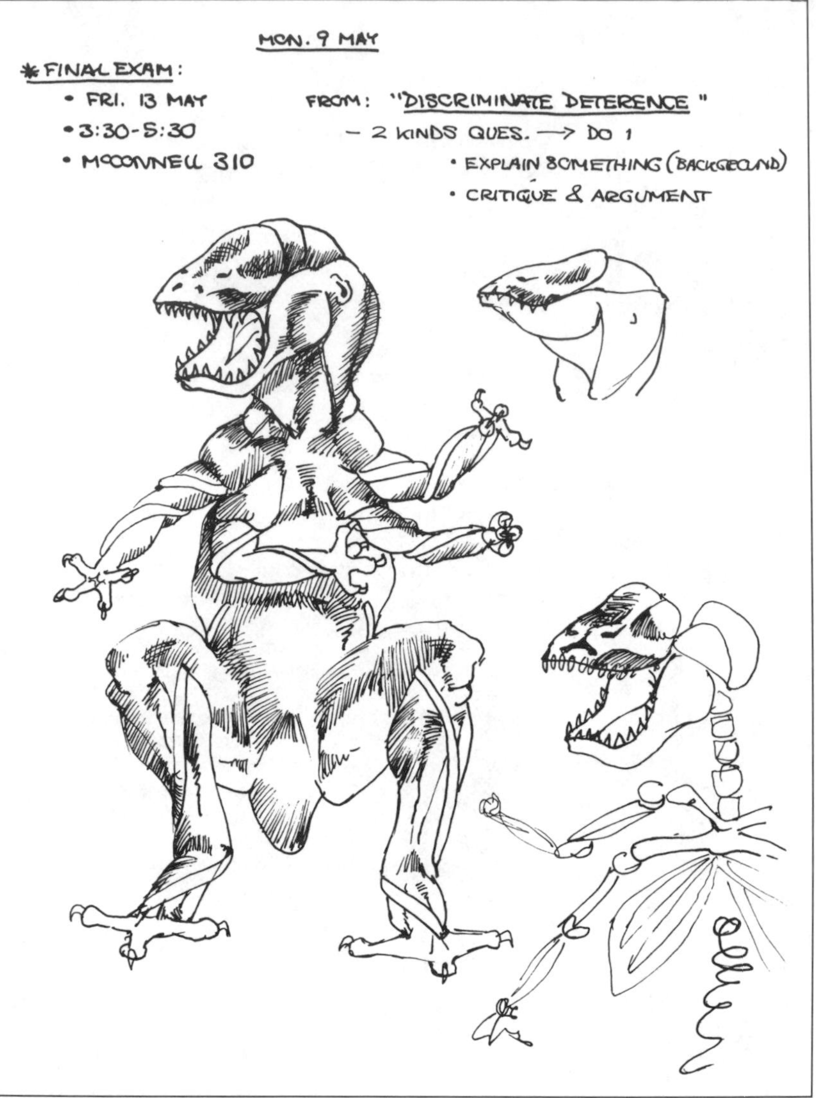

selves, achieves a style that feels more authentic and personal than any writing done for his major. While his diary can be compared to a wide range of writers' journals—from Boswell to Thoreau—who in the male journal tradition assume a public audience, Nick's journal also serves a more intimate purpose. Like many women's diaries, his journal serves as a means for him simply to survive in the university (see Gannett, forthcoming, for 154 further discussion and helpful distinctions about the male/female journal-keeping traditions). Nick struggles in his journal—which includes many sketches and calendars—with making his voice heard within what he sees as the hollow context and content of his academic life. When Nick is encouraged to write a personal statement for Political Science, the paper imitates his own journal form, capturing his aesthetic responses to his own world. Although Nick's journal entries for Prose Writing are far more formal than those of his personal journal, they do allow him to respond to academic reading in the same form he does in his private life. The journal form developed by Nick functions to help him shape his experiences, which as Elliot Eisner points out, is the purpose of all aesthetic forms: "The common function of the aesthetic is to modulate form so that it can, in turn, modulate our experience" (1985, 25). The private literacies of Anna and Nick liberate them but are not often encouraged as resources by university educators, who are wedded to public displays of tested knowledge rather than what Susanne Langer calls the expression that "abstracts aspects of the life of feeling which have no names, which have to be presented to sense and intuition rather than to a word-bound, note-taking consciousness" (Eisner 1985, 35).

Vera John-Steiner, in her interesting analysis of the creative languages of noted artists, writers, dancers, scientists, mathematicians, and musicians, speaks of the diversity of inner thought that contributes to an individual's development of a "dominant inner language of the mind" (1985, 213). Too much emphasis, she, along with Howard Gardner, suggests, has been placed on the dichotomy of the verbal and visual modes of thinking: they urge us to expand our repertoire of learning modes. We need not exclude verbal expression in order to embrace a wider range of literate responses, but, as Elliot Eisner suggests, we need to teach aesthetic knowing as part of the subject matter in our university curriculums, so that students have an opportunity to develop this intimate type of understanding.

An expanded definition of what it means to know through aesthetic experiences invites students to bring their personal literacies into our classrooms to forage together for the intellectual nourishment of the group. The power that is achieved from a diversity of responses within any discipline will allow for the curricular freedom that Maxine Greene describes:

Rather than posing dilemmas to students or presenting models of expertise, the caring teacher tries to look through student's eyes, to struggle *with* them as subjects in search of their own projects, their own ways of making sense of the world. Reflectiveness, even logical thinking, remain important; but the *point* of cognitive development is not to gain an increasing grasp of abstract principles. *It is to interpret from as many vantage points as possible lived experience, the ways there are of being in the world.* (1988, 20) (emphasis added)

Although some of these vantage points may be manifest in writing, we need not always valorize the written word over the many other alternative literacies such as dance, art, sculpture, film, theater, pantomime, music, and song that are available to our students. By enlarging our conception of literacy, we will be able to expand our curricular stance on knowing and, in turn, our students' understanding of possible responses based on their aesthetic sensibilities. Students then will learn to develop their multiple selves with respect to their multiple literacies.

The Discourse of Composition Studies: Constructed Knowing and Collaboration

The real challenge comes from the realization of multiple alternatives and the invention of new models. Aspiration ceases to be a one-way street—from child to adult, from female inferiority to male privilege, from exclusion to full membership— and instead becomes open in all directions, claiming the possibility of inclusion and setting an individual course among the many ways of being human. Even this is not an adequate phrasing, because it suggests the possibility of choosing an existing model and following it toward a defined goal. The real challenge lies in assembling something new.

Mary Catherine Bateson
Composing a Life
(emphasis added)

Mary Catherine Bateson, anthropologist and writer, suggests that men and women need to create new models in education and in our lives based on the diversity of cultures and rapid changes of our enlarged world. Composition studies, in fact, may offer a good place for constructing such a model because, as Patricia Bizzell has recently pointed out, it is a multidisciplinary field with a legacy of interest in teaching and learning (1988, 20). Not only has composition studies been informed and reformed by the thinking from a wide range of disciplines—such as cognitive, clinical, and developmental psychology; education, philosophy, anthropology, literary and historical studies, linguistics, and classical rhetoric— it, too, has greatly been influenced by feminist scholarship and overlaps in a similar desire to design new literacy spaces in classrooms for all students (see Annas 1987, 3–17 on feminist language research and the teaching of writing). Both the interdisciplinary base and the concern with pedagogy explain composition studies' attempts to bring faculty across the disciplines together to consider how written discourse provides the bond for learning within the academic community.

Writing across the curriculum (WAC) as a movement (see Russell 1989a for an historical overview of predecessors to the current WAC movement) offers faculty many literacy/learning strategies for helping students negotiate the complex, discipline-specific discourses that they meet in different fields. Writing consultants and faculty workshops often address the following areas for change with respect to writing: assignment design with emphasis on many short assignments rather than one long paper; more informal writing such as journals, learning logs, and in-class exercises; evaluation procedures such as peer- and self-critiques to augment faculty feedback; techniques for responding to, not just grading, writing; multiple drafting and revision procedures; more explicit ways to connect reading and writing; and reflections on the faculty's own literacy experiences. There is little doubt that if some of these pedagogical suggestions offered by writing specialists were followed, university classrooms would be transformed. But, as Stephen Tchudi points out, such change is not that simple: "When we invite colleagues in other disciplines and fields to teach writing, we are in fact calling for nothing less than a revolution in most of education" (1986, 22).

Many faculty oppose considering new ways of using writing as a way of learning in their disciplines for a variety of reasons (see Russell 1989b for an extended discussion of faculty resistance to WAC programs, which has informed this review). First and foremost, this resistance is due to ignorance, since most faculty have not been trained to view writing as a way of learning for their students, although intrinsically they understand the importance of language within their own professional lives. When Professor Hall concedes that her students' writing problems were "all a matter of language," she had found that the prose style of art history, rather than informing and guiding her students' learning, was shutting them out altogether. As she reflected on how she had personally developed as a writer, she devised new ways to help her students both read and write in the specific prose style of the field. Within a few years, she instituted "writing practices," which aimed to give students some guidance in formulating their written responses as well as providing them with extensive feedback. (See the Epilogue for Anna's comments about her subsequent art history course with Mary Hall.)

Another reason for faculty opposition to writing across the curriculum is explained by the compartmentalization of knowledge in universities and the realization that each discipline has a view of writing that is highly particularized and valued by those working within that field. Moreover, most faculty feel allegiances toward their discipline's discourse conventions and see part of their job as introducing students to that scholarly style. Thus, not only does the faculty's own professional training and practice weigh against making changes in the way they use writing in their classes but so does the view that the job of teaching writing resides mainly within the province of the English department. This position on composition studies as a service course for other disciplines is shared across the curriculum and provides the final resistance to why writing across the curriculum movements often fail.[3]

We have seen in this study that composition studies, as interpreted in Donna Qualley's classroom, did not necessarily represent the goals or functions for the course shared by faculty outside of the field, perhaps not even by those in the English department itself. Prose Writing did not serve to inculcate students into writing for other disciplines, nor did it devote much class time to basic grammar review or issues of mechanical correctness (except in the individual biweekly conferences, in which some time was devoted to editing issues). But consistent with the growing changes in the discipline itself, the Prose Writing class portrayed a social-constructionist and collaborative worldview that was just as value laden as other disciplines. When I entered art history and political science, anticipating that in these classes, we would discuss and explore our personal responses to works of art or share our own political interpretations of the texts under consideration, I called on my own training and background to form these expectations. Gradually I came to realize how foreign Donna Qualley's composition course might seem to an outsider to that field. Composition studies, then, as embodied in this particular classroom, also presented what Geertz has described as a very specific "way of being in the world."

Yet Anna and Nick both valued their membership in the dis-

---

[3] At the time this study took place, the only formal writing across the curriculum program at UNH took the form of voluntary faculty workshops held twice a semester. The following fall a grant-sponsored, university-funded, consultant model for WAC was instituted.

course community created in the Prose Writing course over classes in their majors (they still valued the content of their majors, but not the actual class time). Their appreciation may be attributed to Donna's carefully designed curriculum, which deliberately encouraged communal attitudes toward reading, writing, and knowledge. She saw her role as one of encouraging cooperation in her classroom by getting all students to contribute, to assume responsibility for learning, and to improve as readers, writers, and thinkers. Dewey has pointed out that this kind of learning must be planned: "Community life does not organize itself in an enduring way purely spontaneously. It requires thought and planning ahead. The educator is responsible for knowledge of individuals and for knowledge of subject matter" (1938, 56). This Prose Writing classroom provided a context, a collaborative support system, a dynamic peer group, and collective of members against which and with whom individuals read, wrote, and thought together. As Dewey explained more than fifty years ago, the individuals are not lost or absorbed by the community, but rather use it as the place to refine their own thinking: "Individuals still do the thinking, desiring, and purposing, but what they think of is the consequence of their behavior on that of others and that of others upon themselves" (1927, 24).

Particularly within the collaborative writing project students considered how their ideas, writing styles, and even work habits might affect the others in the group. And it was in their engagement with the group, then, that many students came to understand better their own individual strengths and weaknesses as readers and writers. The wide range of research on collaboration—from specific teaching techniques such as peer response groups and tutoring dyads to the more theoretical reflections of Kenneth Bruffee and John Trimbur—implies that we all collaborate, intentionally or not: "We work together," says Bruffee (paraphrasing Robert Frost's poem "The Tuft of Flowers"), "whether we work together or apart" (Bruffee 1982, 102).

Learning can and certainly does take place in classes in which no sense of community has been established, but for those teachers interested in creating communal classrooms, writing projects like collaborative papers or other written group work can be adapted to help establish a community of learners. Collaborative writing contexts, however, are rare in humanities settings, which tend to foster an atomistic view of writing rather than a view of writing as socially created and shared in terms of its language and knowledge base. Students outside of humanities—engineers and business majors in particular—are often required to do team projects, which mirror the kind of real-world, on-the-job writing situations that they will meet in technical and business positions. Karen Burke LeFevre reminds us that mere lip service is paid in higher education to collaborative group efforts that often do not correspond to the highly individualistic and competitive practices of most of our academic disciplines:

Widely espoused ideals of collegiality and interdisciplinary research are in fact constantly undermined by individualistic assumptions built into the structure of academia in general and the English department in particular. The typical English department faculty member is supposed to be a one-person show who must be able to teach-write-serve-research alone, compete for limited resources, and manage all the while to appear cooperative. Rarely are individuals evaluated on the basis of how well they interact with others to invent or how much they contribute to the inventions of others. (1987, 123–124)

Kenneth Bruffee has argued forcibly for a new way of under-standing what it means to know something by working within the social matrix of a community rather than in isolation. Drawing on the work of Rorty, Bruffee proposes a definition of knowledge as "socially justified beliefs." One of the curricular implications of such a definition would be that "to become liberally educated is to join the *community* of liberally educated people" (1982, 108). Bruffee suggests that one of our responsibilities as educators should be to show our students "how we ourselves became members of the community" (1982, 108). It seems particularly im-portant that students learn how to read and interpret the discourse style and the thinking processes within any academic discipline, particularly those they choose as majors.

Art history and political science classes are not writing courses, nor should they aim to be. I would like to suggest, however, that there are a number of literacy/learning practices, discussed here, that enable all students to earn what Dewey calls "participatory membership" in academic communities. We have already reviewed the types of changes in oral classroom discourse that might affect learning in the university context, as well as the expanded view of literacies outside of written discourse. There are still other specific reading/writing literacy practices that might enable and empower students as learners.

Extensive and demanding reading is at the heart of most liberal arts classes as well as coursework in other disciplines. The close reading of texts, in fact, is an "assumed" college literacy skill, based on very little evidence of students' reading abilities, and with no guidance offered on how to accomplish this. Both

Anna and Nick's experiences showed me that students need more detailed demonstrations, modeling, and class instruction on reading within a discipline. The traditional assign/evaluate model presumes that reading is a purely cognitive, meaning-based activity, rather than an affective and social process. Most college coursework disregards the social aspects of reading, implying that interpretations of texts take place in isolation, ignoring students' background knowledge as an aid to making meaning and discouraging students from working together to construct meanings from texts. Little personal interchange about the course readings even takes place between the teacher and the student; instead, instructors offer their interpretations or readings without much disclosure of how these were arrived at over time. Madeline Grumet describes this process of textual interchange between professors and students: "We pass texts between us. We touch the texts instead of each other and make our marks on it rather than on each other" (1988, 144).

There are simple ways that professors can encourage students to make connections with their course readings through the use of journals, short ungraded or graded responses papers, double-entry notebooks (see Berthoff 1981), reading groups, or student-led discussions. Students can strengthen their engagement with reading by calling upon one verbal system to reinforce another, either by talking about readings or by writing about them, creating what Vygotsky has called "a web of meanings". Finally, learning from texts can be shared within the classroom to display the diversity of responses to reading, to demystify the power of written language, and to enlarge the knowledge base within the community of learners.

Like reading, the main goal of writing in most university classrooms is still limited to the *transmission* of information, from the student to the teacher (who usually already knows it), through the constrictive format of term papers or essay exams. Such transactions use language as the material exchange of words for grades. Writing as "display" or writing as "mastery" posits a passive rather than active view of language and does not encourage the student to explore the wide range of written communicative opportunities: language as exploration, as speculation, as interpretation, as imagination, and, most of all, as expression of previously unarticulated thoughts.

In addition to the limited functions that papers usually serve in humanities classrooms, writing is most often presented as a linear and nonrecursive process. The overall power of writing to discover new ideas, to rethink and revise previous thoughts, is overlooked in the demand for students to produce mechanically correct and technically smooth copy for their teacher audiences. Most classrooms ignore the various stages and cycles that good writing requires by assigning one draft of a paper due sometime near the end of the semester or term. One of the most startling omissions from this model of the writing process is how detached it is from how professionals themselves work and how they know others in their fields write.

In reviewing the types and functions of writing in these three classrooms, I would like to underscore that *more* writing is not the only way to achieve better writing. While most college students do need more occasions for using writing, the range of writing purposes must also be expanded as well as the drafting process that accompanies student texts. The charts in Table 4–1 outline the kinds of writing assigned and the purpose and amount of writing accomplished in three different settings, with Prose Writing not unexpectedly offering the most expansive model for writing and learning.

Table 4–1 ■ *Types, Purposes, and Amounts of Writing in Three Liberal Arts Courses*

PROSE WRITING

Types/Forms	Purpose(s)	Frequency/Amount
Reading journals	Informal, expressive response to readings	Biweekly 5–10 pp.
Collaborative journals	Reflective log Account of collaboration	10–30 pp.
Collaborative project	Problem posing Problem solving	5–15 pp.
Biweekly papers	Discovery Fluency Revision	8 papers 5–8 pp. each
In-class writing	Editing Writing practice Reflection	4 sessions 1–2 pp.
Peer response	Critical writing	4 sessions 1–2 pp.
Self-critique	Evaluation	4–8 times 1 p.
	Total	107–213 pp.

Table 4–1 ■ *continued*

ART HISTORY

Types/Forms	Purpose(s)	Frequency/Amount
Class notes	Memory aid	0 Not required

Midterm exam	Evaluation of
	    understanding
	Integration of
	    lecture and text
		One class
		4–5 pp.

Final exam	Evaluation of
	    understanding
	Integration of
	    lecture and text
		One exam period
		5–10 pp.

Paper proposal	Topic approval	Once ½–1 p.
Final project	Theoretical Integration	10–20 pp.
	Total	19½–35 pp.

POLITICAL SCIENCE

Types/Forms	Purpose(s)	Frequency/Amount
Class notes	Memory aid	0 Not required
Response papers	Answer questions Integrate readings	5–8 papers 2–3 pp.
Final project	Open format	Personal response and integration 5–10 pp.
	Total	15–26 pp.

In addition to Prose Writing providing the most writing practice and range of written forms, what really distinguishes these three courses with respect to writing is the amount of feedback and response given to the student work. The multiple-drafting, conferences, revision, and peer workshops that provide guidance and support in Prose Writing could be adapted for other coursework as well. The student papers in all courses could have been shared to allow for students to serve as what Karen Burke LeFevre calls "resonators" for each other's work. Sharing writing enriches the classroom dialogue with the voices of peers, instead of limiting it to antiphonal conversations between teachers and students.

There are many other possible ways of using writing, both

informally and formally, even within the course structure of lectures. Most of the suggestions I have for changing the way writing
and reading are practiced in higher education imply shifts in the
whole process of university teaching. One of the positive aspects
of the writing across the curriculum movement is that although
teachers come together to discuss writing assignments, they end
up talking about pedagogical issues. By joining together to try to
make the climate for learning a richer one for university students,
professors of all disciplines have begun to discuss literacy practices
in particular fields and to consider how changes might be made.
When Hall began to reflect on her own experiences as a writer in
her profession, she began to see the necessity of offering practice
and preparation for writing for her own students. Just as Donald
Schön suggests in *The Reflective Practitioner* (1983), Hall challenged
her own practice through "reflection in action".

The most far-reaching change for writing at the university
level that I can envision has been posed by Karen Burke LeFevre:
the creation of a universitywide writing portfolio (1987, 137).
Such a plan would involve institutionalization of some aspects of
writing across the curriculum by requiring students to write in
most of their courses. Students would then be required to collect
papers throughout their careers and submit a portfolio within
their majors as part of their degree requirement. Portfolio evaluation is now being considered in some state educational systems
at the elementary and secondary levels, (Vermont, California,
New York), in arts programs across the country (Harvard's Project
Zero and National Arts Education Research Center at N.Y.U.), and
is being developed by Educational Testing Services as an alternative to testing. Portfolio evaluation has the potential for giving
students at the university level some reason for engaging in
thoughtful writing as they take courses across the disciplines.
Although such a program would need careful thought and im-
plementation, it should offer an improvement on the current system
of "doing papers" and then discarding them, which represents a
great deal of wasted intellectual resources both on the part of
students and their teachers.

Conclusions

In this ethnography I have looked at some overlapping spheres of
academic discourse that liberal arts students might encounter in
their university experiences. I have suggested that the university

curriculum encourages the separation of students' private and public selves through the compartmentalization of disciplines that establish boundaries around their knowledge bases and discourse conventions. I have raised some questions about how academic discourse communities might rethink the literacy structures they hold in common across the curriculum, so that classrooms may become the kinds of places where students are empowered as learners. And in this final chapter I have considered some very general suggestions for curricular revision based on my detailed look at the literacies of two college students.

Such change concerns the overall construct of discourse models in the university, which are embedded in patriarchal practices and conventions. Recognition of women's preferred learning styles, new forms of speech, writing, and epistemologies, will invite women students to participate more fully in higher education. In writing, emphasis needs to be placed on alternative discourse forms both for male and female students: exploratory, generative forms, such as autobiography, journals and diaries, narrative and reflective writing, should be added to the current staple of the argumentative/persuasive papers, the traditional essay, and the term paper. In speech, the role that silence plays for women students needs to be better understood both in its positive and negative terms: first the value of silence as providing a potential transforming and creative space for female students to work, but alternately the negative role of silencing that stems from women's discomfort with agonistic speech.

There is great potential for change in curriculum development based on our understanding of the multiple literacies— "multilinguality" (Maxine Green) or "multiple intelligences" (Howard Gardner)—that students bring into our university classrooms. Team-taught interdisciplinary courses in history and music, literature and art, dance and mythology, politics and media studies invite students to respond to several modes of instruction and see the interconnectedness of all knowledge. Allowing students to sketch pictures, build sculptures, create videos, write songs and musical scores, make quilts and wall hangings, and work in multiple genres and mediums will stretch the seams of our disciplines to include different types of learners and thinkers. By expanding ways for students to share their learning, we may begin to challenge the academy's overemphasis on verbal understanding and propositional knowledge.

Along with anthropologist and cultural critic Clifford Geertz, I think it is important for scholars themselves to cross disciplinary boundaries and hold conversations about knowledge making and thinking in other fields. It is not an easy task to see the world through another pair of glasses, but it is not impossible either. Some of the most interesting moments for me in this study occurred as I began to analyze the forms of discourse used in another field and started to really understand the habits of mind being fostered there. Had I spent time in the life sciences, in engineering, or business, I would have still found that each discipline's way of considering the world is embedded in the ways that reading, writing, and talk are used by scholars, that these contribute to their "ways of being" in the world.

Further Research

I agree with Virginia Woolf's observation that "books continue each other, in spite of our habit of judging them separately" (1981, 84). It is my hope that, just as my research has grown from the rich bounty of other studies, I may leave some seeds here to germinate future plantings. Some of the many possibilities include the following:

1. More ethnographies of college students' literacies. I would look at the literacies of students of various ethnic backgrounds in a range of college settings and across the academic disciplines, particularly in the sciences, engineering, and business.
2. Research on gender and discourse. I would select one topic of interest, such as a case study of gendered interactions in a reading or writing group, and follow this in depth.
3. An ethnography of one college student, throughout all four years of education, considering every reading and writing assignment given.
4. A survey of the use of portfolios in tutorial and other settings, such as studio art, to suggest possible models for a collegewide writing portfolio requirement.
5. Case studies of college teachers who use extended writing in their classrooms, focusing on disciplines outside of the humanities. How do university professors put into practice many of the ideas that come from the writing across the curriculum movement?
6. Research on feminist teaching pedagogies and their impact on composition studies. There continues to be important work in both fields that overlaps.

7. Collaborative research to design a teaching course open to all faculty in a university, which would consider integrating reading, writing, group work, and gender-related issues into the university curriculum movement.
8. Continued exploration of the ways that high school curricula and college curricula can connect, so that high school students receive more practice and preparation for the kinds of writing they will actually encounter in college coursework.
9. Interdisciplinary coursework between the humanities and the arts, encouraging student responses in mediums outside of writing, and encouraging portfolio evaluation.
10. Continued study and support of the writing across the curriculum movement to share the ways, both pedagogical and administrative, that it has proved successful on different campuses.

Using the Prose Writing class considered here as an example, I think that those in Composition Studies as a discipline need not worry so much about preparing students for reading and writing in other discourse settings. Instead, we might ask how other disciplines are preparing their classrooms to get the most out of literate students like Anna and Nick and other such multiliterate students: how are other disciplines creating contexts for such students to read, write, and talk in creative, critical, and personally engaging ways? Maxine Greene, in her fine book *The Dialectic of Freedom* (appropriately initiated as a John Dewey Lecture), suggests that educators must create "new spaces" in our schools and invite fresh ideas into them so that intellectual freedom can again thrive.

Academic discourse communities cannot flourish without real dialogue, without engaged reading, without committed writing, without an extension of the private literacies that are an inherent part of many students who inhabit our classrooms. We must allow ourselves to integrate into our classrooms those literacy/ learning practices that will enable students both to belong to and participate in many discourse communities during their university careers and finally in their lifetimes.

Epilogue

*A*nna and Nick both dropped out of college the
following fall. Although they eventually graduated,
these students were so uncertain about their academic and career goals, that they both felt the
need to take time off before completing their degrees.

Nick also left school because he was too broke to pay
for his last semester of coursework. He earned the necessary money by cooking in various seacoast restaurants,
landing a steady job in the jazz club that Anna wrote about
in her final paper for Prose Writing. When Nick finally
accumulated enough money to enroll for his last term of
courses, it was a mishmash of leftover general education
requirements, which did little to stimulate him. Nick's
"durable" mother attended his overdue graduation and,
while celebrating afterwards, they ran into Nick's old
girlfriend Erica. The encounter proved less painful than
Nick expected: they forgave one another for all that had
passed between them in a hug and moment of understanding. After this, Nick reported that he felt "healed"
somewhat and more optimistic that people can actually get
over a disastrous relationship. His experience with Erica,
he confessed, had tainted all the others he had tried,
because he feared an eventual breakup and possible
aftermath.

After graduation, Nick bought his first used car and began saving for a trip to Greece, still earning his way as a cook. When we met to catch up on news, he showed me a political comic strip that he was drawing for his friends (see Figure E–1) and assured me that he was still keeping his personal journal. He said, however, that he could not imagine either art or writing being part of his eventual job. He found art with a capital *A*, as in critics and magazines, phony, commercialized, and exclusionary: "Regular people don't get exposed to the full range of art, and that's too bad—textiles and photography and all that." And Nick still spoke bitterly against education, which he said was too bureaucratic and tracked. His advice for educators in general was to consider the "garbage" they dish out to students who were capable of so much more. "Education," Nick criticized, "is just another capitalist consumption market. We're always asked to produce something that's a thing of value. There are never enough students producing something for themselves."

Figure E–1   ■   *Nick's Cartoon*

Anna moved to San Francisco to live with an old high school friend and enrolled part time in a design institute in which she studied layout and photography, supporting herself by working in a poster-framing shop. Renewed by her studio art courses, she discovered that she was really quite adept and skilled at much of the work. When she came east at the holidays and we met for lunch, she showed me her photography projects from her growing art portfolio. After a year in San Francisco, she traveled during the summer in Europe, living in youth hostels, but finally returning to New Hampshire for her last semester of coursework. Anna had to catch up on some of the same general education requirements that Nick had taken, but mainly she took art history courses to complete her major. She enrolled in an upper-level course, Contemporary European Art, with Professor Hall and was excited about studying with her again. When she shared her course syllabus with me, I saw that Hall had made some real changes in the way she approached writing. On the syllabus she described "preparatory exercises," which were intended to provide writing practice for students before they took formal exams on the same material. Hall promised "immediate feedback" on these exercises and folded a holistic evaluation for the informal exercises into the final grade. Anna's final art history courses all proved important for her, and she said that finally she felt part of the art history department, although for her it came too late. After graduation Anna planned to return to San Francisco and earn another B.A. degree in studio art, focused mainly on design. When I asked why she didn't just pursue a master's degree, Anna said that she felt she really didn't need one, that she had discarded any notions of being part of academic life. She said that once she had been attracted to intellectuals, explaining that her art history professors all seemed "to have their own worlds, their own discourse: they are so into it," but that in the end she realized that they were mainly "just talking to one another," and she didn't see the point to it. Since her travels to the West Coast and to Europe, Anna confessed she now feels that "there are lots more interesting people to talk with than academics."

Donna Qualley married an elementary school teacher the year after my work in her classroom was completed. They held a summer celebration for their friends on the lawn of their home, complete with a potluck dinner under a yellow tent and with music and games like horseshoes, badminton, and volleyball. Relatives and friends attended the informal event, eating and drinking long into the perfect summer afternoon. Donna continues to teach writing at the university, sometimes designing special course sections or teaching in-service writing courses to high school teachers. She has recently enrolled in a doctoral program.

One of my new responsibilities is as a writing consultant for faculty under a writing across the curriculum grant funded by the university. In this position, I support faculty who are interested in integrating writing into their courses in new ways. I have met with varying success. Some faculty members are open, as was Hall, to considering how writing can be used to help students learn the material in their disciplines. Others resist, displaying a reluctance to take class time away from coverage for writing, claiming that students need more time to acquire background knowledge, not to write. Mainly though, I have found real changes in both the way the process of writing is viewed and in the types of writing projects encouraged: I have seen poetry-writing options for soil science; peer response groups in chemical engineering; multiple drafting in occupational therapy and forestry; journal writing in entomology, animal science, and human nutrition courses; collaborative projects in ecology and electrical engineering. What started as a simple inquiry on my part about how students view writing in disciplines outside of the English department has given me many new understandings about literacy and learning in higher education. The journey has been insightful.

Appendix
Prose Writing Syllabus

A

ENGLISH 501/sec. 09
Fall 1987
Donna Qualley

TEXT: David Bartholomae and Anthony Petrosky, *Ways of Reading*. "Lab Ticket": $5.25 to cover the cost of duplicating papers

---

English 501 is an advanced writing and reading course, and a prerequisite to all other writing courses in this university. In this section we will explore the essay as a way for helping us construct new understandings about issues we find important. We will use reading and writing to help us find out what we have to say—what we think—about a subject.

The class consists of a series of rituals: papers, journals, reading groups, writing groups. Toward the end of the semester, we will adapt these activities to a new task—a longer project on a collaborative paper.

Papers ■ On Thursdays (see schedule) you will hand in a 4–5 page (typed, double-spaced) draft of a paper you have been working on. You will need two copies of this paper: one for me and one for you to continue working on, to use in conference the following week (so we both have a copy) and to use for editing purposes in class. I will not accept poetry or fiction. On the copy of the paper you hand to me, you should note any questions or concerns you have. This is your paper prior to talking about it. What do you see that is working? What areas do you think need work? I would like to know what help you need from me. And I want to know that you have thought about what's happening with your paper prior to conference.

Writing Groups ■ Writing groups allow you to receive feedback about your work in progress from a larger audience than just me. They serve the dual role of providing you with experience in reading-writing process (rather than just finished products—this is but another "way of reading"). This in turn allows you to look at your own developing drafts more critically. When you present a paper to writing group, you, the writer, will determine just what kind of help you need from members of the group. After each writing group session, the readers will take the papers home and do a further written response to the writer and give it to them the following class. The writer will then talk in her journal about the kinds of help she received and what she planned to do next with the paper.

Reading Groups ■ Four times during the semester you will meet in a reading group. Each time, one person from the group will choose a selection from *Ways of Reading* to have other group members read. Before the reading group meets, everyone will read the piece and write a journal response—thus, everyone will have thought about the essay prior to the group. The person leading the discussion will bring up issues that caught her/his eye—issues that surprised, perplexed, intrigued her or him. The idea of the reading groups is to have everyone enhance their first reading of the piece by hearing other reactions. Following the group, everyone will go back to the piece and write a second journal response—about how their reading changed as a result of the group. These group meetings will last about 20–25 minutes each time.

Journals ■ The Tuesday following reading groups (and once prior to reading groups) you will hand in a journal to me. The journal should contain your responses to the selections in Bartholomae (reading group selections and selections that I ask you to read), your writer's response to writing groups, and your written reaction following every conference you have with me. This reaction will basically contain the following:

What help you wanted from conference.

What help you received.

What you plan to do next as a result.

These journals may be handwritten informally (but with pen please so I can read them). I will collect them and talk with you in them; that is, respond to what you have to say. Basically we will be carrying on a conversation about reading and writing. I imagine these journals will be fairly substantial—7–10 (or more) pages. The journals represent the guts of your thinking; they are the playground for you to monkey around with what you think. I am looking for active, engaged, insightful responses.

You will also do a specific journal for the collaborative paper project.

Collaborative Paper ■ This will be explained in class, but, briefly, this project allows you to work with a couple of other people on a paper. This is a complex undertaking and will consist of your finding material (essays, short stories, news articles) in the library, doing journal responses, and then deciding as a group which of your articles will be used to trigger a paper. The group will have to decide how to write it. They will keep a journal of their reactions to the whole collaborative process. The group will meet for a conference with me and then the final paper is due Dec. 3rd along with each of your journals (thus, each member could receive a different grade, since your journal will be counted as about 40 percent of this grade), but more in class ...

Attendance is Mandatory ■ The class works through interaction. There is no way to make up things:

Miss more than two classes, the grade drops by a full letter.

Miss more than four classes, you fail the course (this applies to sickness, any reason).

Miss a conference (without rescheduling), your grade drops by a letter.

Miss two conferences, you fail.

Evaluation ■ You are evaluated on the basis of your serious, sustained work—that means active involvement in what you are doing. I look for curious, questioning minds, risk takers, people who will challenge themselves so they can grow as readers and writers. Grades usually boil down to a decision between what is adequate work (a "C") and what is excellent work (an "A"). If you do all the work (on time), attend all classes, this is adequate. You must show evidence of growth to earn a higher grade. Your grade will be based on the following:

Collaborative paper + journal

Two papers

Journals (includes reading responses, writing group stuff, conference reactions)

Exact percentages to be decided later.

Time ■ This course is intense. There is always something that needs working on. Spread your reading and writing out. Time away from a paper or in-between readings of an essay is one of the most helpful things you can do for yourself. But you can't do it if you just go for the last-minute cram, or try to write a paper (from genesis of idea to final copy) in one sitting. For novice as well as professional, writing and reading are slow plodding work. Making meaning does not occur quickly.

SAVE EVERYTHING: ALL NOTES, JOTTINGS, SCRIBBLES, DRAFTS, PAPERS—ALL OF IT.

Appendix *B*
Collaborative Writing Project

Collaborative Project
Fall 1987/English 501

Most people still conceive of writing as an individual act. Oh, sure, writers will bounce their ideas off other people — they will use readers — but the final act is still the writer doing his or her soliloquy on that blank page. Indeed, most of your own experience with writing (usually in school) has been just this: "your own work." You have been warned against cheating, "looking on someone else's paper"; or plagiarism, "stealing somebody else's ideas." However, your experience in this class with discussion, reading and writing groups, and conferences may begin to suggest something different. We do not write in a vacuum. Our ideas are shaped by others. Even the ideas we think are all ours are, in many cases, a synthesis of all the bits and pieces we have picked up along the way from our encounters with other people. A good part of the writing done outside of school, especially in an organizational setting, is collaborative. Members work together to produce reports, recommendations, policy statements, business plans, rules, and other documents. Over the next month or so, we will engage in some collaboration of our own. This is how it will work:

Basically—Individually you will look at writing from four different areas and make journal entries on each one. Your will then select one piece of writing you think you partners and you could use to spark an idea for a paper. You and your collaborators will switch articles, read each other's choices, and then come to an agreement about which of these articles you will use. Then you must decide how you will collaborate on writing a paper triggered by some idea in the piece you have chosen. The logistics of the collaboration will be up to you; the important thing is that each member contribute to the actual writing of the paper. You will keep a journal on the whole process (selecting the article to writing the paper).

The Readings

1. Go to the library and look through the following magazines for an essay (and you know what an essay is by now) that you find especially thought provoking—something that you can really sink your teeth into, something that raises some interesting questions in your mind. Plan to spend some time locating this essay. The first piece you identify as an essay may catch your attention, but continue to peruse and see what else is available, until you are sure you have a good one. During the initial search, you will not need to read everything word by word; you will probably read the first few paragraphs for the possibilities and scan the rest. But once you have decided on an essay, read it thoroughly. Don't just soak up the information like a passive sponge—actively question. Wonder. Criticize. Argue. Applaud. I suggest xeroxing the piece if it is not too long so that you can read pen in hand. This will make the journal entry easier later. Include quotes and ideas from the text that have triggered your reaction in your journal entry. Be sure to include all bibliographic data in your journal entry: Author, title (of magazine and article), pages, date.

   I have particularly selected these periodicals for their meaty articles. If you check with me, I may allow you to choose another publication, but certainly no *People, Glamour, Sports Illustrated, Readers Digest*, etc.:

Harper's	*Nation Review*
New Yorker	*Commentary*
New Republic	*Ms.*
Scientific American	*Discovery*

2. Select a "feature" or editorial from an issue of the *New York Times, Christian Science Monitor*, or *Washington Post*. Take your time in finding something that strikes you as "interesting" and follow up with a journal article. Again, include all bibliographic data. Current copies of newspapers are located on the first floor of the library and back issues are on the second floor in the microfilm room. The *New York Times* dates back to the 1800s—you may want to look for something historical.

3. In the periodical room on the second floor, look through the current displays for some of the literary review magazines that carry short stories (*Aegis, Southwest Review*, etc.). They are easily identifiable on sight. You want to find a complete short story—not an excerpt from a novel, nor a poem. This may take some time, because you will need to read the story to see if it provokes a strong reaction from you. Respond in a journal. Note your reactions to content, language, style, or fiction in general—anything that strikes you, makes you think or connect. Note bibliographic data.

4. Choose a handout, chapter, or section from a text of one of your other classes that has sparked your thinking, extended it in some way. You will have probably read this once already. Read it again. What does it make you think about? What ideas or questions does it raise? Obviously the piece you select will need to be something you can take issue with. If you choose a section entitled "Rules and Procedures for Dissecting Grass-hoppers," it should be because you want to comment on the procedures or ethics of all this. In other words, I'm interested in your thinking about these things, not what they say necessarily. Of course your journal entry will need to refer to the text. Include all bibliographic data.

5. Now that you have four journal entries in response to four readings, you should select one of these you feel might provide a good trigger for a paper. In your journal, discuss why you chose this particular reading and not the others—I am interested in your reasons for your choice. Bring copies of the article for each member of your group. After you exchange and read each other's articles, as a group you will need to select which one you will actually collaborate on. In the journals, people should discuss their reasons for why they chose the article they did and how the group arrived at a consensus.

The Writing

6. As a group, you must now decide what you will write and how you will write it. In what way will each person contribute? Will you jointly make a list of ideas for the paper, have someone rought out a draft, and have the group revise it? Will you each write sections of the paper and then try to unify them? How you write these papers may depend on how you have reacted to the reading. Some papers may be argumentative, debating some issue you have identified. Maybe the collaborators take opposite sides and the paper turns out to be a discussion of why this happened. (You can use your imagination—in fact I am looking for innovative approaches. I am thinking of Siskel and Ebert, the movie critics who rarely agree. ...) Papers may depend on the strengths and interests of the writers—humor or dialogue, perhaps. You will not have a great deal of time and this will probably involve several meetings but it should prove "interesting." In your journal, note everything you can about the process of collaboration you are going through. What are your thoughts and feelings about this—how does it differ from writing on your own (may make socialists out of you. ...)

7. After you have a draft, you will meet with me for a group conference and then meet back with each other to decide on revisions and editing. Although the paper will have been written jointly, it still must appear unified and coherent. ...

8. After finishing the paper, you will need to do a final journal entry. What have you learned or noted about collaboration? What worked and what didn't? What might you do differently? How does it compare to other kinds of writing you have done? Your individual journals and the group paper will all be turned in. Each person will receive the same grade for the paper, but will be graded individually on their journals, thus each group member could end up with a different grade.

Time Table

11/3   Library—to work on articles.

11/5   Writing group.

11/10 Library (you will need more than two classes for this probably).

11/12   Reading group (last)—collaborative groups meet and exchange articles for each to read.

11/17   No class, but collaborative groups should meet (either at this time or at a prearranged time, to decide which article to use to trigger a paper).

11/19   Collaborative groups meet to work on writing.

11/23, 11/24, 11/25 Sign up for a group conference. First draft should be completed before Thanksgiving (choose one of these days).

12/3   Collaborative paper (final for grading) plus journals due.

12/10   Two papers and journal selection (last class).

Appendix C

Methodology: The Handwork of the Field Investigator

Ethnography is the study of lived experience. ... One could say, then, that the point of ethnographic research is to examine how, in the course of fabricating their lives, individuals also weave their material cultures.

Linda Brodkey
Writing Ethnographic Narratives

As Linda Brodkey's textual/textile quote suggests, ethnographers are concerned with how participants "fabricate" their lives from the cloth of their own cultures (1987A, 25–26). Drawing further on the fabric metaphor, I found that conducting an ethnographic study is a great deal like doing handwork, like piecing together an intricate and carefully designed garment that is intended for practical use. Because the narrative power of an ethnography allows the reader to become engrossed and at ease in the world being described, the findings and conclusions appear to emerge seamlessly from the study, causing some critics of educational ethnography to misunderstand its often invisible methodology.

For every ethnography, there is a story behind the making of the story; how I come to know what I know is the most revealing part. I would like to share how I conducted this study by turning my garment inside out, showing how the original pattern was cut, the pinning and stitching done, and the fitting accomplished.

The Research Question: "Making Your Own"

My initial research interest was to understand how students interpret the literacy demands made on them in academic settings; what it meant from their vantage point to be literate in a university. My hypothesis for this study was, then, nothing more than a belief that college students have far greater literacy than has previously been documented, that Hirsch and Bloom and other educational critics have a restricted view of college students' literacy.[1] An ethnographic design seemed most appropriate for my purposes because it is concerned with the informant's world-view. Whatever else a methodology may be, suggests Paul Diesing, "it should at least be adequate to the particular thing described and should not distort it" (1972, 141).

My research began with a clear need to locate a setting within the university to start my work as well as a desire to find informants, but with only a foreshadowing of what my focus might become. As I lumbered along, I lived mainly in a state of ambiguity, because, as Michael Agar points out, ethnographers "grow their own questions" (1980, 197) as they conduct their research. Over time, new research concerns gradually replaced old ones; for example, I added the roles of both reading and talk in facilitating literacy to my original concern with academic writing. Midway into my study (about six months), the research question became more focused so that I could articulate it as "What are the literacy/ learning structures within a college classroom that contribute to the student's sense of an academic community?" This homemade question helped me shape the rest of my project.

Negotiating Entry: Prose Writing

My data gathering officially started in the setting of Donna Qualley's Prose Writing course, which she volunteered to have me visit during the first week of classes (September 1987) to see if it

---

[1] The most valuable research I drew upon about a college students' literacy was Lucille McCarthy's ethnography of a college student, Dave, *Stranger in Strange Lands* (1985). In her study, she shows Dave writing in three different settings across the curriculum and examines the various rhetorical demands made upon him by the requirements of disciplines such as biology, literary studies, and freshman writing.

would be suitable for my research. I came on the second day of her class and stayed for the entire semester (the class met twice a week for one and a half hours for fourteen weeks). I was not surprised that Donna's classroom became my initial context for the study. My previous connection with her in graduate seminars brought us together in a natural teacher-researcher collaboration to learn how students viewed classroom literacies. Initial fieldnotes indicate my attraction to her class:

Love Donna's laugh and red shoes. Very high quality of discussion, lots of participation on only the third day. Reading an essay in class makes it possible to talk immediately afterward. Like the idea of the reading conference, want to tape it. Many possibilities of students who said they would work with me. Need to discuss time, commitment, interest. Feel very good about the class and about working with Donna. Good possibilities here. Notice that I pay more attention to the students than to Donna.

Entering this setting was facilitated by my own background as a writing teacher, by Donna's ability to present me as a colleague, and by the students' receptivity to having a participant-observer in their classroom. As the semester wore on, students made occasional references to me as "the researcher" or to "Elizabeth's research." Many students brought me writing assignments from other courses throughout the semester, affirming for me the researcher status they had accorded me within their classroom.

As colleagues, Donna and I were able to establish a collaborative relationship in which we exchange my field notes, with her adding any observations she wished to mine. From the beginning, it was clear that, although the work of the research was to be mine, I valued her insights as well. Sometimes we would both pore through transcripts, fascinated by what her students had said.

Selecting Informants: Getting the Students' Perspective

Although some readers of this study may insist that the students I described are not "typical" state university types, perhaps I might suggest that there are no completely "typical" student volunteers for a project such as mine. I would also argue that we have not looked closely at enough college students to fully understand the range of literacies they bring to our classrooms, probing beneath what on the exterior seems unassumingly ordinary. My process for selecting student informants was simple: I asked for volunteers, willing to talk with me weekly, who were also enrolled in majors that required extensive writing.

All the students in Prose Writing class initially appeared interesting to me. I knew I had to limit my choices, because I wanted to include extensive interviews and I would need time to establish a collaborative relationship with key informants. My six original informants included two women: Anna, who did a great deal of writing in her art history major, and Connie, whose major of outdoor education itself attracted me. Nick was such an articulate student that I asked him to volunteer. Carlos, enrolled in a Russian literature course, offered the perspective of the returning, part-time student. Tim was learning disabled and felt that talking about his writing projects in other courses would help him. Randy, whose major was leisure, management, and tourism, was involved in campus politics, a fraternity, and a small Bible group. Together these students presented a wide range of potential perspectives on academic literacy: different majors, different genders, different skill abilities, different interests. My eventual selection process was thus based on hunches, chemistry, and the search for diversity.

I paid each student a small university-funded stipend for their involvement with my project (CURF Grant). Once when Nick was so broke that he didn't have enough money to photocopy some of his writing for me, I joked that he was probably involved in the project just for the pay. He reminded me that he had recently worked in a local cable factory where he made considerably more in hourly wages. Since none of my informants ever asked to drop out of the study, I felt that they were learning as much as I was.

The combined perspectives of these students led me to alternative ways of considering academic literacy. Connie, for instance, helped me see that the academic skills developed in college might be tied to more than a classroom or even a major: literacy could be intertwined with a personal construct of the self. I learned this through her invitation to attend the Club meeting, at which she was presenting a talk on the use of the journal in experiential education. This student-operated club provides leadership experiences in planning and taking small groups of students on wilderness or nature trips. My field notes from that night indicate what I learned:

Connie gave group members a journal made especially for them and asked us all to find a quiet spot and write about something significant that happened in our day's activities. On the blue cover of the journal was written: "We all climb the same mountain together but we each get something different out of it." I was given a journal as well and knew that I would be expected to share my writing. We wrote for about twenty minutes and then reconvened and read parts of what we had written. There was a long discussion on the use of journals in adventure experiences, both individual and group journals.

Connie showed me that I might need to look outside the college classroom to reflect on the literacy behaviors that I saw taking place inside these settings. Each student in my study was able to teach me something very individualized about his or her private literacy during the course of this study, which informed and expanded my understanding of public literacies.

Like most ethnographers, I collected more data than I would be able to use and found the process of eliminating material rather painful. Second semester I followed only four students—Connie, Anna, Carlos and Nick—to courses in their majors. Tim had no writing in his second-semester coursework and Randy's major duplicated one of Connie's two majors (leisure, management, and tourism). I began with six students, worked down to four by second semester, and finally wrote only about two, Anna and Nick. Such decisions were mainly guided by the quality of data I was collecting, my personal engagement with students, and a sense of their own commitment to my project.

Family Member/Guest: The Design

According to Wilcox, the overall aim of an ethnographer is to "combine the view of an insider with that of an outsider to describe a social setting" (1982, 462). In each of the several academic settings in which I worked, I was able to achieve both the insider and outsider perspective. During the first phase of data collection, I had a rich supply of data sources from Prose Writing class: from Donna, from the six target students, and from the whole class who treated me more like a family member in their Prose Writing class. My goal for this part of my fieldwork experience was to make the familiar setting of a composition classroom strange, to see Prose Writing from the perspective of an outsider, using key students to inform me.

The second phase of my data collection took me into foreign territory, into disciplines that I had either never studied before or that now seemed alien to me. My goal for this part of the study was to make the unfamiliar setting familiar to me, drawing on the expertise of the student informants who were declared majors and supposedly insiders in these disciplines. My sources of data were more dependent upon my informants during the second phase of research, because I was treated as more of a guest in these classrooms than as an accepted member of the community, as I was in Prose Writing.

As a guest, I began by gaining formal invitations to visit these classes. Here are my field notes from when I was trying to gain entrance to Carlos's Russian course:

I slush my way across campus to the Russian department to see if I can join Carlos in his Dostoyevsky course. I find Professor R., with his back to the door, immersed in reading and eating his lunch, which includes onions and brie. Even sitting down beside him I can tell that he is a very short man. He wears a sweater vest, striped shirt and heavy glasses.

Quickly we begin to talk about the course. He shared that using journals in his classes helps him "keep in touch" with his students' thinking but that he had 45 students and fell behind in reading them. In the Dostoyevsky course he plans to give 60% of the grade for class participation, hoping that the oral involvement will take the place of a journal. If writing is valued in the university, he said, then classes must be smaller.

As a guest, I relied on good manners in acquiring writing samples or oral transcripts from students in these other disciplines who never fully understood my status in their classes. And like a polite house guest I tried to reciprocate the hospitality of the instructors by giving them some ideas, when asked, about how their classrooms might become more effective learning contexts through the use of writing. In the courses attended with my two case studies, both instructors elicited my advice about writing: one considered my suggestions and acted upon them.

Looking and Listening:
The Ethnographer's Tools for Data Collection

The major techniques for acquiring ethnographic data are through participant observation by collecting "thick descriptions" (Geertz 1973) in the form of field notes and by holding interviews with informants (Spradley 1979), although photographs, writing, and personal artifacts are also used. Lofland and Lofland stress the "mutuality" of intensive interviewing and field observations for the naturalistic investigator (1984). At the outset, field notes might include everything from the angle of the sun or the smell of a classroom to the verbatim talk that goes on there as well as clothes worn and gestures used by the speakers. When the question is still hazy, my notes are often prolific and unfocused. Here's a snip of my September field notes, revealing an eclectic and unorganized mixture of recording that I do, jumping from my methodology to the class dynamics to the key students:

I should have taped this session but feel the use of a tape recorder would be too intrusive this early on. Tried to capture and summarize the conversation. Class began with Donna taping up a big poster that Holiday Inn ladies gave her when she graduated from college. The poster shows the student in four years of college. In sequence two, the head is severed and then in sequence four it is filled with sand. She asks why the poster seems appropriate to their discussion of Freire and then jokingly suggests, "Everything I say today is just a bag of sand."

Anna came in late. I noticed that Nick writes with a fountain pen, very unusual for a student. Carlos showed me a new appointment book he bought to organize his life. Tim held some exchanges with Laurie about her boyfriend. Randy's perfunctory remarks about readings put me off.

These field notes go on for seven more pages with most of the space devoted to recording verbatim classroom conversation. In later notes from this class, I develop more concise note-taking skills, writing less, saying more, mainly because I have begun focusing: such culling of field notes starts as soon as possible. At the base level, then, data analysis is just a way of sorting through different types of notes taken. In late September (1987), I began to code my notes, adapting a technique outlined in Schatzman and Strauss. Notes are coded as ON (observation note) or TN (theoretical note) or MN (methodological note) or PN (personal note). From early in the study, here's a page of my coded field notes:

ON: When I came into class Randy was talking with Donna about how he didn't have his paper ready due to computer problems. Andy said, "You can't rely on technology." After the class assembled, Donna announced that Allie was running for Miss New Hampshire and that the class could go together as a field trip if the fee wasn't $25 a person. Students ask Allie questions about the contest.

A paper was due in class today and Donna asked them to write about what they felt was working best in their papers.

Question: Can we write about what is not working?

Donna: Yes, most writers look at the negative. Write about any concerns you have.

Neil: Where, at the end?

Donna: Anywhere, I'll read your *self-evaluation* of the paper as I read the paper. Make comments throughout if you want.

MN: While the class writes, I pass out three pages from *Peanuts* cartoons about writing. I am trying to establish some silent rapport with them as a group. I notice that when they stop writing (11:20), they pick up the cartoons and amuse themselves until the rest of the class is finished. Some students smile at me in acknowledgement of my gift.

ON: Donna: I'd like you to *evaluate* your paper each week when you hand them in: it guides my reading. Now I'd like you to look at what Hoagland says about the essay form and *reread your own essay*. Look at your paper and on a separate sheet, respond. How do you see your paper through his eyes? (The essay is called "What I Think, What I Am" by Edward Hoagland from *On Essays: A Reader for Writers*).

TN: This in-class reading of one text (student) against another (professional) creates a distancing effect. Some students write without rereading their essays, others go back and forth. Everyone seems absorbed as they work between two texts, creating *intertextuality*.

PN: Donna seems relaxed, always gives enough time in class for students either to write or read. Anna looks tired and disheveled; Randy seems tense. I realize that I've seen them all in a kind of equal way that I will never see them again after I read these first papers.

Several months later, when I return to these coded field notes, I highlight the ideas of *self-evaluation* and *intertextuality* to form one of my emerging data categories on how writing is used in this classroom. This initial coding makes the ensuing search and support of analytic categories more systematic.

In all, I collect 114 typed pages of coded field notes on the Prose Writing classroom, which I keep in a salmon-colored loose-leaf binder. When I share these notes with Donna, we discover that my observations and interpretations about what is going on in her class are sometimes different from her own, adding another perspective to my data through this collaborative process. Mainly Donna and I do not disagree, but, as the following example shows, we extend each other's thinking. When, for example, I reread a transcript from one of Donna's writing groups, I wonder why so much of the student discussion centers on differences in forms of writing, differences between, for example, the essay and story. I insert a theoretical note for myself in the transcript:

(T.N.: Is this an unnatural discussion of form that wouldn't be ongoing in this class if Donna hadn't set them up to think about form through readings such as Hoagland's "What Is an Essay?")

When Donna reads the transcript and my note, she responds in the margin saying, "Probably, but we can't help the discussions that occur in our classes. A history is being created, a context is in process, a conversation unique to this class, and to any class." Although I am the primary researcher in this context, I use Donna's perspective to corroborate or disconfirm some of my findings.

Structured Conversations: Informant Interviews

While I am busy recording field notes on the classrooms, both in Prose Writing and later four other field sites, I also hold weekly interviews with each of my student informants. These interviews turn my focus away from descriptions of what is happening in particular settings to individual perceptions and interpretations of literacy events and encounters through the perspective of my informants. First semester I spend an hour or more with them, either before or after their writing conferences, usually tape-recording our interviews. Second semester, when I audit a course with each student, our interviews are more informal and often take place before or after class. Both terms, we review reading and writing assignments and talk about what is happening in the courses I am observing. General interview guides were constructed (see Spradley 1979 for questioning techniques) so that over the course of two semesters I would get approximately the same information from each student. But more than acquiring the same data for each student, these interviews become the major source for my understanding the students' perspective on their own literacy.

What takes place over time in our interview sessions is called by Elliot Mishler "the joint construction of meaning." Mishler explains that rather than conducting interviews with a completely predetermined format, the interview proceeds "through mutual reformulation and specification and questions, by which they take on particular and context-bound shades of meaning" (1986, 53). My weekly interviews with students sound like informal conversations as I attempt to follow the individual thinking patterns of each student. When Anna says that she has certain things that follow her around in all her coursework, I try to probe for these elusive "things"; when Nick shares that the women students' responses in his writings group are pretty "gritty," I need an interpretation for this word; when Carlos says that he writes primarily for himself, I try to understand the range in his concept of audience; and when Connie suggests she can't learn in one of her classes unless she understands how to "use" the information, I have to get at her meaning for "applied knowledge." In my interviews, I assume very little, as I try to make explicit the literacies that empower or short-circuit students' learning processes. And together we arrive at shared meanings of particular terms, of life stories, of ongoing events, so that meaning is grounded in our actual shared conversations.

Here is a portion of an important interview with Connie, in which she explains why she is having trouble with her "foods and dudes" course, a large (300-student) lecture-style, general elective course with a lab component. In this interview, Connie talks about the papers written for the course, both her diet analysis and the most recent paper on a computer-simulated experiment about the diet of chickens.

Elizabeth: You say you've found Dr. White a very satisfying lecturer. And then you say that you wish you had a better way of *connecting* his lectures. Did this assignment [on the chickens] help?

Connie: I think the diet analysis could have *connected* it for me but you only had a week to do it. If we had looked at our diets over the whole semester, I think that would have been a lot better. I don't think this chick study has anything to do with humans. Why do we want to know about diets of chickens? We're not chickens—this is a food and people course, not a foods and chicks class.

Elizabeth: They do offer a course in animal nutrition, I know.

Connie: Maybe abstractly he's saying that these same nutrients are important to people, but you already know that from class. It would have been better to show that these nutrients are important when looking at your own diet. I think the diet analysis could have been a project to help connect all the information for each person because each person has different dietary needs. I don't know what mine are. I know from the diet analysis that I'm lacking in iron. But I don't know why I'm lacking in iron.

Elizabeth: Are you saying that these assignments just scrape the surface?

Connie: Right. You can say all these things, and he's got, he's got much information. *You can give back all this information but it doesn't mean anything unless you can internalize it, unless you can use it yourself. And then you can begin to use it for other people as well.*

Weekly interviews probed students' own constructs for their literacy and learning patterns in an attempt to discover what most helps the learner. In Connie's case, she suggests that she needs to apply or "connect" her learning for it to be meaningful. My folders bulge with data as I record both general and specific information for each student about college literacy demands. I file and code these separate interviews as well (using different colored binders for each student), attaching notes on possible categories or themes that come out of our extended conversations, my classroom observations, and my analysis of their writing in all their course work. Each folder tells a different story of students' literacy experiences in college. Each folder could be read as kind of a patchwork quilt.

Validating Patterns: The Analytic Memo

During the first semester, I draw on still another source of information to verify data that I gather in individual interviews — those
are transcripts of Donna's writing conferences. With each informant's permission, I tape, listen to, but do not always transcribe
these conferences. Carlos, for instance, has a dramatic conference
with Donna after she has read his paper *Oblomov*, which Carlos
has volunteered to share with the class to model writing group
responses. Donna is baffled by his paper; Carlos is defensive.
Here's the initial part of the ten-page transcript, which guides me
in my subsequent interview with Carlos and becomes part of my
first analytic memo:

Donna: Why did you want do this paper with the group?

Carlos: Why? Well, because I've only done two for you. This is the second
and I like it better than the first one.

Donna: I had a hard time with this.

Carlos: You had a hard time with it?

Donna: I don't know what "oblomov" is.

Carlos: That's *Oblomov* right there (points to his Penguin paperback).

Donna: Thanks. You assume that ...

Carlos: Everybody knows who Oblomov is.

Donna: Yes. Help us out.

Carlos: Well ... I've developed my own character here and he's spun
right off of this guy's ... that book right there ...

Donna: "Penguin says."

Carlos: It's a classic, trust me. The reason it's a classic is because the
character's timeless. He could have existed anytime, he could have
existed twenty thousand years ago ...

Donna: Okay, well, that makes all literature classic. For that very reason.

Carlos: Okay. I figured what would he be like in the twentieth century.
But there's more than that. What this paper represented is me,
what's happening with me and myself.

Using this conference transcript, my own interview with Carlos,
and a taped transcript of the class discussion of Carlos's *Oblomov*
paper, I wrote an analytic memo to myself about Carlos's confusion over his two audiences of Prose Writing and Russian class.
The analytic memo (Schatzman and Strauss 1973, 104) pulls together a number of pieces of information around a theme or
event and forces the ethnographer, who is so busy collecting
data, also to reflect on it. The analytic memo thus becomes a kind

of internal dialogue. Here is an excerpt from the memo I wrote to myself on Carlos's confusion of audience. What I am finally after is not just my perception of this event but Carlos's.

Analytic Memo 2

As I work with this student, I began to sense his confusion over a "sense of audience" in writing for these two different courses, Russian literature and Prose Writing. Instead of writing about the relatively unknown Russian novel *Oblomov* for Russian class, Carlos wrote the paper for English 501. His submission of this paper for Donna's course began an interesting thread of events which I will describe below.

When Carlos volunteered to let Donna use his *Oblomov* paper to demonstrate how writing groups should work, she never anticipated the full range of responses that would emerge. The paper ended up not providing a good model of writing group response, because Carlos had misjudged the background and knowledge of his audience. He has written no papers yet for Russian, only journal entries, and did not intend this paper for Russian but for English 501. The question of Carlos's understanding of audience will be an interesting one to follow this semester, since it has been firmly set in motion in this course.

The data that I am considering here include:

1. Carlos's Prose Writing paper, which requires prior knowledge of an unfamiliar Russian novel, *Oblomov*.
2. The transcript of Carlos's workshop when the whole class read and responded to his paper.
3. Donna's conference with Carlos about the novel.
4. My conference with Carlos about all these events.
5. A note from a student in Russian class who read Carlos's paper at his request.
6. Journal entries from students in Prose Writing who responded to the whole-class workshop.
7. Carlos's own journal entries, which display his continued confusion over differing audiences.
8. Carlos's paper written for Russian class on an entirely different novel.

In this memo, after setting up my topic and listing the sources of data I considered, I then discuss what Carlos himself has said about audience in our interviews:

Carlos has used some very unusual words to talk about audience. At one point he said that his English papers in Freshman English were very "popular"—particularly with women students. He also felt that his *Oblomov* paper would probably "threaten" his readers. Yet when I ask him about who his imagined audience is for his writing, he says; "I just write to please myself," which is contradictory to the idea of writing that is either "popular" or "threatening."

The next paper Carlos writes for Prose Writing he describes as a very "impersonal" topic about buying American products over foreign imports. Does he think that neutral topics are safer and less "threatening" for this class?

This memo sets me up to watch for connecting threads in my talks with Carlos as well as in classroom observations. In October, Carlos suggests in an interview that his *Oblomov* paper was a mistake: "It's like you're coming in on the middle of a moving merry-go-round or something like that." He goes on to write well for both his courses, never again confusing his audience, often talking explicitly about audience expectations. He also drops the guise that he writes only for himself.

Analytic memos, written on any topic or event that the ethnographer is concerned with, pull from multiple data sources to arrive at interpretive frames. Later, when I am ready to write my descriptive chapter on Prose Writing, I am able to draw from this memo to describe a significant classroom event.

Data Analysis: Model Building

The processes of reflecting on and writing about the growing data sources in an ethnography help move the research from anecdotes and personal insights to the stage of analysis, to constructing interpretative models. What sounds suspiciously unscientific to the quantitative researcher—that the themes or categories arise from patterns in the data—actually describes a very rigorous comparative method that involves "joint coding and analysis" to generate theories for further testing (see Glaser and Strauss 1967, chapter 5).

For example, since I am not a linguist, I never intended to enter the territory of discourse analysis: I never intended to count male/female turntaking in transcripts of group work as I eventually did. But my study drew me into considering the ways talk supported reading and writing in Donna's classroom. As early as the first week of observation, I wrote in my field notes: "It is the talk that is so exciting." Innocently enough, I started to tape small reading and writing groups and to transcribe Donna's writing conferences as well as my own interviews with students. In rereading these many transcripts, I began to see patterns related to both gender and power in the classroom context. I turned to the work of sociolinguists, feminists, and conversational analysts to inform me about these emerging patterns (Aries 1987; Thorne and Henley 1975; Thorne, Kramarae, and Henley 1983; Frank and Treichler 1989). I am still not a linguist, but a teacher researcher who is convinced that the way conversations take place in classrooms plays an important part in how and what students learn.

Language use emerged as one of the key categories that I felt contributed to students' sense of community within the college classroom. I relate this not to confess that I'm a novice at discourse analysis but rather to show that ethnographers go where their findings point them, not where preconceived hypotheses suggest that data will be found. Ethnographic theory is not built from a priori categories, but from the ground up as Paul Diesing describes:

The holist uses evidence to build up a many-sided, complex picture of his subject matter. He accomplishes this by using several kinds of evidence, each providing a partial or limited description that supplements other partial descriptions.(1972, 147)

There was no stage more frustrating than the analysis of my massive data into workable analytic categories. For one month, I drafted and redrafted versions of Donna's classroom, pure descriptions, without any ordering principle for the reader. Donna patiently read and reread each draft, but finally suggested that although the data were fascinating—after all, it was her classroom—she didn't know what she was looking for as she read. My researcher journal reflects my reliance on Donna as a supportive reader:

I finally got the first fifteen pages of the Anatomy section right. I have, according to my file dates, been working on these pages every day for three weeks. One day I spent two hours drafting two sentences. I could actually hear my heart beating while I wrote, so anxious was I to get it right.
Donna has been my best reader so far. After reading four preliminary drafts of my narrative about her classroom, she wrote back that it would help her a great deal if she knew what she was looking for as she read the narrative. What a simple thing for her to say: how do I know what all this mess means?

May 1988

Four categories in my massive data from two semesters of field notes were able to account for how the sense of an academic community grows within a college classroom. Although those four categories are there, embedded in the data, supported and reconfirmed by many different sources, and although they explain how college classrooms may become literate communities, they remain my constructed and superimposed view of how these college students' literacy works. Another researcher, sifting through the same piles, would not come up with the same categories; another researcher would not have the same lived-through experiences with these informants or these settings. Ethnographer Andrea Fishman warns against transplanting another researcher's organizing categories:

In fact, it is probably the ways these organizing categories work that make the results of this study seem at all polished or complete. And while I don't know how I would have finally written up my research without them, I would caution any reader against trying to transplant these categories to another setting or to assume that my findings may be found intact anywhere else. (1988, 211)

The most difficult test of my data will have to be whether or not my accounts of these students' literacies and the categories constructed to explain them prove useful to others who read this ethnography. The seams of this study are now visible, maybe even a bit ragged from this detailed discussion of conducting an ethnographic study. It is my hope that, in sharing my handwork, another tailor might design an ethnography suitable for her own fabric.

Bibliography

Agar, M. 1980. *The professional stranger: An introduction to ethnography*. New York: Academic Press.

Aisenberg, N., and M. Harrington. 1988. *Women of academe: Outsiders in the sacred grove*. Amherst: University of Massachusetts Press.

Annas, P. 1987. Silences: Feminist language research and the teaching of writing. In *Teaching writing: Pedagogy, gender and equity*, ed. C. Caywood and G. Overing. Albany, N.Y.: State University of New York Press, 3–17.

Atwell, N. 1985. Writing and reading from the inside out. In *Breaking ground: Teachers relate reading and writing in the elementary school*, ed. J. Hansen, T. Newkirk, and D. Graves. Portsmouth, N.H.: Heinemann.

———. 1987. *In the middle: Writing, reading, and learning with adolescents*. Portsmouth, N.H.: Boynton/Cook.

Au, K. H. 1980. Participation structures in a reading lesson with Hawaiian children: Analysis of a culturally appropriate instructional event. *Anthropology and Education Quarterly 11*: 91–115.

Bardwell, J. 1984. *Images of a university: A photographic history of UNH*. Durham, N.H.: The University of New Hampshire.

Barnes, D. 1976. *From communication to curriculum*. Harmondsworth, England: Penguin.

Bartholomae, D. 1985. Inventing the university. In *When a writer can't write: Studies in writer's block and other composing processes problems*, ed. M. Rose. Guilford Press, New York.

Bartholomae, D., and A. Petrosky. 1987. *Ways of reading: An anthology for writers*. New York: St. Martin's Press.

———. 1986. *Facts, artifacts and counterfacts: A theory and method for a reading and writing course*. Portsmouth, N.H.: Boynton/Cook.

Bateson, M.C. 1989. *Composing a life*. New York: Atlantic Monthly Press.

Baugh, J. 1983. *Black street talk*. Texas: University of Texas Press.

Belenky, M., B. Clinchy, N. Goldberger, and J. Tarule. 1986. *Women's ways of knowing: The development of self, voice and mind*. New York: Basic Books.

Berry, W. 1977. *The unsettling of America: Culture and agriculture*. San Francisco: Sierra Club Books.

Berthoff, A. 1981. *The Making of Meaning: Metaphors, models and maxims for writing teachers*. Portsmouth, N.H.: Boynton/Cook.

Bissex, G. 1987. *Seeing for ourselves: Case study research by teachers of writing*. Portsmouth, N.H.: Heinemann.

Bizzell, P. 1986. What happens when basic writers come to college? *College Composition and Communication 37*, 294–301.

———. 1988. How do discourse communities change? Paper presented at the Mind in Society conference, University of New Hampshire, Durham, N.H.

Bizzell, P., and B. Herzberg. 1986. Writing across the curriculum: A bibliographic essay. In *The territory of language*, ed. D. McQuade. Carbondale: Southern Illinois University Press.

Bloom, A. 1987. *The closing of the American mind*. New York: Simon and Schuster.

Brodkey, L. 1987a. Writing ethnographic narratives. *Written Communication 4*: 25–50.

———. 1987b. *Academic writing as social practice*. Philadelphia: Temple University Press.

Broude, N., and M. Garrard. 1982. Introduction: Feminism and art history. *Feminism and art history: Questioning the litany*, 1–17. New York: Harper and Row.

Bruffee, K. 1982. Liberal education and the social justification of belief. *Liberal Education 68*: 95–114.

———. 1984. Collaborative learning and the conversation of mankind. *College English 46*: 635–52.

———. 1986. Social construction, language, and the authority of knowledge. *College English 48*: 773–90.

Bruner, J. 1986. *Actual minds, possible worlds*. Cambridge: Harvard University Press.

Burnyeat, M.F. 1985. Sphinx without a secret. [Review of Studies in Platonic Political Philosophy by Leo Strauss] *New York Review of Books*, May 30, 30–36.

Calkins, L. 1985. Forming research communities among naturalistic researchers. In *Perspectives on research and scholarship in composition*, ed. McClelland & T. Donovan. New York: Modern Language Association.

Cambridge, B. 1987. Equal opportunity writing classrooms: Accommodating interactional differences between genders in the writing classroom. *The Writing Instructor 7*: 30–39.

Cayton, M. 1988. Women's initiation into academic discourse communities. Paper presented at the annual meeting of the Conference on College Composition and Communication, Seattle, Washington.

Caywood, C., and G. Overing. eds. 1987. *Teaching writing: Pedagogy, gender, and equity*. Albany, N.Y.: SUNY Press.

Cazden, C. 1980. *Classroom discourse: The language of teaching and learning*. Portsmouth, N.H.: Heinemann.

Cheatam, A., and M. Powell, 1986. *This way daybreak comes: Women's values and the future*. Philadelphia: New Society Publishers.

Chiseri-Strater, E. 1987. Lost Voices. Education Resources Information Center.

———. 1984. The case of the reluctant reviser. In Composing in context: Case studies of the revision strategies of freshman writers. Master's thesis. University of New Hampshire.

Cooley, C.H. 1964. *Human nature and the social order*. New York: Schocken Books.

Cunningham, M. 1985. *The dancer and the dance*. New York: Marion Boyars.

Dewey, J. 1927. *The public and its problems*. Denver: Allan Swallow.

———. 1938. *Experience and education*. New York: Collier Macmillan.

Diesing, P. 1972. *Patterns of discovery in the social sciences*. London: Routledge and Kegan Paul.

Durham Historical Society. 1976. *History in an oystershell*. Durham, N.H.

Eiseley, L. 1971. The brown wasps. In *The night country*. New York: Scribner. 227–36.

Eisner, Elliot. 1985. Aesthetic modes of knowing. In *Learning and teaching the ways of knowing: Eighty-fourth yearbook for the national society for the study of education*, ed. E. Eisner. Chicago: University of Chicago Press.

Elbow, P. 1973. *Writing without teachers*. London: Oxford.

Emig, J. 1977. Writing as a way of learning. *College Composition and Communication*, *28*: 122–128.

———. 1983. *The web of meaning: Essays on writing, teaching, learning and thinking*. Portsmouth, N.H.: Boynton/Cook.

Fishman, A. 1988. *Amish literacy: What and how it means*. Portsmouth, N.H.: Heinemann.

Flynn, E. 1988. Composing as a woman. *College Composition and Communication 39*: 423–35.

Frank, F.W., and P. Treichler, eds. 1989. *Language, gender and professional writing: Theoretical approaches and guidelines for nonsexist usage.* New York: Modern Language Association.

Freire, P. 1970. *Pedagogy of the oppressed.* (trans. M.B. Ramos). New York: Continuum Press.

Gannett, C. 1991, forthcoming. Gender and journals: Diaries and academic discourse. Albany: SUNY Press.

———. The stories of our lives become our lives: Journals, diaries and academic discourse. Manuscript.

Gardner, H. 1983. *Frames of mind: A theory of multiple intelligences.* New York: Basic Books.

Gee, J. 1987. What is literacy? Paper presented at the Mailman Conference on Families and Literacy. Harvard Graduate School of Education, Cambridge, Mass.

Geertz, C. 1983. *Local knowledge: Further essays in interpretive anthropology.* New York: Basic Books.

———. 1988. *Works and lives: The anthropologist as author.* Stanford: Stanford University Press.

Gere, A., and R. Stevens. 1985. The language of writing groups: How oral language shapes revision. In *The acquisition of written language,* ed. S.W. Freedman. N.J.: Ablex.

Gilligan, C. 1982. *In a different voice: Psychological theory and women's development.* Cambridge, Mass.: Harvard University Press.

Ginet, S. McConnell, 1989. The sexual (re)production of meaning: A discourse-based theory. In *Language, gender, and professional writing,* ed. F. Frank and P. Treichler. New York: Modern Language Association.

Glaser, B., and A. Strauss. 1967. *The discovery of grounded theory: Strategies for qualitative research.* New York: Adeline Publishing Co.

Graves, D. 1983. *Writing: Teachers and children at work.* Portsmouth, N.H.: Heinemann.

———. 1989. Process communities. Speech presented at the conference, Process in Practice, Fall 1989. Durham, N.H.

Greene, M. 1988. *The dialectic of freedom.* New York: Teachers College Press.

Grumet, Madeline R. 1988. *Bitter milk: Women and teaching.* Amherst: University of Massachusetts Press.

Harris, Joseph. 1989. The idea of community in the study of writing. *College Composition and Communication 40*: 11–22.

Hatch, D. 1988. Reaching the general through the specific: writing and thinking in art history. Paper presented at the annual meeting of Conference on Composition and Communication, St. Louis, Mo.

Heath, S.B. 1983. *Ways with words: Language, life, and work in communities and classrooms.* New York: Cambridge University Press.

Hirsch, E.D. 1987. *Cultural literacy: What every American needs to know*. Boston: Houghton Mifflin.

Hoagland, E. 1981. What I think, what I am. In *On essays: A reader for writers*, ed. Paul H. Connolly. New York: Harper and Row.

Hubbard, R. 1989. *Authors of pictures, draughtsmen of words*. Portsmouth, N.H.: Heinemann.

Hugo, R. 1979. *The triggering town: Lectures and essays on poetry and writing*. New York: Norton.

John-Steiner, V. 1985. *Notebooks of the mind*. Albuquerque: University of New Mexico Press.

Langer, S. 1959. *Feeling and form*. New York: Charles Scribner.

LeFevre, K.B. 1987. *Invention as a social act*. Carbondale: Southern Illinois University Press.

Lippard, L. 1983. *Overlay: Contemporary art and the art of prehistory*. New York: Pantheon Books.

Lofland, J., and L. Lofland, 1984. *Analyzing social settings: A guide to qualitative observation and analysis*. Davis, Cal.: Wadsworth Press.

Martin, J.R. 1985. *Reclaiming a conversation: The ideal of the educated woman*. New Haven: Yale University Press.

McCarthy, L. 1986. A stranger in strange lands: A college student writing across the curriculum. Ph.D. diss.: The University of Pennsylvania.

Mishler, E. 1986. *Research interviewing: Context and narrative*. Cambridge, Mass.: Harvard University Press.

Morton, Kathryn. The storytelling animal. *New York Times* Book Review Section, December 23, 1984, 1–2.

Murray, D. 1982. Teaching the other self: The writer's first reader. In *Learning by teaching*. Portsmouth, N.H.: Boynton/Cook.

———. 1984. Reading while writing. In *Only Connect*, ed. T. Newkirk. Portsmouth, N.H.: Boynton/Cook.

Neilsen, L. 1989. *Literacy and living: The literate lives of three adults*. Portsmouth, N.H.: Heinemann.

Noddings, N. 1984. *Caring: A feminine approach to ethics and moral education*. Berkeley: University of California Press.

North, S. 1987. *The making of knowledge in composition: Portrait of an emerging field*. Portsmouth, N.H.: Boynton/Cook.

Olsen, T. 1978. *Silences*. New York: Delacorte Press.

Ong, W. 1978. Literacy and orality in our times. *ADE Bulletin 58*: 1–7.

Penelope, J., and S. Wolfe. 1983. Consciousness as style: Style as aesthetic, In *Language, Gender and Society*, ed. Thorne, Kramarae, and Henley. Rowley, Mass.: Newbury House.

Perry, W.G., Jr. 1970. *Forms of intellectual and ethical development in the college years: A scheme*. New York: Holt, Rinehart and Winston.

———. 1981. Cognitive and ethical growth: The making of meaning. In *The Modern American College*, ed. A. Chickering. San Francisco: Jossey-Bass.

Phillips, S. 1972. Participant structures and communicative competence: Warm Springs children in community and classroom. In *Functions of language in the classroom*, ed. C.B. Cazden et. al. New York: Teachers College Press.

Pirsig, R. 1974. *Zen and the art of motorcycle maintenance*. New York: Bantam.

Polyani, M. 1958. *Personal knowledge: Toward a post-critical philosophy*. Chicago: University of Chicago Press.

Porter. J. 1986. Intertextuality and discourse community. *Rhetoric Review* 5: 34–47.

Qualley, D. 1987. A new beginning place: Examining theory with theory. Manuscript. Durham, N.H.: The University of New Hampshire.

Rich, A. 1979. When we dead awaken. In *Lies, secrets and silence*. New York: W. W. Norton.

Rodriguez, R. 1982. *Hunger of memory: The education of Richard Rodriguez: An autobiography*. Boston: Godine.

Rose, M. 1989. *Lives on the boundary: The struggles and achievements of America's underprepared*. New York: The Free Press.

Rosenblatt, L. 1978. *The reader the text the poem: The transactional theory of the literary work*. Carbondale: Southern University Press.

Rosenblum, R. 1969. The abstract sublime. In *New York painting and sculpture 1940–1970*, ed. H. Geldzahler. New York: Dutton.

Russell, D. 1989a. The cooperation movement: Language across the curriculum and mass education, 1900–1930. *Research in the teaching of English 23*: 399–423.

———. 1989b. Writing across the curriculum in historical perspective: Toward a social interpretation. *College English 52*: 52–73.

Sadker, M. 1987. Gender communications quiz. Reported in B. Cambridge, Equal opportunity writing classrooms: Accommodating interactional differences between genders in the writing classroom. *Written Communication 7*: 30–39.

Schön, D. 1983. *The reflective practitioner: How professionals think in action*. New York: Basic Books.

Schatzman, L., and A. Strauss, 1973. *Field research: Strategies for a natural sociology*. Englewood Cliffs, N.J.: Prentice-Hall.

Selden, E. 1935. *The dancer's quest: Essays on the aesthetic of the contemporary dance*. Berkeley: University of California Press.

Showalter, E. 1981. Feminist criticism in the wilderness. In *Critical inquiry*, Winter: 179–205.

Spender, D. 1985. *Man Made Language*. 2nd ed. London: Routledge and Kegan Paul.

Spradley, J. 1979. *The ethnographic interview*. New York: Holt, Rinehart and Winston.

Stone, R., ed. 1989. *Essays on the closing of the American mind*. Chicago: University of Chicago Press.

Taylor, D., and C. Dorsey-Gaines. 1987. *Growing up literate: Learning from inner-city families*. Portsmouth, N.H.: Heinemann.

Tchudi, S. 1986. The hidden agendas in writing across the curriculum. *English Journal 75*: 22–25.

Thorne, B., and N. Henley, eds. 1985. *Language and sex: Difference and dominance*. Rowley, Mass.: Newbury House.

Thorne, B., C. Kramarae, and N. Henley, eds. 1983. *Language, gender and society*. Rowley Mass.: Newbury House.

Trimbur, J. 1985. Collaborative learning and teaching writing. In *Perspective on research and scholarship in composition*, ed. B. Mc-Clelland and T. Donovan. New York: Modern Language Association.

University of New Hampshire Undergraduate Catalog. (1987–88) Durham, N.H.: Office of University Publications.

University of New Hampshire. *Admissions News*. (April, 1987). Durham, N.H.: Office of Admissions.

Vygotsky, L.S. 1978. *Mind in society: The development of higher psychological processes*. Cambridge, Mass.: Harvard University Press.

Watson, J., and R.J. Potter. 1962. An analytic unit for the study of interaction. *Human relations 15*: 2.

Wells, G. *The meaning makers: Children learning language and using language to learn*. Portsmouth, N.H.: Heinemann.

Wilcox, K. 1982. Ethnography as a methodology and its applications to the study of schooling: A review. In *Doing the ethnography of schooling*, ed. G. Spindler. New York: Holt, Rinehart and Winston.

Williams, R. 1973. *The country and the city*. New York: Oxford University Press.

———. 1976. *Keyword: A vocabulary of culture and society*. New York: Oxford University Press

Woolf, V. 1981. *A room of one's own*. (Rpt 1929) New York: Harcourt Brace Jovanovich.